Transformismo

"Alas" ("Wings") by Diarenis Calderon Tartabull

Transformismo

Performing Trans/Queer Cuba

M. MYRTA LESLIE SANTANA

University of Michigan Press
Ann Arbor

Copyright © 2025 by M. Myrta Leslie Santana
All rights reserved

For questions or permissions, please contact um.press.perms@umich.edu

Published in the United States of America by the
University of Michigan Press
Manufactured in the United States of America
Printed on acid-free paper
First published February 2025

A CIP catalog record for this book is available from the British Library.

Library of Congress Cataloging-in-Publication Data

Names: Santana, M. Myrta Leslie, author. | Michigan Publishing (University of Michigan), publisher.
Title: Transformismo : performing trans/queer Cuba / M. Myrta Leslie Santana.
Description: Ann Arbor, Michigan : University of Michigan Press, 2025. | Includes bibliographical references (pages 181–190) and index.
Identifiers: LCCN 2024034587 (print) | LCCN 2024034588 (ebook) | ISBN 9780472077168 (hardcover) | ISBN 9780472057160 (paperback) | ISBN 9780472221974 (ebook)
Subjects: LCSH: Drag performance—Social aspects—Cuba. | Drag performance—Cuba. | Gender expression—Social aspects—Cuba. | Gender identity in music. | Transgender people—Cuba—Social life and customs. | Gender-nonconforming people—Cuba—Social life and customs. | Women, Black—Cuba—Social life and customs.
Classification: LCC PN1969.D73 S36   2025 (print) | LCC PN1969.D73 (ebook) | DDC 792.7/2097291—dc23/eng/20240921
LC record available at https://lccn.loc.gov/2024034587
LC ebook record available at https://lccn.loc.gov/2024034588

An earlier version of chapter 4 was published in part as "Transformista, Travesti, Transgénero: Performing Sexual Subjectivity in Cuba," *Small Axe: A Caribbean Journal of Criticism* 26, no. 2 (68). Copyright 2022, Small Axe, Inc. All rights reserved. Republished by permission of the Duke University Press.

This book will be made open access within three years of publication thanks to Path to Open, a program developed in partnership between JSTOR, the American Council of Learned Societies (ACLS), University of Michigan Press, and The University of North Carolina Press to bring about equitable access and impact for the entire scholarly community, including authors, researchers, libraries, and university presses around the world. Learn more at https://about.jstor.org/path-to-open/

Cover photograph: Deyanira performing at Apocalipsis, in Havana, Cuba (2017). Photograph by M. Myrta Leslie Santana.

*For my mother
and for hers*

Contents

LIST OF ILLUSTRATIONS	ix
ACKNOWLEDGMENTS	xi
PREFACE: WHY CUBA?	xv
Introduction: Transforming Cuba	1
1 Las Vegas: Transformismo and Cuba's Capital	19
2 Apocalipsis: Transformismo at the End of the World	49
3 El Mejunje: Provincial Transformismo	75
4 Transformista, Travesti, Transgénero: Performing Trans/Queer Subjectivity	105
5 Transformismo masculino: The Social Project of Havana's Drag Kings	133
Coda: The Future of Transformismo	157
TOWARD A GLOSSARY	167
NOTES	171
REFERENCES	181
INDEX	191

Digital materials related to this title can be found on the Fulcrum platform via the following citable URL: https://doi.org/10.3998/mpub.12410823

Illustrations

	"Alas" ("Wings") by Diarenis Calderon Tartabull	*frontispiece*
1	Alberto, the drag persona of Black lesbian feminist activist Argelia, ready to march in the Jornada Contra la Homofobia y la Transfobia	2
2	Advertisements for cabaret performances from *Show* (1958), including an image of Madame Musmé	24
3	Devora, a celebrated young transformista from Havana, performs at the gay nightclub XY	38
4	Blankita, one of the best-known comedic transformistas in Cuba, performs at Karabalí in Havana	41
5	Esmeralda performs at Apocalipsis	50
6	Alberto and Dany perform together at Apocalipsis	58
7	Adela performs at El Mejunje, with Carmita, the drag persona of Silverio	81
8	Adela, Carmita, and Cinthya (out of drag) discuss the significance of El Mejunje	83
9	Blaccucini performs at El Mejunje while Adela looks on	86
10	Silverio introduces the show Proyecto Yo Me Incluyo in rural Remate de Ariosa	90
11	Laura Marlen, a veteran transformista, performs in Remate	91
12	Zulema, a prominent young transgender transformista from Santa Clara, performs in Remate	92
13	Dany performs in the Peña de Olga Navarro at Cabaret Las Vegas in Havana	123
14	Deyanira performs at Apocalipsis in Havana	127

15 Alberto performs with his quartet at a house party
    in Havana   137
16 One instantiation of El Cuarteto Habana performs at
    La Cecilia in Havana   141

All photographs except where noted in the captions are by the author and Kerry White.

Acknowledgments

Primero, y antes que nada: A toda mi gente en Cuba, gracias por haberme hecho una familia en la isla de mis ancestras. Gracias, Argelia, por ser mi amiga y mi hermana y por invitarme a ser tu fan todos estos años. Gracias a Afibola y Diarenis por enseñarme tanto y acompañarme a través de varias transiciones. Gracias, Olorun, por escogerme, por jugar tantos juegos conmigo y por contarme muchos cuentos buenísimos. Gracias, Ayamey, por hacerme reír tan profundamente y por confiar en mí. Gracias a Sayné y Austin por ser mi familia y por aguantarme todos estos años. Gracias a Max y a Nomi por haberme mostrado lo que es ser una mujer trans bella, lista y poderosa. Gracias a Katiuska por haberme tratado como una hermana desde el principio y por ser tan linda conmigo y con Kerry. Gracias a mi familia de origen, a todxs lxs primxs que me han acuerpado en mi tiempo en Cuba, brindándome amistad, compañía, comida y mucho más, por haber resucitado un vínculo sanguíneo con la isla. Gracias a todas mis amistades en Cuba que me han acompañado desde que empecé a ir a Cuba.

Muchas otras personas en Cuba me facilitaron mi tiempo, vida e investigación en la isla. Sobre todo, gracias a todxs lxs transformistas quienes compartieron conmigo su tiempo, su arte y sus historias. A Blaccucini, Deyanira, Dany, Kiriam, Esmeralda, Zulema, Laura, Cinthya (que en paz descanse), Lara, Víctor Víctor, Dévora, Blankita, EC, Z, N, D, K, N y muchxs más. Sin ustedes, no habría libro. Gracias a todxs lxs artistas, intelectuales y activistas que me enseñaron durante mi tiempo en Cuba: a Cyann, Norma Guillard Limonta, Norge Espinosa, Henry Heredia, Roberto Zurbano, Tomás Fernández Robaina, Víctor Fowler, todas las trabajadoras del departamento de música de la Casa de las Américas, Alejandro Zamora, Ulíses Padrón Suárez, Damián Sainz, Ramón Silverio Gómez, P, NP, AA, L y AD. Gracias a todxs lxs demás que formaron parte de mi familia trans/queer en Cuba: a JE, CM, J, F, A, L, A, R, V, M y muchxs más.

I am honored to have the drawing "Alas" ("Wings") by my dear friend Diarenis Calderon Tartabull as the frontis image for *Transformismo*. In "Alas," I see *las plumas* (the feathers) that signify femme queerness in the Spanish-speaking Caribbean and the *plumofobia* (femme-phobia) we femmes endure in the Americas. Moreover, I see the flight that Cubans have had to withstand for centuries, from the forced migration of Atlantic slavery to the departures of generations of Cubans since the Revolution, my family included, who are trying to find ways to live despite the ongoing violence of US imperialism. But I also see the flights that bring me and other diasporic Cubans back to the island and into relation with people like Diarenis as well as the ways that Cubans manage to make lifeways that go beyond, that escape the limitations that surround them. By putting "Alas" at the front of this book, I mean to foreground the labor of Afrofeminist/trans/queer artist-activists in Cuba, including Diarenis, who work to make life better on the island and have influenced every page of this book.

This book emerges out of the dissertation I wrote while I was a PhD student at Harvard University. My committee there—Ingrid Monson, Kay Shelemay, Alejandro de la Fuente, and George Paul Meiu—offered me tremendous support and guidance in my studies, research, and writing. Sindhu Revuluri was my most steadfast mentor, and without her I would not have finished my PhD. The staff of the Department of Music are legendary, and I am particularly grateful to Kaye Denny, Nancy Shafman, Eva Kim, and Lesley Bannatyne. Other mentors and teachers throughout the university held me up through the difficulties of graduate study, especially Lorgia García Peña, Michael Bronski, Robin Bernstein, Ajantha Subramanian, Vincent Brown, and Sophia Roosth. I was blessed to have the cohort of the century, known to each other as the Femmebassy: Etha Williams, Pei-Ling Huang, Grace Edgar, and Alana Mailes. Harvard was also where I met the sisters who became the Diasporic Femme Collective—Laurie Lee, Krystal Klingenberg, and Tamar Sella—who continue to inspire me and lead my thinking and writing. Laurie teaches me how to be a stronger sister, thinker, and writer whenever I get to spend time with her. Krystal is the best co-conspirator and a truly gifted maker of community. Tamar, like Laurie and Krystal, is a diasporic sister par excellence: she carried me through fieldwork and sees me in the deep way we all need. I was beyond fortunate during my PhD to meet Kareem Khubchandani, who has supported and championed my work ever since while serving as the best auntie role model I could hope for.

UC San Diego has been a challenging but inspiring place to bring this book to fruition. Amy Cimini has been the greatest colleague and sister a girl can dream up, and keeping Sarah Hankins in my corner since graduate school has been a blessing. Their animal offspring Raftery, Puppy, and Dusty have all provided hugs, scratches, and love for years. Ben Cowan and his partner Mark have given me that elusive sense of home in a state so very far from my upbringing. I am lucky to have colleagues and friends in San Diego like Lera Boroditsky, Julie Burelle, Anthony Burr, Eric Geiger, Barbara Jackson, Sara Johnson, Lorena Mostajo, Ivan Ortiz, and Jade Power Sotomayor. Our staff in the Department of Music and at the Center for Faculty Diversity and Inclusion have helped my work at the university run smoothly. I am personally, intellectually, and politically inspired by my students every day, and I thank all of them, especially my graduate advisees Max Schaffer and Alejandrina Medina, who are—fortunately for them—light-years ahead of me in so many ways.

Much of the intellectual formation for this book took place at the University of Michigan, where I did undergraduate and graduate studies in violin performance. Nesha Haniff, Ruth Behar, and Larry La Fountain-Stokes introduced me to Caribbean studies and transformed the way I see myself, the Caribbean, and the world. Christi-Anne Castro, Karen Fournier, and Chuck Garrett were exceptional role models as I began to envision the possibility of musical study. Dean Hubbs was my closest mentor during work on my Doctor of Musical Arts degree and became a dear friend; she and her work are the reason I ever considered pursuing a PhD in music. So many friends at Michigan provided further intellectual, political, and spiritual sustenance, especially Jason Amos, Darci Sprengel, Vivian Luong, Steve Lett, Erika Boysen, and Rocky Block.

I am thrilled, then, that this book is being published by the University of Michigan Press, with whom it has been an absolute delight to work. Sara Cohen has been a dream of an editor, supporting each step of the process and offering keen and transformative feedback along the way. I am deeply indebted to my not-so-anonymous readers Larry La Fountain-Stokes and Susan Thomas, both of whom not only improved the manuscript but bolstered my confidence in finalizing the book.

I have been very fortunate to have been supported in higher education by incredible thinkers and teachers. Susan McClary introduced me to feminist and queer musicology during my master's at the Cleveland Institute of Music, starting me down the path that led to this book. Guidance, support, and letters of recommendation have been provided by none other than Maureen Mahon, Ellie Hisama, Shana Redmond, Deborah Wong, Susan Thomas, Matthew Morrison, Alejandro Madrid, and Tavia Nyong'o. Camaraderie aplenty has been doled out by Ruthie Meadows, Eva Pensis, Marysol Quevedo, León García Corona, Project Spectrum (especially Clifton Boyd, Lissa Reed, Anna Gatdula, and Catrina Kim), Amarilys Estrella, Aurelis Troncoso, Beshouy Botros, Cordelia Rizzo, and Esther Kurtz. My small group from the Faculty Success Program of the NCFDD—Olivia Johnson, Kamahra Ewing, and Frankie Kung—has been with me from the very beginning of the tenure track and continues to hold me up. I have treasured the guidance of my padrino José Irizarry at critical junctures over the past several years.

Finally, this book would look nothing like it does were it not for my family. My *abuela* and *abuelo* who helped raise me instilled in me the *cubanidad* that lingers throughout these pages. My brother Bobby was my first friend and is still my best, and he has brought me some of my favorite beings on this planet: his wife Courtney, their children Jack and Owen, and their dog Penny. Growing up with my aunt Mayda; my cousins Tim, Megan, and Mia; and my uncle Sergio and his wife Carmen afforded me a childhood full of stories and laughter. Early chosen family like Maggie Carlin, Jeff Wunderman, Ryan Callahan, and Roberto Sinha started teaching me to craft what I need. My father and his wife Nancy have always provided a loving second home in New York. But there are no words to capture the debt of gratitude I owe my mother, to whom this book is dedicated. *Transformismo* is an attempt to better understand her and our ancestors and to be closer to her and her mother. Without her, simply, there would be nothing.

I am blessed beyond belief to have not only the family described above but also the family I am making now. I met my wife Kerry in Havana in May 2016, and my life has never been the same since. In the ensuing years, she brought me a kind of love and complicity for which I wouldn't have previously even dared to hope. She knocked me out of a deep denial, led the way in our transitions, and loved me at my absolute worst. There is not a word in this book that has not been touched and made better by her presence, her care, and her intellect, and my gratitude for her is boundless. Coparenting our fabulous dog Chus together has made our life even sweeter. Chus has saved my life more than once, and she teaches me every day that I am, first and foremost, an animal.

Preface

Why Cuba?

Por eso siempre permaneceré al margen,
una extraña entre estas piedras,
aun bajo el sol amable de este día de verano,
como ya para siempre permaneceré extranjera,
aun cuando regrese a la ciudad de mi infancia.
Cargo esta marginalidad inmune a todos los retornos,
demasiado habanera para ser neoyorkina,
demasiado neoyorkina para ser,
—aun volver a ser—
cualquier otra cosa.

This is why I will always remain on the margins,
a stranger among the stones,
even beneath the friendly sun of this summer's day,
just as I will remain forever a foreigner,
even when I return to the city of my childhood
I carry this marginality, immune to all turning back,
too *habanera* to be *newyorkina*,
too *newyorkina* to be
—even to become again—
anything else.
 —Lourdes Casal, "Para Ana Veltfort"
  Translated by David Frye

Is it arrogant to return to a place you've never been?
 —Noor Naga, *If an Egyptian Cannot Speak English*

On a typically warm day in February 2018, my wife Kerry and I made our way to the Virgen del Camino neighborhood in Havana, Cuba, to interview the Afrofeminist lesbian artist-activist Diarenis Calderon Tartabull.[1] Our journey started from our apartment in the coastal neighborhood of El Vedado and followed the zigzagging southeasterly route of the P1 bus. We passed through El Cerro and Luyanó before entering the San Miguel del Padrón municipality that is home to Diarenis's neighborhood, Virgen del Camino. Once we arrived at our stop, we ambled down the Calzada de Güines, running into Diarenis's partner at the time at a nearby gym, who told us she would catch up with us shortly at Diarenis's house.

When we arrived at Diarenis's door, she invited us in and offered us some tea while we waited for her to finish up some housework. Her house was full of the books and memories befitting someone who has spent a lifetime advocating for her communities.[2] I was eager to speak with her about her work, but I was also a bit apprehensive. Though we had coincided at various events around the city, we didn't yet know each other well, and it was not my practice to conduct interviews like this with activists with whom I did not yet have a relationship. But, with a visa expiring in a few short months, I did not feel I had the luxury to take things as slowly as I once did.

At that time, I had already been doing research in Cuba for nine months, but Diarenis was the first person to turn the interview back on me. When she finally sat down with us, before I turned on the recorder, she engaged me about my work and why I was doing it. As a Black lesbian feminist activist in Cuba, she had become accustomed to being an ethnographic subject, and she wanted to get some more clarity before she consented to do so again. "Do you identify as a white man?" she asked me. (To be clear, though I now present rather obviously as a trans woman, at the time my gender subjectivity was less clear.) "No," I replied, "I am a queer person, and in the US I would call myself Latinx."[3] "See?" Diarenis's partner, freshly arrived from the gym, interjected from the kitchen, "they think differently there."[4] Diarenis went on, asking me why I cared and wanted to know more about Afrofeminism and Afrofeminists in Cuba.

I fumbled through an answer: Transformismo (drag performance) as a performance complex, putatively my object of inquiry, demands an analysis that is as attentive to racial formations and political economic transformations as it is to gender and sexuality. It lives at the intersection of long histories of racial impersonation on the island, the shortcomings of postsocialist reform projects, and renegade genealogies of trans/queer worldmaking. Afrofeminism is perhaps the only political and intellectual project in Cuba that takes all of these seriously together in their interlocking ways. My own intellectual orientation, too, like that of anyone who claims trans/queer-of-color critique as their toolkit, is beholden to transnational histories of Black, woman-of-color, and Third World feminisms, which shape the way I see myself, Cuba, and transformismo. So, I wanted to get to better know the current trajectories of Afrofeminism on the island.

If my answer was clunky or unclear, Diarenis still let the interview go on for some reason, recording it for herself just as I did for me. Our conversation ranged widely, encompassing Diarenis's previous social projects and their aims, the textures of the Afrodescendant movement in Cuba, and the shortcomings and exclusions of LGBT rights in Cuba. In particular, we talked about the persistence of racist ideology within mainstream LGBT spaces and the kinds of people who remain left out: bisexuals, *travestis*,[5] trans people, women, Afrodescendants.

When we decided the interview had ended, Kerry and I lingered to share a meal with Diarenis, her daughter, and her partner, over which we primarily talked about our diverse upbringings on and off the island. At one point, Diarenis's partner suggested that my worldview, beholden to Black feminism despite the fact that I am not Black, was inflected by my having been raised in the US. "If you had been born in Cuba," she said, "we would be having a very different conversation." "No," Diarenis interjected, "if you had been born in Cuba, we would not be having this conversation at all."[6]

I begin *Transformismo* here to answer a question that often gets asked of ethnographers with regard to their "field sites" of choice: Why Cuba? I am supposed to answer this question in some intellectually appropriate way, by telling you about Cuba's especially fraught place in relation to US imperialism, the Caribbean's history of feminist activism and thought steeped in Black life, or the social potency of the particular work of my interlocutors on the island. While all of those are important and will be addressed in the pages of *Transformismo*, here I want to say plainly that the only reason I started doing research in Cuba, the only reason I am writing this book, is because my mother was born in Havana.

By this I mean that I went to Cuba, as Marcia Ochoa said of her queer diasporic ethnography in Venezuela, "to learn about the conditions of possibility for my own existence" (2014, 235). As a translesbian diasporic Cuban, I knew very well what it was like to be a trans/queer Cuban in the US. But where had this trans/queer *cubanidad* come from? And what was it like to be a trans/queer person in Cuba today? These are the questions that hang over the rest of *Transformismo*.

This diasporic subject position engenders certain possibilities for the researcher, collaborator, and co-conspirator. Lila Abu-Lughod has suggested that we feminist and "halfie" ethnographers trouble anthropology's investments in "a fundamental distinction between self and other" (1991, 137) and complicate facile renderings of ethnographic positionality, making it clear that "every view is a view from somewhere and every act of speaking a speaking from somewhere" (141). If our reflexive, personal writing is always at risk of being labeled as little more than solipsism, Ruth Behar argues that it can also generatively halt the ethnographic imperative to report, leading readers into "the enormous sea of serious social issues" (1996, 14).

Reflecting on the narrative about my interview with Diarenis, I think the diasporic subject position also makes certain solidarities possible that often remain out of reach otherwise. To me, Diarenis's suggestion that had I been born on the island we would not be in dialogue reflects the fact that white queer people in Cuba,[7] just like white queer people in the US, are poised to balk at the suggestion that racial formations meaningfully structure trans/queer space and relationality. I have seen, for example, white lesbians in Cuba angrily shout down Black lesbians for positing that white supremacy and the long wake of slavery still shape Cuban society, including its trans/queer corners.

Diarenis seemed to suggest that, for me, the process of diaspora had engendered a possibility of coalition. To the extent that such a possibility exists, it comes, I would say, from a history of movement that racialized me and my family in the US in a particular way and thus moved me to look for explanations that would account for my experience.[8] Those I found in classes with Caribbean intellectuals in my undergraduate studies, like Nesha Haniff, Lawrence La Fountain-Stokes, and Ruth Behar, and also in the work of diasporic Cubans whose political and intellectual consciousness was inspired by radical social movements in the US—e.g., Black, Chicano, Puerto Rican, and gay liberation—like Lourdes Casal, José Esteban Muñoz, and Juana María Rodríguez.[9] From them, I learned that there was no way to understand my trans/queer diasporic subject position without reading Black feminism.

This diasporic solidarity, however, is always on the brink of failure. Reflecting on the presence of Black Cuban poet and cultural critic Víctor Fowler at a conference celebrating the publication of her trans-diasporic edited collection *Bridges to Cuba* (1995), Ruth Behar noted his "impatience with the heroic Cuban-American stories of return, of bravely flouting parental and exile community authority to go back to the island, of feeling linked to lost worlds, dreams, and affections" (1996, 158). What do our flowery narratives do to unsettle the imbalance of power and resources between us and our island-based counterparts? Fowler had arrived in the US with "the clothes on his back, a T-shirt and jeans," while "[a]ll the Cuban-Americans were dressed casually but well; lots of good wools, silks, and leather jackets" (Behar 1996, 158).[10]

I do not offer this reflection on my diasporic femme ethnography, then, to suggest that it is a salve or a solution.[11] In the end, a text like *Transformismo* may win a place for a diasporic author in the US academy, but it will not secure the better material futures being sought by the author's interlocutors. In many ways, in fact, I am poorly situated to write the book that follows, not having grown up in and lived the island's particularities. I begin here to lay bare my motivations and orientation in writing *Transformismo*, which is, after all, an account of how one trans/queer diasporic Cuban made sense of her "return to a place [she's] never been" (Naga 2022), the "city of [her mother's] childhood" (Casal 1976, 1995). I want this to color how you read the rest of the book, my complicities and my *desconocimientos*, my desires and my arrogance.

Overall, I agree with Jafari Allen when he says that "though writing a book will never un-punch or de-rape, will never reverse the court decision, people should know that they are free and that they deserve study, a record of some of the highlights of how this freedom is performed" (2016, 622). *Transformismo* is meant to be such a record. Perhaps other trans/queer diasporic readers will find inspiration in it, as I have in all of the work and people I cite and refer to above.

Introduction

Transforming Cuba

You would have had to look very hard to see the only *transformista masculino* (drag king) who performed at the 2016 Conga Contra la Homofobia y la Transfobia (Conga Against Homophobia and Transphobia) in Havana, Cuba. Alberto, the drag persona of the Black lesbian feminist artist-activist Argelia Fellové Hernández, was tucked away in La Piragua, the open plaza next to the grand and storied Hotel Nacional.[1] As we waited for the Conga—Cuba's version of the gay pride parades that dot the globe in the summer months—to begin, Alberto posed for me to take a picture that would capture his baseball cap, his painted-on mustache, and his short-sleeved button-down shirt and tie (see figure 1). His right hand encircled a bottle of water, while his left kept a gentle hold on the massive Cuban flag he and dozens of his fellow trans and queer Cubans collectively marched down Calle 23, the main artery of Havana's queer nucleus, just in front of an identically sized rainbow flag with a similar escort.

Alberto encouraged me to take a spot next to him, and I was happy to do so, excited to be participating in the Conga for the first time. I thought about my abuelos as we marched down La Rampa, a nickname for this section of Calle 23, a main artery of Havana's ritzy El Vedado neighborhood and its trans/queer epicenter. We were just blocks from the apartment my abuelos lived in when they got married. What would

Fig. 1. Alberto, the drag persona of Black lesbian feminist activist Argelia, stands ready to march in the 2016 Jornada Contra la Homofobia y la Transfobia.

they think about their translesbian diasporic *nieta* returning to the island to walk in this Conga, shouting "¡Socialismo sí! ¡Homofobia no!" in concert just a few yards away with the likes of Dr. Mariela Castro Espín, the niece of Fidel Castro, a man my abuelos had raised me to revile? To my other side was Kerry, the fellow researcher I had just met, who would eventually become my wife. Along with Alberto and countless fellow transgender and queer Cubans, we took up all the street, slowly making our way from Havana's iconic Malecón to the Pabellón Cuba, the sprawling event space where the rest of the days' festivities would take place.

Argelia and I had met the first time I went to Cuba in June 2015, through a connection made by the Afrofeminist psychologist Norma Guillard Limonta. At the time of the 2016 Jornada Contra la Homofobia y la Transfobia (Conference Against Homophobia and Transphobia), the two-week event of which the Conga is a part, I was just beginning to understand the barriers that Argelia was facing as a transformista masculino, and the distinctly Afrofeminist and Afroqueer motivations and social foundations of her work.[2] In her efforts to promote the visibility of Black lesbian women in Cuba, for example, Argelia had tried to insist on greater participation of transformistas masculinos in the various events of the Jornada, but the event's organizers had not acquiesced. So, she took her performance to the streets, marching the Cuban flag down Calle 23 in drag, representing a country and an LGBT-rights movement that had not adequately addressed her needs or those of her fellow Black feminist lesbian artist-activists.

By contrast, *transformistas femeninas* (drag queens) figured prominently throughout the two weeks of the Jornada. They rode alongside Dr. Castro Espín, the director of the Centro Nacional de Educación Sexual (National Center for Sex Education, CENESEX) as she arrived at La Piragua in a convertible classic car.[3] They performed at the Pabellón Cuba following the Conga, and later at the Fiesta por la Diversidad (Party for Diversity) at the nearby La Gruta nightclub. And they were featured in the nationally televised Gala Contra la Homofobia y la Transfobia that had taken place the previous evening at the iconic Teatro Nacional José Martí, sharing the stage with Spanish pop diva headliner Marta Sánchez. The veteran comedic transformista Margot emceed the Gala alongside famed Cuban actress Laura de la Uz. The dynamic transformista Imperio performed to Spanish singer Mónica Naranjo's "Mi vida por un hombre," filling up the stage with a larger-than-life outfit comprised of a long black gown, a sculptural cape that looked like a giant spider web extending outward from her neck, and a tall blond wig that looked like a flame trying to lick the rafters. In a show that also featured the eternal cabaret star Juana Bacallao, Cuban-American singer Cucu Diamantes, and the plus-size dance troupe Danza Voluminosa, fellow transformistas Sahira and Angela Nefer gave performances lip-synching to songs by Black and Latin American divas like Whitney Houston and Gloria Trevi. The spectacle was moving and fabulous, impressive in the way that trans/queer people were able to speak for a state that not long before had imprisoned them for *peligrosidad social*, for social danger. Nevertheless, I was unsettled seeing Argelia—who had come to transformismo masculino through her work with CENESEX and had championed the practice as a form of Black lesbian activism, a critical element of any trans/queer movement in the hemisphere—seated in the audience, a spectator, not a performer.

Transformismo tells a story about how trans/queer performance has been accommodated in Cuba's social and political mainstream despite intense persecution in recent history, about who remains left out of such aboveground scenes and discourses, and about what *those* people are doing to cultivate a future Cuba in which all trans/queer people can thrive.[4] To be sure, this is a particularly Cuban story, one that emerges out of the island's response to economic struggles since the fall of socialism, the state's shifting attitude toward sexual diversity in the last fifteen years, and the exclusions of these interlocking social and economic transformations. *Transformismo*, then, is about the futures people like Argelia are making possible for Cuba and the ways those visions see beyond the limitations of mainstream LGBT rights discourses on and beyond the island, which include discourses of racelessness, a tainted pact with the tourism economy, investments in respectability, and intractable lesbophobia.

In this way, *Transformismo* is also an American story, in the hemispheric sense, one that relies on the racial-sexual-economic legacy of slavery, the history and present of settler colonization and US imperialism, the ongoing intensification of global racial capitalism, and the uneasy fates we face as trans/queer people.[5] Throughout the hemisphere, LGBT movements and spaces suffer from the same limitations I describe above. Trans/queer studies scholars have already told us about the political dead end of accommodationist LGBT rights approaches (e.g., Cohen 1997; Spade 2015) and the inadequacy of even revolutionary nationalist projects to apprehend Black/queer existence (e.g., Ferguson 2003, 10, 140–41, 146). *Transformismo* documents these shortcomings of dominant LGBT rights and revolutionary politics in the hemisphere and the contours of a possible trans/queer liberatory future.[6]

Since the 1990s, many authors have offered compelling accounts of sexual diversity that contend with Cuba's history of revolutionary nationalism and the racial and political economic formations that trans/queer Cubans have had to navigate since Cuban independence.[7] It has been less common, however, for these texts to center the work and ideas of culture workers—this despite the fact that the tremendous importance of the arts in Cuban civil society has been documented by a number of interdisciplinary thinkers.[8] *Transformismo* enters here to attend to trans/queer politics through close ethnographic attention to the perspectives and interventions of trans/queer performers on the island.

Transformismo is not, however, a treatise on the music of trans and queer performance in Cuba, despite my training as an ethnomusicologist. While such a project might be interesting or illuminating, it would not do enough to document or advocate for the urgent work of trans/queer liberation in Cuba or anywhere. Instead, I take a sideways approach to music, a performance-studies approach to music, one that Alejandro Madrid has suggested "asks what music does or allows people to do" (2009). Though music is everywhere in *Transformismo*, my attention is not on the musical object; instead, I consider "what happens when music happens" (Blau 2009). Throughout, for example, I am attentive to the ways transformismo, as it did in the Gala above, stages foreign music to imagine life off the island and relies on Black vocal labor for its affective force. My claims, however, are not about that music, but rather about the social and political possibilities engendered by the performances of trans and queer people.

In proceeding this way, I mean to contribute to the unsettling of music studies' dogged investment in a woefully parochial understanding of what music is and what its analysis might look like. I write, then, alongside a long line of primarily feminist, queer, and racialized music-studies scholars who have suggested that a more capacious approach to musical study would allow us to more directly address the most pressing social and cultural problems related to our work.[9] I offer *Transformismo* in the hopes that it might help to encourage and legitimize a more socially and politically relevant and engaged music studies.[10]

Transformismo is neither an exhaustive history of transformismo nor a systematic overview of its contemporary manifestations in their totality. Like Alexandra Vázquez's analysis of Cuban music in *Listening in Detail*, *Transformismo* is "an interaction with, rather than a comprehensive account of" (2013, 9), transformismo. Though more historical or general approaches to transformismo would be a useful and welcome addition to the literature, *Transformismo* is more accurately an account of what contemporary gender performance and performers in Cuba have to say about social and material transformation on the island more broadly. This is, to me, what is most urgent in a Cuba that desperately tries to hold on in the wake of the COVID-19 pandemic, intensifying imperialist US foreign policy, and the ensuing material scarcity brought by both.

In calling this work *Transformismo*, then, I am referring as much to the relationship between trans/queer performance, sexual subjectivity, and social and political transformation as I am to gender performance in particular. Cubans use the terms "transformismo" and "transformista" to refer to what would be called "drag performance" and "drag performer" in the United States. The word plays on the "transformación" ("transformation") from one gender to another while calling to mind "travesti" and "transgénero," categories I discuss in chapter 4. "Transformismo" is also one Spanish term for the theory of evolution, and some trans/queer activists in Cuba do indeed call for an evolution of the Revolution, which I will touch on in chapter 3. Scholars of postsocialism, meanwhile, will probably think of Gramsci's *trasformismo* when they see the title of this book, and indeed some observers understand the Cuban state's about-face with regard to trans/queer performance as an example of that Italian strategy of political containment.[11]

Most directly, I offer this study of trans/queer performance and social transformation in Cuba as an entry in the ongoing elaboration of what could be called trans/queer studies *en las Américas*. This transdisciplinary formation contends with the historical and transnational meanings and flows of categories of sexual subjectivity; their relationship to broader racial, colonial, and imperial formations; and the political strategies we trans/queer people deploy toward our own liberation.[12] Within it, *Transformismo* contributes an embedded, ethnographic account of trans/queer life and art/world-making in the Caribbean. Like many works in this and adjacent intellectual and political universes, then, I take gender and sexuality to be historically and socially produced categories, ones that have surprising ruptures and continuities both over time and throughout the hemisphere, disrupting the rigid categorization of our social lives that informs so much of liberal LGBT rights discourse.[13] Perhaps unusually, however, I will dwell here on the activist work of artists and the artistic work of activists, offering attention to the important work that performance and art do in shaping our subjectivities, in transforming political and economic realities in the hemisphere, and in providing spiritual and psychic sustenance and leadership in struggle.[14] In doing so, *Transformismo* aims to unsettle the boundaries imagined between performance and subjectivity, gender and sexuality, and sex and the broader social and political economic sphere within which it exists.

Researching Transformismo

The methodological and theoretical orientation of *Transformismo* likewise reflects my broader investments in trans/queer liberatory movements throughout the hemisphere. The relationship with the island that I elaborated in the preface; the critical, performance, and collaborative ethnographic methods I will describe here; and the book's foundation in the various race/sex theories I will discuss below all evince a primary desire not to make truth claims or produce knowledge about Cuba, nor to translate the island to North American academics, but rather to participate meaningfully in efforts to transform Cuba and the hemisphere.

The particular materials I analyze as I do so come from a lifelong relationship with Cuba, long-term ethnographic research on the island, and ongoing communication with artists, intellectuals, and activists in Cuba and its diaspora. Most of the ethnographic data in *Transformismo* comes from eleven months of research in Cuba conducted between May 2017 and April 2018. During this time, I participated actively in trans/queer nightlife in Havana, formed trans/queer community on the island, traveled twice to Santa Clara, and became familiar with a broad network of artists, intellectuals, and activists. I conducted more than two dozen formal interviews with transformistas, audience members, and trans/queer activists, and I had more than a dozen less-formal conversations with prominent Black, feminist, and trans/queer intellectuals. Just as importantly, I made a life with my friends and family (both chosen and of origin), sharing in the joys and frustrations of living and getting by in Havana and Cuba.

Numerous episodes from before and after my long-term research in 2017–2018 also inform and appear in this book. In some ways, having been brought up in the Cuban diaspora, I have been conducting research for this project since I was born. Cuba looms large in the narratives and lives of diasporic Cubans, and I have been trying to make sense of the island for as long as I can remember. Reading and working in Cuban and Caribbean studies with Ruth Behar and Lawrence La Fountain-Stokes during my undergraduate studies and with Alejandro de la Fuente during my PhD all contributed further to my understanding of Cuba and its and my place in the world.

Regular travel to Cuba since 2015 has been a critical way to better understand the island and my relationship to it. Three preliminary research trips to Cuba in 2015 and 2016 shaped the course my later writing would take. Beyond meeting Argelia and Kerry, I met my grandmother's cousins and their descendants for the first time, became acquainted with life on the island, and began to understand the place of transformismo in contemporary Cuban culture. Travel to Cuba since 2018 has provided critical follow-up to my primary research and illuminated the precarities faced in the wake of COVID, civil unrest in July 2021, and increasingly harsh US sanctions. Though so-called "research" trips have long blended into visits with my chosen family and family of origin, I always encounter things in Cuba that inform my work. COVID robbed me of several years of such visits, but I have returned to Cuba four times since 2018 and intend to do so for the rest of my life. Perhaps more importantly, I stay in touch with a number of people on the island for reasons as much personal as professional, remaining up-to-date on social life in Cuba through contact with trans/queer sisters and brothers, transformistas, and members of the Afrofeminist/trans/queer movement.

The texture of these interactions is informed by traditions of performance, critical, and queer diasporic ethnography. Like Marlon Bailey, I learned from Dwight D. Conquergood's elaboration of coperformative witnessing, an "approach [that] requires one to perform and lend one's own body and labor to the process involved in the cultural formation under study, particularly when it involves a struggle for social justice" (Bailey 2013, 22). Sometimes, this meant offering my musical abilities as a violinist at *peñas de transformismo, cumpleaños de santo*, or a birthday, funeral, or wedding.[15] Much more often it meant showing up, lending a hand, marching with my people, or helping to get in the way of sexist and racist abuse. In this way, my project drew from critical ethnography insofar as it began "with an ethical responsibility to address processes of unfairness or injustice within a particular *lived* domain" (Madison 2005, 5). Throughout *Transformismo*, I aim to be the kind of author who "takes us beneath surface appearances, disrupts the *status quo*, and unsettles both neutrality and taken-for-granted assumptions by bringing to light underlying and obscure operations of power and control" (Madison 2005, 5).

As I described in the preface, these investments are not merely or even principally intellectual or scholarly, but rather emerge from my own position as a translesbian diasporic Cuban. My political and intellectual orientation to researching and writing this project has always been based in trans/queer-of-color critique, itself emerging from long histories of Black, woman-of-color, and Third World feminisms. In this way, *Transformismo* for me has always been a "race/sex project" (Allen 2013, 552), one that begins from the understanding that "we cannot understand the dimensions and dynamism of the social character of human being without thinking gender, sexuality, race, class, and nation as they are lived—simultaneously" (Allen 2016, 617–18).[16] The book is aligned, then, with Black/queer ethnographers who examine the racial-sexual-economic legacies of slavery, colonialism, and US imperialism in the Caribbean (e.g., Alexander 2005; Wekker 2006) and fellow Cuban diasporic critics who have been inspired by histories of race/sex thinking in the US and the Caribbean and its diaspora (e.g., Muñoz 1999, 2009, 2020; Rodríguez 2003, 2014, 2023).

Even more directly, my analyses in *Transformismo* are inspired by related intellectual traditions in Cuba that understand race and sex together (e.g., Rubiera Castillo and Martiatu Terry 2011; Fowler 1998; Guillard Limonta 2016), especially Cuba's Afrofeminist/trans/queer movement.[17] This artistic, activist, and intellectual movement insists on the interrelationship between historical and contemporary racial and sexual formations. It emerges from long histories of Black feminism on the island while responding to the inequities that have grown since the fall of socialism, which I will further elaborate here.[18] The practice of transformismo has both explicit and indirect ties to Afrofeminist/trans/queer critique: In the case of Argelia, who opens this introduction, her work as a transformista masculino comes directly out of her involvement with Afrofeminist artist-activism. More subtly, however, Afrofeminist/trans/queer criticism on the island helps to make sense of transformismo's complex entanglements with long histories of racial impersonation, gender subversion, and foreign influence in Cuba.

By toggling back and forth between Cuban Afrofeminist/trans/queer analyses and Black/queer criticism from the US, I do not mean to translate Cuban movements for North American readers, but rather to recognize the inherently transnational nature of these projects and their aims, as much in Cuba as in the US and throughout the hemisphere. In the edited collection *Afrocubanas*, editor Inés María Martiatu Terry (2011, 2–3) connects their conception of Afrofeminism to Caribbean and Latin American thinkers like Agustín Lao-Montes and Sueli Carneiro as well as Black feminists in the United States, especially Audre Lorde. This mode of citation is cyclical, to be sure; recall that Lorde herself came out of the Caribbean diaspora and that so many of her fellow Black, Third World, and woman-of-color feminist writers, too, shared diasporic roots.[19] Contemporary Afrofeminist/trans/queer critics in Cuba and its diaspora, too, articulate a transnational vision for trans/queer liberation, situating their struggle in relation to that of Black people, women, and trans/queer people throughout the hemisphere.[20] Thus, *Transformismo* adopts a hemispheric race/sex approach in the chapters that follow.

Finally, all of the research in this book was not conducted alone, but rather in partnership with my wife Kerry White. When I met Kerry at the 2016 Jornada, she was doing research for her master's thesis in Latin American studies at the University of Florida, and I was starting research for the dissertation that would become an early basis for this book. Serendipitously, Kerry found herself able to accompany me for my year-long research trip, an idea about which I was initially apprehensive. It would be amazing to have Kerry with me in Cuba, but would she hinder my ability to do the research I needed to do?

Indeed, Kerry's presence did affect how I was perceived in Cuba, always interpellated as a foreigner as I walked next to a six-foot-tall fair white femme. Much more profoundly, however, Kerry provided sorely needed support during the more difficult periods of research and invaluable intellectual dialogue at critical moments. It was uniquely beneficial, for example, to have a fellow Cubanist by my side, especially one who has, frankly, a much better command of Cuban and Latin American history than I. Or to have a fellow researcher with me to listen and offer feedback as the earliest versions of the chapters that follow started to take form.

More critically, Kerry afforded a more meaningful relationship with the interlocutors who would eventually become our chosen family. Looking back, I think that our femme-for-femme relationship brought us into community with the Black lesbian women who became our closest interlocutors, as we shared a sense of what family might look like, in a way that would perhaps have been impossible had I been in Cuba by myself. Had I been perceived as a lone gay male ethnographer, a somewhat well-trodden subject position, perhaps I would have been more easily interpellated into the broader context and relational paradigms of sex tourism. Now, as Kerry and I articulate ourselves more clearly as trans lesbians, I see that being with Kerry has always meant being in lesbian community with these brilliant and committed activists I now call family and continue to learn from daily.

Why is it, then, that when I tell fellow academics that Kerry spent my research year with me they sometimes see it as an ethical dilemma, one I must resolve through reflection and writing in the project? To some extent, I think certain researchers feel that this weakens the necessary assertion that I did this work *on my own*, that this is indeed a single-authored monograph. This, to me, is a fiction. If you look at the classic ethnographies that PhD students are required to read in their training, you will find—almost always tucked away in the dedication or acknowledgments—the presence of kin at the research site and in the writing process. Take, for example, Alan Merriam's reference to his wife Barbara in the acknowledgments for *The Anthropology of Music*: "I am as certain as any man can be that Barbara has enjoyed the writing of this book almost as much as I, and that we stand firmly together in the sharing of whatever may have been achieved by it. She has taken full part in all field research, and read and criticized this manuscript" (1964, x).

This is no exception, to be sure, and you can recall, as well, Valetta Swann and Bronisław Malinowski in Mexico or the many ethnographic spousal duos, including Brenda and Charles Seligman, Bambi and Edward Schieffelin, and Michelle and Renato Rosaldo.[21]

In being transparent about Kerry's presence and impact, then, I mean to intervene in what Renato Rosaldo has so thoughtfully described as the "myth of the Lone Ethnographer" (1993, 30–34). The Lone Ethnographer, informed by "'his native' sidekick," passed on a "complicity with imperialism, a commitment to objectivism, and a belief in monumentalism" (Rosaldo 1993, 31). I don't mean to suggest that merely living with Kerry in Cuba or even reflecting critically on her presence accomplishes Rosaldo's aim of "remaking social analysis." Instead, I reflect on Kerry's presence—in concert with my relationship to Cuba and my commitments to critical and performance ethnography—to write from a place not of ethnographic authority but rather of sisterly complicity with Cuba's trans/queer culture workers, people who work every day to make life in Cuba more livable.

Transforming Cuba

The contours of transformismo in Cuba today depend on histories of economic transformation in the wake of the fall of the Soviet Union, liberal reform since the transfer of power between Fidel Castro and his brother Raúl Castro, and shifting official approaches to LGBT rights since at least 2008. Here, I will elaborate some of these processes and the ways they have been apprehended by critics on and off the island. This social and historical context will provide a foundation for understanding the observations about transformismo I will make in the chapters that follow.

The fall of socialism continues to structure everyday life in Cuba and the ways Cubans understand their material and political economic realities. Most immediately, the collapse of the Soviet Union led to the punishing scarcity of the Período Especial en Tiempos de Paz (Special Period in Times of Peace). In response to this crisis, the Cuban state began a process of dollarization, first accepting US dollars for payment and later creating a currency pegged to the US dollar. These processes gradually led to a system that continues to today in which Cubans' life chances and experiences vary drastically based on their access to foreign currency or lack thereof.

The liberalization efforts of the Cuban state further intensified under the leadership of Raúl Castro. This has been particularly felt in the growth and development of the tourism sector of Cuba's economy. Beginning roughly in 2006, as part of their "Actualización del modelo económico cubano" ("Update of the Cuban Economic Model"), the Cuban state turned more aggressively to foreign investment and tourism as a way to procure hard currency. Hotels were built in partnership with foreign corporations and took over entire coastal areas on the island as they also began to dot Cuba's major cities. A sprawling network of *casas particulares* and *paladares*—independently owned guest houses and restaurants, respectively—also developed over the last thirty years, and along with it a more informal economy grew to shuttle tourists about and attempt to capture some of their hard currency, too.

Critics of Cuba's postsocialist economic reform have linked these changes to the increasing racial, sexual, geographic, and economic inequity that has befallen Cuba over the last twenty years. Cultural critic Roberto Zurbano, part of a broader Afrodescendant movement on the island, argued that Cuba's dual economy—one operating in the local currency and the other in foreign ones—created "two contrasting realities," one in which white Cubans enjoyed access to capital from abroad and another where Black Cubans saw "a reversal or paralysis of the great social mobility that propelled them from 1959 to 1989" (2014, 71). Indeed, as tourism and remittances became the largest sectors of Cuba's economy, those with property and family abroad—who are overwhelmingly white—enjoyed relative prosperity, while those relying on the domestic economy (of whom a majority is Black) struggled to afford basic needs (see Espina Prieto 2010, 29–31). Cuban political economist Ailynn Torres Santana (2020, 12), moreover, has shown that while there is near gender parity in the state sector in Cuba, women are dramatically underrepresented in the much more lucrative private sector.

Cuba's Afrofeminist movement has provided holistic racial, sexual, and economic analyses of these reform projects that take aim at the historic and contemporary inequities that characterize Cuban society (Benson 2020, xix). Historian Devyn Spence Benson explains that groups like the Afrocubanas Project—a grassroots, community-based working group of Black and *mulata* women—emerged to "strategize about how to tackle the economic difficulties and racial discrimination that emerged during Cuba's economic crisis of the 1990s" (2020, xviii). "Black women in particular," she suggested, "were denied sought-after positions in the newly opened hotels because of their looks, and many were assumed to be prostitutes as sex tourism expanded on the island with white male foreigners looking to explore sexual fantasies with women of African descent" (Benson 2020, xix). At the same time, the imagery of Black and mixed-race women was used to sell Cuba to foreigners (Berry 2016, 25–26).

Almost coterminously with the expansion of the private sector, the Cuban state transformed its approach to LGBT rights as well. In 2008, CENESEX began to develop a more public presence advocating for LGBT social acceptance and political reform. They spearheaded the first Jornada, to coincide with the International Day Against Homophobia (IDAHO) in May, and unrolled their "campaña por el respeto a la libre orientación sexual" ("campaign for respect toward free sexual orientation"). This campaign, sometimes informally referred to as Cuba's "sexual revolution," involved various efforts to provide resources for trans and queer people, educate the public about trans/queer issues, and curb police repression of gender nonconformity. The recent passage of the new Código de la Familia in September 2022—which legalized same-sex marriage and single- and same-sex-parent adoption on the island—can be seen as part of the long arc of this campaign.

Critics of Cuba's so-called "sexual revolution" have suggested that it either coopts earlier grassroots trans/queer activism as its own or has less noble motivations than may be initially apparent, such as sanitizing Cuba's homophobic image to attract more tourism and foreign capital. Members of the Cuban hip-hop movement have argued that CENESEX ought to thank Afrofeminist culture workers, in particular the hip-hop duo Krudxs Cubensi, for introducing the social and ideological ingredients of sexual transformation on the island before they did (Saunders 2015, 297–99).[22] Other queer critics of Cuba and the Caribbean have suggested that the state-backed LGBT-rights movement is little more than a ploy to accumulate formerly ostracized Cubans within the aegis of the state or to rehabilitate Cuba's homophobic image abroad as it expands its tourism sector (e.g., Negrón-Muntaner 2008; Sierra Madero 2014).

Transformismo in particular offers a window into the ways the above transformations—both political economic and social—are linked. The spaces that host transformismo in coastal Havana, the subject of chapter 1, are both private and state-run establishments that cater to tourists and Cubans with access to foreign capital. By effectively decriminalizing trans/queer performance and bringing it above ground, then, the Cuban state has also turned it into a source of foreign capital. Simply put, the kinds of official transformismo spaces I will describe in chapter

1 would not be able to exist as they do without the tourism economy as it exists today.

Throughout *Transformismo*, I understand these kinds of spaces as part of an LGBT mainstream that includes but is not reducible to the state's "sexual revolution." This would certainly describe CENESEX and other state sexual diversity outfits, but it also encompasses the private establishments that cater to queer Cubans and foreigners in coastal Havana, the purveyors of LGBT-oriented tours and experiences in Cuba through platforms like Airbnb, and the discursive and aesthetic contents of other aboveground events and spaces.

In this way, the dominant LGBT terrain in Cuba begins to resemble its counterparts throughout the hemisphere: There is a kind of mainstream that coincides with the interests of the state and of capital, which in the Caribbean is inherently linked up with tourism economies. There is a familiar hierarchy between trans/queer people in this realm: white people, people with access to capital, and cisgender gay men see the benefits of these movements, while Afrodescendants, lesbians, poor people, geographically marginalized people, trans people who do not conform to respectable gender presentations, and others find themselves underrepresented, left behind, and left out.

Much as in the rest of the hemisphere, then, there are trans/queer people and organizations outside of the mainstream who are advocating for a more holistic liberation in the face of interlocking oppressions. Cuba's Afrofeminist/trans/queer projects in particular have spoken out about the shortcomings of mainstream approaches to LGBT rights on the island. In a profile of the group NOSOTRXS, for example, cofounder Afibola Sifunola explained that the collective emerged out of the cofounders' uneasy fit as Black nonbinary lesbian women within existing antiracist and LGBTIQ projects (*IPS Cuba* 2020). "Una gran parte de la comunidad LGBTIQ queda fuera," Sifunola explained; "se deja detrás a personas gordas, negras, más humildes, que viven en barrios periféricos, a quienes es necesario dar espacio y representatividad" (*IPS Cuba* 2020; "A large part of the LGBTIQ community is left out; fat people, Black women, poor people, those who live in peripheral neighborhoods are left behind, and they need to be given space and representation").[23]

In the face of these exclusions, NOSOTRXS articulates an alternative social, material, and political vision for the island. Cofounder Diarenis Calderon situated their Afro/queer feminist work within a broader context of social projects seeking to transform Cuba, describing their "visión ecológica, de paz y bienestar, orgullo de la comunidad, haciendo alianzas, identificando y denunciando actitudes patriarcales, racistas y fundamentalistas, y estableciendo puentes con otros proyectos y experiencias, brindando nuestra plataforma como escenario para sus quehaceres y procesos de formación" (*IPS Cuba* 2020; "ecological vision of peace and well-being; pride in community; forming alliances; identifying and denouncing patriarchal, racist, and fundamentalist attitudes; and establishing bridges with other projects and experiences, offering our platform as a stage for their work and development").

Throughout *Transformismo*, I am curious about the ways that trans/queer people create meaningful possibilities in the face of racial, sexual, spatial, and economic inequity that mainstream LGBT spaces, movements, and discourses fail or refuse to address. The majority of *Transformismo* documents these efforts, which provide resources for trans/queer Cubans on the margins of the tourism economy and offer new ways of understanding race, space, capital, and gender/sexuality.

Charting Transformismo

Transformismo is organized around the shortcomings of dominant LGBT spaces and discourses in Cuba and the kinds of possibilities that are engendered on the social, spatial, and economic margins of trans/queer life on the island. In chapter 1, I position the contemporary aboveground transformismo scene in coastal Havana in relation to Cuba's expanding tourism economy, offering both historical context and an elaboration of its contemporary forms. A brief genealogy of transformismo in Cuba since the 1950s shows that transformismo has long been caught up with negotiations with foreign capital, racialized performances of gender, and trans/queer world-making in the face of homo/transphobia. I then narrate a semifictional composite show that offers a window into the social, material, and aesthetic contents of the aboveground, official transformismo scene in coastal Havana. By coming with me to this show, you will gain further insight into the overlap between this scene and Cuba's tourism economy, both of which extract value from Black femininity while precluding Black women themselves from enjoying the profits generated in these sectors.

In chapters 2 and 3, I turn away from the tourism economy to see what work transformismo is doing in spaces oriented toward Cubans themselves. Chapter 2 focuses on transformismo in Havana's *repartos*, or peripheral neighborhoods, where I suggest that transformistas are providing affordable social and material sustenance to their fellow Cubans that affirms their racial, sexual, and economic positions on the island. I narrate three performances from two different parties in the region: one prominently and lovingly stages Afrocuban folkloric and religious performances for its patrons, another places value on—rather than extracting it from—trans/queer sociality and aesthetics, while a third stages performances of class that resonate with its local audience. All of them cater to the needs of Cubans of typical means, asserting their dignity in a context of increasing scarcity and precarity.

Chapter 3 moves to Villa Clara Province in central Cuba to discuss the ways transformistas there are blending Revolutionary discourses with trans/queer liberatory ideas to form unique and potent coalitions that exceed the limitations of mainstream LGBT spaces on the island.[24] First, I tell the story of El Mejunje, Cuba's oldest queer cultural organization, situating it and the work of its transformistas within the city of Santa Clara, the province of Villa Clara, and broader discussions about regionalism in Cuban and trans/queer studies. I then take you to a handful of performances in Villa Clara Province: A night at El Mejunje elaborates the ideological underpinnings that inform Santa Clara's transformistas, while a show in rural Remate de Ariosa demonstrates how they build solidarity between the city and the rest of the province. Performances at a new party in the center of Santa Clara and at a sparkling outdoor nightclub on the city's periphery further show how the ideas that shape El Mejunje radiate outward to encourage intergenerational coalitions that offer vital trans/queer lifeways.

Chapters 4 and 5 discuss the work of Black transgender and lesbian transformistas, respectively, to consider how they are thinking beyond the limitations of mainstream understandings of sexual subjectivity and politics in Cuba. In chapter 4, I draw on the self-narrations of three Black transgender transformistas to describe how their conceptions of trans subjectivity exceed dominant understandings through their flexibility and fluidity, their reliance on performance and labor, and their relationship to racial and economic formations. I offer some background regarding the terms of trans/queer subjectivity on the island, and I locate debates about the relationship between transformismo and transness within broader discussions about gender and sexuality as categories. I suggest that transgender transformistas' creative negotiations of existing categories offer novel ways of navigating and understanding sexual selfhood for trans people.

Chapter 5 considers the work of Havana's transformistas masculinos, positioning their Black lesbian feminist vision within broader trends of Afrofeminist/trans/queer artist-activism that challenge dominant antiracist and LGBT rights discourses in Cuba. I elaborate Argelia's trajectory as a transformista and discuss her collaborative work with other Black lesbian and transmasculine performers in Havana. In particular, I describe the ways transformistas masculinos are promoting Black lesbian women's visibility in Cuba, cultivating sorely needed space for Black lesbian women, and articulating a coalitional politics that connects the demands of Black lesbian women to broader efforts toward social and economic equity on the island. I suggest, then, that their work resonates with Afrofeminist and Afrolesbian activism in the Caribbean and throughout the Americas.

Finally, in the coda I fast forward and zoom out to discuss the futures that have come thus far for the transformistas who populate this book and suggest that their work offers insight into some possibilities for a hemispheric trans/queer liberation that exceeds the limitations of dominant LGBT rights discourses. I describe the ways that the COVID-19 pandemic, the July 11 protests, and the explosion of immigration out of Cuba have affected Cuba's transformistas. Then I situate their work within related efforts elsewhere in the Americas that narrate a trans/queer politics that is always tethered to broader investments in racial, sexual, and political economic transformation throughout the hemisphere. In all, I ask what trans/queer people throughout the hemisphere might learn from Cuba's transformistas as we try to foment more liberatory trans/queer futures.

Before we go on, however, I want to reflect briefly on some of the work that I intend for *Transformismo* to do. More than anything, I have written *Transformismo*, as one mentor counseled, with a younger version of myself in mind. I hope that young diasporic trans/queer readers will see themselves and their questions reflected here, and that the book will serve as one helpful tool in their own political and intellectual conscientization. In particular, *Transformismo* suggests that social and political leadership is likely to come from places that dominant forces will say lack value or relevance. Mainstream liberal discourses might tell us that trans people, Black people, or poor people are an inconvenience or a nuisance. Some diasporic Cubans will suggest that there is nothing worth looking for back on the island. Indeed, all of these are precisely the sites *Transformismo* looks to for guidance on trans/queer liberation.

This suggestion does not just resonate in the diaspora, however, but has work to do on the island as well. So often I see queer people in Cuba question and critique Afroqueer activists, unwilling to contend with the racial history of their island. Just as often, others have told me that there is nothing of value in the queer nightclubs I was going to or especially the parties in the repartos. *Transformismo* demonstrates that vital work is being carried out by such people in such spaces, work that has the capacity to overcome dominant LGBT rights discourses' inabilities to answer for the complexities of postsocialist economic policy, trans/lesbophobia, the legacy of slavery, and the pall of US imperialism as they pertain to everyday life in Cuba. In *Transformismo*, I turn in particular to the Afro-feminist/trans/queer movement for an autochthonous and grassroots mode of critique that apprehends Cuba's history while striving to make real, embedded interventions that promise better futures to all Cubans.

CHAPTER 1

Las Vegas

Transformismo and Cuba's Capital

I felt like a bit of a star myself, standing next to the gorgeous and towering Devora, the transformista who seemed to be performing everywhere in Havana at the time. She had invited me and Kerry to join her and her boyfriend at Cabaret Las Vegas after our interview with her in October 2017. There we were, lingering in the back of the club, chatting and watching the show, when about halfway through Maridalia took the stage. One of the most enduring transformistas in Cuba, Maridalia has been working as a transformista for more than 30 years. You can see her in her early days in the now-classic documentary *Mariposas en el andamio* (1995), and just as she did back then, Maridalia still carries around a live mic for her performances so she can sing along with her formidable voice when she wants to, booming over the recorded artist. That day at Las Vegas, this was the Mexican pop singer Yuridia and her version of "Así fue," originally written by Mexican icon Juan Gabriel to be sung by Spanish diva Isabel Pantoja.

Early in the song, Maridalia descended from the stage to work the audience. She inched gingerly down the handful of steps, gathering one side of her long, dark brown dress to expose her low heels. Once a slight vixen, she is now a full-figured veteran. Her gown showed off a tasteful amount of her chest, lace covered her shoulders and her arms to the wrist, and her dark brown wig was gathered in a sizeable updo.

Everywhere—neck, ears, wrists, fingers—sparkling jewels caught the stage lights. With the mic to her lips, Maridalia sang along with Yuridia while walking around to perform to each of the men seated in the front row. Like many of Juan Gabriel and Pantoja's collaborations, "Así fue" was a popular song among transformistas in Cuba, capturing both the *balada's* recollections of transnational *bolero* and Pantoja's flamenco-inflected vocal stylings to reflect both Cuba's place in Latin America and its European aspirations. The lyrics speak to a lover who has moved on and is urging her ex to do the same. In the context of a state-run gay nightclub in a city where not long ago transformismo was hotly persecuted, it almost seemed as though Maridalia was imploring her homeland to get over its own tortured relationship with trans/queer people.

Standing next to Devora, who was at the forefront of the younger generation, I appreciated the massive transformation that had taken place so that we could all be in this establishment as we were. If, in the days of *Mariposas*, Maridalia practiced her art under the constant threat of police repression and jail time, here she was performing as a marquee artist at a state-run nightclub. Back then, merely having lipstick in your possession as a *maricón* (faggot) was justification for arrest; that night, Devora could safely walk to Cabaret Las Vegas done up beautifully, with a long curly wig, full face makeup, a revealing dress, and us—her trans/queer retinue—in tow.

Still, something was amiss. Next to us, a young, dark-skinned femme was seated with a gruff, older Italian man in what seemed to be a primarily economic arrangement. The charge for the cover and the drinks at the establishment was far beyond the means of ordinary Cubans. Moments earlier, two other transformistas had performed a number that relied on Afrocuban religious performance as the butt of a joke, offering a little local culture to make the predominantly foreign audience laugh. And the place is, to be fair, a bit of a dump. How did we get here, and—wherever we are—is this really progress?

In this chapter, I ask how a space like Las Vegas came to exist and describe the social place of nightclubs like Las Vegas in contemporary Cuba. I suggest that mainstream transformismo spaces—much like the tourism economy that makes them possible—rely on the labor and creativity of racially, sexually, and economically marginalized people while reproducing the same racial, sexual, and economic exclusions and inequities that have characterized Cuba since the fall of socialism. First, I offer a genealogy of the contemporary scene that draws from the queer historiography of Cuba, accounts by Cuban cultural critics, and my own ethnographic research. This historical narrative highlights the ways that transformismo has long vacillated between underground and official spaces, always doing different kinds of social and political economic work in each.

I then turn to the mainstream contemporary scene, weaving together a composite show that draws from my participation in twenty or so *fiestas gay* in the nightclubs that dot Havana's coastal neighborhoods. This night out demonstrates the ways that, while this scene does indeed sanction trans/queer space in the center of Havana, transformismo in mainstream shows is also often caught up with the exploitative imagery and economic exclusions of the tourism economy. To attend to the interlocking racial, sexual, economic, and aesthetic dimensions of this scene, I rely on insights from trans/queer-of-color critique and Black music criticism: The former provides a framework for understanding both the social exclusions that structure gay space (Bailey 2014, 490) and the shortcomings of revolutionary nationalism as a vehicle for trans/queer liberation (Ferguson 2003, 3–4). The latter situates transformismo within a hemispheric context in which Black women's voices define national culture while Black women themselves are disregarded in national projects (e.g., Tate 2003, 4).[1]

Though I offer in-depth readings of particular performances, these are not meant to be indictments of the specific artists I introduce. Instead, they are intended to situate these performances within the broader social context and political economy of transformismo, which is irrevocably tied up with Cuba's tourism economy, its racial and sexual imagery, and the inequity it extends. This chapter, then, provides the social, aesthetic, and historical backdrop against which the people and scenes I describe in the rest of the book, ones that emerge and work primarily outside of the tourism economy, ought to be understood.

Transformismo's Roots and Routes

Let me begin again, almost sixty years before the show that opened this chapter, on another night at Cabaret Las Vegas. In May 1958, Oscar took Mirta out for an early celebration of her twenty-seventh birthday. Mirta's mother Amparo came over to watch their two kids at their apartment on Calle Humboldt, and they all had dinner together at home before Oscar and Mirta took the short walk to Cabaret Las Vegas on Calle Infanta. Oscar put his arm across the small of Mirta's back as they turned onto

Calle P just one block from the nightclub, and he kissed her reflexively as they got in the short line outside the entrance. Once they made their way to the host, they asked for their friend Julio, the busboy who had agreed to get them in at a reduced price. Though Oscar made enough money to support them by working for a US oil company, there wasn't an abundance left over after the costs of raising two children and paying rent in El Vedado.

Before long, Julio ushered them past the bar and seated them with another couple at a table at some remove from the stage. Oscar ordered a rum for himself and a light Cristal beer for Mirta while they made small talk with their tablemates. Just after 1 a.m., the orchestra started to ready itself, and then the sinuous trumpet sounds of the band's leader Rolando "El Ruso" Aguiló rose above the ensemble. Aguiló had been born in Matanzas in the same year as Mirta, and he had just played in the orchestra at the famous Cabaret Tropicana for the tremendously popular visits of Nat King Cole to the island's capital. The reedy voice of Juana Bacallao complemented his brassy horn, as she launched in to her eponymous guaracha "Yo soy Juana Bacallao."

Over the applause at the end of the number, the emcee—comedian Eddy Cabrera—welcomed the audience to the show. He announced the night's cast: a singer, a burlesque performer, a couple of dancers, and, finally, "el transformista chino" Madame Musmé. Cabrera did some light crowd work, asking a foreign couple where they were from, and another Cuban couple what they were celebrating. Mirta and Oscar were far enough away from the stage that they escaped his attention. Then she came on.

La China Musmé, as she was sometimes known, was one of the most celebrated transformistas of the 1950s in Havana. Arriving at the nightclub as a slight Chinese Cuban man with his pants above his waist, he would transform backstage into an enviable beauty (Ramírez 2010a). That night, he sang with his own voice over Aguiló's capable band, his soaring countertenor enchanting with the lilting bolero "Flor de Yumurí" by Cuban pianist Jorge Anckermann.[2] The bass player complemented Musmé with a gentle habanera rhythm as she sang, "Flor de Yucayo, la bella / al nacer me ha copiado / Yumurí en su cristal" ("Flower of Yucayo, the beautiful / Yumurí copied me at birth / in its crystal").[3]

This semifictional narrative, this critical fabulation, recalls the vibrant transformismo scene of Havana in the 1950s, underscores the centrality of performances of racialized gender to transformismo historically, and situates myself within the study at hand.[4] Though I don't know whether my abuelos Mirta and Oscar went to Cabaret Las Vegas in May 1958, they did go to other nightclubs in their neighborhood in El Vedado, and Musmé really did perform at Cabaret Las Vegas that month in a show that sounded a lot like the one I narrated (*Show* 1958, 74; see figure 2). There is a strange continuity, then, between my ancestors' presence and mine, Musmé and Maridalia, Yumurí and Yuridia. Here, I offer an overview of what happened in between, with attention to the ways transformismo has persistently moved between underground and official spaces, serving distinct social, political, and economic roles in each. A thorough history of transformismo is beyond the scope of this book; instead, I insert transformismo in the already-developed queer historiography of Cuba. In doing so, I show that transformismo has a long history of providing sustenance to marginalized trans/queer Cubans during times of persecution. At the same time, transformismo has at various points come aboveground, too, and there it tends to become entangled with foreign capital and the complex influence it has had throughout Cuba's history.

Long before Musmé, as in other parts of the Americas and the world, travestismo—or cross-dressing—was a prominent feature of various artistic scenes in Cuba in the late 19th and early 20th centuries. Jill Lane (2005, 117) discusses José Candiani's cross-dressed performance as a "comic, crass guajira" in the plays of Juan José Guerrero in the 1870s. Early in the next century, the rumba craze that swept through Cuba was launched by Rita Montaner's performance of "Ay Mamá Inés" in the zarzuela *La Niña Rita o La Habana en 1830*, for which she was not only in blackface but also cross-dressed as the stock character of the "negrito."[5] And Cuban historian Abel Sierra Madero (2020) has discussed the warm reception in the magazine *Social* of cross-dressed Peking opera performer Mei Lanfang in the 1920s.

Notice, then, how the history of travestismo in Cuba is caught up with racial formations and political economic transformation: The plays Lane analyzes were part of a broader fabric of *teatro bufo* that was acting out Spanish colonialism, Cuban independence, and the persistence of slavery.[6] Blackface, Lane further explains, "is the frame through which Asians enter representation in Cuba" (2008, 1729). During my research for this book, numerous cultural critics, transformistas, and audience members offered each of these scenes, as well as Carnaval and Afrocuban religious performance, as origin stories for transformismo—it, too, is imbricated in Cuba's history of colonization, slavery, and coerced migration.

Though travestismo was an acceptable element of turn-of-the-century

PALERMO Club

Amistad y San Miguel. Teléfono M-5058. Orquesta Alfredo Farach, dirigida por Carlos Argibay, Jr. Horas del Show: 11:30 p.m. y 2:30 a.m. Elenco artístico: La exquisita cancionera Marta Rabell; Ana María Guerra, vedette; Noemí y Marianela, pareja de danzas típicas y la animación a cargo del imitador Delio Otero.

Casino NACIONAL

San Rafael y Prado. Tel. M-9296. Gran orquesta dirigida por Peruchín y Conjunto de Nelo Sosa. Horas del Show: 10:30 p.m. y 1:30 a.m., los sábados, a las 10:30 p.m., 12:30 y 2:30 a.m. Elenco artístico: Una revista de Gustavo Roig titulada "El Último Cuplé", con el aporte estelar de Wilfredo Fernández, Rosa Elena Miró, Imperio Aragón, la pareja típica Nancy-Guille y la de género español Lolita y Reyes, coro y modelos.

PANCHIN Club

Playa de Marianao. Teléf. B-7794. Orquesta California Swing, dirigida por Arturo Mesa. Horas del Show: 11 y media p.m. con excepción de los sábados a las 12 de la noche y el segundo show invariablemente a las 2 y media a.m. Elenco artístico: El notable actor Luis Cabeiro con sus imitaciones humorísticas y animador del espectáculo; la pareja típica Kary y Miguelito; Lourdes Torres, magnífica cancionera; Lilliam Vasallo, escultural vedette y el debut del gran transformista Madame Pompadour.

SIERRA Club

Concha y Cristina. Teléf. X-2928. Orquesta Habana-Arias, dirigida por Pablo Arias y Conjunto "Sierra Club". Horas del Show: 12:40 y $10 a.m. Elenco artístico: Celeste Mendoza, cantante de estilo original, en sus interpretaciones del auténtico guaguancó; Thaís solista de género español; Luis García, cancionero; Hermanos Torres, acróbatas; Doris and Robert, sensacional pareja de bailes internacionales y el Tony's Trio, cultores de danzas típicas.

ALI BAR Club

Avenida de Dolores y Carretera de Lucero. Orquesta Antillana de Moisés Alfonso. Horas del Show: 12:30 y 3:30 a.m. Elenco artístico: Benny Moré, el Bárbaro del Ritmo; Roberto Faz y su Conjunto; Orlando Vallejo, cancionero; Fernando Alvarez, cancionero; Conchita Fuster, cancionera; Marta Castillo y Rolando Espinosa, famosa pareja típica; Ñico Menviela, cancionero, y Roberto Jaramil, animador y cantante.

RUMBA Palace

5ª Avenida y Calle 116 (Playa de Marianao). Teléf. B-7880. Orquesta de Raúl Diñigo. Horas del Show: 10:30 p.m. y 1:30 a.m., los sábados y domingos, 10:30 p.m., 12:15 a.m. y 2 a.m. Elenco artístico: Wilfredo Rosabal, cancionero; Loreta Quintana, cancionera; Omar Ferrán, transformista; Rubén Duval, transformista; Los Juniors, Trio de bailes internacionales; Manela y Carlos de Granados, pareja española y la aplaudida pareja típica Gladys y El Kid, dos colosos del mambo y de la rumba.

PENNSYLVANIA

Playa de Marianao. Cabaret y Restaurant. Tel. B9-1044. Orquesta de Rafael Rivero. Horas del Show: 10:15, 1:30 y 2:30 de la madrugada. Elenco artístico: Lina Hernán, vedette; Imperio y Rodolfo Quirós, estampas españolas; Mario y Pitucha, pareja de género típico, y Manolo Barnet, cantante y animador.

LAS VEGAS Club

Infanta y 25. Orquesta de Rolando Aguiló con su cantante "Cuchungo". Horas del Show: 1 y 4 a.m. Elenco artístico: Madame Musmé, transformista chino con sus cantos y bailes; Juana Bacallao, vedette; Eddy Cabrera, animador y scketchs cómicos; Roxana, strep; Tony and Daisy, pareja típica y la dirección artística a cargo del coreógrafo Joseíto Suárez.

74—SHOW

Fig. 2. Advertisements for cabaret performances from *Show* (vol. 5, no. 51 [May 1958]). In the bottom right, an image of Madame Musmé. Transformistas Omar Ferrán, Rubén Duval, and Madame Pompadour are mentioned throughout. (Courtesy of the Cuban Heritage Collection, University of Miami.)

theater, Cuba's narrating class was certainly not accommodating of queerness and gender nonconformity in everyday life.[7] Gender inversion, in concert with blackness and miscegenation, was a source of considerable medical and juridical panic in 19th-century Cuba (see Sierra Madero 2006, 23–52; Blanco Borelli 2016, 18, 35–36).[8] The case of Enriqueta Favez, a lesbian woman who lived her life as a man and was sentenced to four years in a psychiatric hospital in 1823 and later deported, is evidence of how Cuban officialdom treated gender transgression.[9] And in the 1920s, while writers in *Social* were praising Mei Lanfang, others in mainstream magazines like *La Semana* and *Carteles* pronounced themselves against the phenomena of *pepillismo* and *garzonismo*, gender nonconformity in men and women, respectively (see Sierra Madero 2006, 81–138).

At the same time, sites of travestismo were forming outside of mainstream theater scenes, sometimes with specifically queer contours. Sierra Madero tells the story, for example, of the Bataclán Universitario, a performance troupe active in the 1920s that was made up of students from the University of Havana. In their frequent use of travestismo, Sierra Madero suggests, they cultivated a queer space, and the extant texts from their performances "ridiculizan la subjetividad burguesa e instituciones como el matrimonio, al turista estadounidense y hacen guiños constantes a la cultura francesa y europea" (2020; "ridicule bourgeois subjectivity and institutions like marriage, US tourists, and they wink constantly to French and European culture"). By the 1930s, transformistas were even included in certain variety shows in the popular cabarets in Havana, while still others cross-dressed and performed undetected as models or members of the choruses in these shows (Ramírez 2010a). In her brief but substantive history of transformismo in Cuba, feminist journalist Marta María Ramírez (2010a) recalls one of her interlocutors seeing cross-dressed men in Havana's Carnavales in the 1940s as well.

If these early examples of transformismo remained somewhat clandestine, by the 1950s transformistas had become a fixture of Havana's prominent cabaret scene. Ramírez (2010a) quotes singer Lourdes Torres, who was active during this time, as saying, "Era raro cabaret de segunda—que no era un tugurio—que no tuviera un transformista en su elenco" ("It was unusual for a mid-level cabaret—that wasn't a total dive—*not* to have a transformista in its cast"). In his anthology dedicated to Cuban nightlife from 1920 to 1960, Cuban musician Bobby Collazo (1987, 324–25) lists ten active transformistas during the 1950s, separated into those who primarily sang and those who primarily danced. Magazines from the era like *Show* and *Carteles* list transformistas as part of several well-known shows in the city, often featuring pictures of them in drag. As you already know, famous among them was Madame Musmé.

In the wake of the Cuban Revolution, these shows were shuttered by the new government, seen as a prominent symbol of the bourgeois, capitalist, and exploitive excesses of US imperialism on the island. Literary scholar Emilio Bejel (2001, 97) suggests that this era was characterized by a "purging of vices" on the part of government officials, aimed purportedly at tackling corruption on the island spurred on by US power. In practice, however, the threat of US imperialism "lent itself perfectly to abuses of power by *machistas* obsessed with power and control" (Bejel 2001, 97). At the same time that the government offered economic opportunities for sex workers, who they depicted as victims of US exploitation, it also cracked down on queer people.[10] As Bejel notes, "[p]rostitution, drug addiction, and homosexuality were strongly associated with one another in the Cuban cultural imagination, and several revolutionary leaders exploited this situation for their own political objectives" (2001, 97). Musmé herself fled Cuba in 1961 in the midst of this context (Ramírez 2010b).

This wave of repression culminated in the creation of the Unidades Militares de Ayuda a la Producción (UMAP, Military Units to Aid Production) in the central Cuban province of Camagüey in 1965. The Revolutionary government sent various figures deemed to be outside the realm of social acceptability—including trans/queer people, religious people, and Afrodescendent intellectuals—to these Soviet-style reeducation centers in which, not unlike in the gulag system, they would do hard agricultural labor in order to transform their unfavorable orientations.[11] Bejel (2001, 100) describes conditions that were so dismal that officials responsible for them were later executed.

If the UMAP camps were in many ways the height of trans/queer oppression at the hands of the Revolutionary government, they were also the site, according to Ramírez (2010b), for the renewal of transformismo as a theater of resistance. There, trans and queer people would use whatever they could get their hands on to put on shows that, like the cabarets of the 1950s, included an opening number, singers, models, dancers, an announcer, an invited artist, and a grand finale (Ramírez 2010b). Exiled playwright Héctor Santiago explained to Ramírez that "toallas, sábanas, mosquiteros y sacos de diferentes materiales se convirtieron en copias de glamorosos vestidos" (2010b; "towels, sheets, mosquito nets, and sacks of different materials became copies of glamorous dresses"), dyed with mercurochrome or gentian violet. Ropes turned into wigs, and makeup was either brought in on family visits or improvised from bricks, talc mixed with annatto powder, or shoe polish turned into mascara (Ramírez 2010b). Musical accompaniment was provided in the form of vocals supported by a percussion section of wooden boxes, aluminum cans, spoons, agricultural tools, and sticks (Ramírez 2010b).

One unintended impact of the UMAP camps, then, was to bring the cabaret shows outside the realm of capitalist excess and into a trans/queer underworld. Moreover, queer Cuban critics have suggested that the UMAP camps fomented a kind of social and political consciousness among queer people on the island. Ramírez describes the camps as a zone of interclass contact, where "[h]omosexuales marginales, procedentes de clases medias, bajas y pobres o del mundo carcelario, se unieron a la homosexualidad educada, refinada e instruida" (2010b; "marginal homosexuals, middle- and low-class and poor, or from the carceral world, gathered with the educated, refined, and informed homosexual class"). Tomás Fernández Robaina asserts that while certain political, intellectual, and artistic elites were spared confinement in the UMAP camps, the centers did unite those who had tried to hide their sexual preferences as well as those who were more openly queer. As a result, Fernández Robaina suggests, "en la mayoría de los homosexuales surgió un sentido de pertenencia, de identificación absoluta con su sexualidad, con la comprensión y el convencimiento total, en muchos de ellos, que de nada valía el ocultamiento, la simulación" (2005; "there arose in the majority of the homosexuals a sense of belonging, of absolute identification with their sexuality, with the total understanding and conviction, in many of them, that nothing was worth hiding, pretending").

When the UMAP camps closed in 1968, in the face of international criticism, the Revolutionary government shifted to other tactics for queer containment and control. Historians of race and sex in Cuba associate the 1970s with the "quinquenio gris" (gray or dark five years), which saw the "parametración," the marginalization or ostracism, of elements seen to challenge the dominant ideology of the Revolution, especially Afrodescendants and trans/queer people.[12] In effect, this time period turned to social marginalization in much the way that the UMAP camps had deployed material marginalization. Fernández Robaina (2005) explains that homosexuality during this period was treated as an illness at odds with Cuba's socialist project. In 1968, the Primer Congreso de Educación y Cultura (First Congress on Education and Culture) stated clearly that homosexuals in the artistic and cultural sphere constituted a threat both to the nations' youth and to the moral image of the Revolution abroad, leading to the removal of many queer people from official posts and the flight of many queer people from the island (Fernández Robaina 2005). That same meeting vilified "the work of black intellectuals, like Walterio Carbonell, who had fought to insert the history of Africa and blacks in Cuba into the public school curriculum" (Benson 2016, 235).

As such, transformismo stayed underground for these years, flourishing in private house parties on the outskirts of the city (Ramírez 2010c; Pérez 1996). As in the UMAP camps, transformistas converted household items into the primary materials for blush, eyeshadow, and eyeliner (Pérez 1996, 3C). Cuban diasporic journalist Daniel Fernández cites two documentaries from this period—*El discreto encanto del transformismo* and *Un episodio en la vida de Truca Pérez*—and recounts that, in a testament to the climate of this era, both films were confiscated from him by state security in Cuba in 1978, and he was sentenced to four years in prison for having them in his possession (Pérez 1996).

But the end of the 1970s also saw certain openings in official discourses around sexual diversity. After having formed as a subgroup of the Federación de Mujeres Cubanas (Federation of Cuban Women, FMC) in 1972, the Grupo Nacional de Trabajo de Educación Sexual (National Working Group on Sex Education, GNTES)—which would eventually form the basis for the establishment of CENESEX in 1989—became its own state organization in 1977. Radical East German literature on sexual diversity influenced the group, which started adopting attitudes and strategies toward transness and queerness that, for a state institution, were ahead of their time (see Roque Guerra 2011, 222). This, too, faced tension within the Revolutionary government. Though Cuban surgeons performed the first gender-affirming genital surgery in 1986, pressure from the state in the face of possible public backlash halted further efforts (Castro 2017, 105–6).[13]

The 1980s brought new episodes of trans/queer fugitivity and sequestration. During the Mariel boatlift, in which roughly 124,000 Cubans immigrated to the US, Fidel Castro used the idea of gender-nonconforming people to animate a picture of the kinds of 'undesirables' who had abandoned the Revolution (Capó 2010). Among those who left was Cuban transformista Julie Mastrozzimone, who would become a key presence in the drag scene in Miami (Peña 2013, 160–64).[14]

Then, in 1986, to mitigate the global HIV/AIDS epidemic, the Cuban state enforced a compulsory quarantine for HIV-positive individuals, which lasted until 1994. The institutions in this national network of sanatoriums, too, became "verdaderos centros de transformismo" (Ramírez 2010c; "veritable centers of transformismo"). The Los Cocos sanatorium—in Santiago de las Vegas, situated on the outskirts of the province of La Habana—served as the capital city's site, and it was there that the nurse Guillermo Ginestá began impersonating Gunilla von Bismarck, the German countess known for her participation in Spanish social life. Ramírez (2010c) credits Ginestá with the rebirth of transformismo, breathing life into the performance complex that would sustain it in the coming decades.

Just as Cuba was navigating the HIV/AIDS epidemic, however, the fall of the Soviet Union irrevocably transformed Cuban society. As I discussed in the introduction, Cuba entered what is known as the Período Especial (Special Period) during which it saw devastating economic shrinkage and punishing material scarcity.[15] Everyone I know who was in Cuba during the Special Period has some harrowing story they retell with a mixture of trauma and humor: some people raised hens clandestinely on their rooftops for eggs, others fried grapefruit rinds in place of pork cutlets, while others recall buying pizzas with condoms arranged on top in place of cheese. As you will recall from the introduction, the economic crisis of the Special Period paved the way for economic liberalization and the state's eventual turn to tourism for hard currency.

Paradoxically, transformistas today routinely describe the Special Period as the golden era of transformismo, and the 1990s and early 2000s saw a veritable explosion of artists, venues, and culture surrounding the performance complex. During this period, a semi-clandestine network of trans/queer parties featuring transformismo sprouted all over Havana. Trans and queer people would spread the word about so-called "fiestas de diez pesos" (ten-dollar parties) in barely secret locations where they would gather.[16] By 1993, Ramírez (2010c) estimates that roughly 100 transformistas were active in Havana, grouped into various performance troupes. Beyond Havana, this era also saw the birth of El Mejunje, Cuba's first queer cultural center, in Santa Clara, which I will discuss in depth in chapter 3. In 1996, the Miami Spanish-language newspaper *El Nuevo Herald* suggested, in fact, that "En todas las provincias de Cuba se celebran, con gran aplauso del público, y bajo 'la vista gorda' de las autoridades, los festivales de travestismo" (Pérez 1996, 3C; "in all the provinces of Cuba, to great applause from audiences, and under 'the blind eye' of the authorities, festivals of transvestism are celebrated").

This era was rife with contradictions: The transformismo movement—with all of the fabric, accessories, and sound equipment it required—

flourished in a time of extreme material scarcity. Its scale meant it was an open secret, and yet the scene was under constant threat of police repression. Nevertheless, transformistas today lovingly recall the performances and aesthetics of this time period. During my research for this book, it seemed as though the bonds formed by facing repression together and the exceptional creativity in the face of scarcity lent a lasting golden aura to this moment.

The documentary *Mariposas en el andamio* (1995) offers a window into the shape and meaning of transformismo in this era. When the police shut down a house party featuring transformismo in the Black, working-class La Güinera neighborhood, a worker at a nearby construction site arranged to have them perform at the workers' cafeteria.[17] The improvised cabaret led to surprising solidarities between faithful Revolutionaries and the trans/queer subjects the Revolution deemed unworthy. The aesthetics of the scene—improvised material culture, boundless drama, local music, and transnational longing—all continue to shape transformismo today. Watching *Mariposas*, you get a sense of the punishing social stigma transformistas faced as well as the intricate and life-affirming networks they nonetheless built.

The 1995 Festival de Transformismo Gunilla further demonstrated the tensions between transformistas and Cuban officials during this time. For that competition, thousands of people gathered outside of the centrally located, 1,700-seat Teatro América to watch nine transformistas compete for the title Miss Gunilla, in honor of the aforementioned Ginestá, who had died that year with AIDS. Major state-sanctioned artists served as the jury: Miguel Barnet, author and winner of the Premio Nacional de Literatura in 1994; Senel Paz, author of the short story on which the classic queer film *Fresa y chocolate* (1993) is based; and the singer Soledad Delgado (Ramírez 2010c). An official from the Ministerio de Cultura opened the event, suggesting that the "travesti movement" could not be ignored by the Revolution (Pérez 1996, 3C). But as soon as the multi-night event had started, it was shut down without explanation (Pérez 1996, 3C). Other parties were subject to frequent raids by the police, and indeed every transformista I spoke with who was active during this time recalled running from the police with her heels in one hand and her wig in the other. In 1997, the underground gay club El Perequitón in the Marianao neighborhood was memorably raided on a night when Spanish filmmaker Pedro Almodóvar, Spanish actress Bibi Andersen, and French fashion designer Jean Paul Gaultier were in attendance (Ramírez 2010c).

In response to this repressive environment, and in the absence of sustained official support for trans/queer social life, grassroots movements grew to address the social and political persecution of trans/queer people. Tomás Fernández Robaina (2005) recalls the pathbreaking work of the Organización Nacional de Entendidos (ONE), which would organize parties that featured transformismo throughout Havana and published the quarterly magazine *Hola Gente*. That organization collapsed in 2001, however, when one of its members was picked up in a routine detention by police officers, who confiscated materials that revealed its existence and the location of its events (Fernández Robaina 2005). That same year, the iconic transformista Kiriam protested outside of CENESEX along with 42 other travestis demanding that they act in the face of this kind of police repression of trans/queer people. Kiriam went on to found the Proyecto TransCuba that year, which she ran until 2007 and through which she taught roughly twenty travestis to perform as transformistas as an economic alternative to sex work.

Cuba's hip-hop movement, too, was a site for pathbreaking trans/queer political action and worldmaking. In particular, the work of Krudxs Cubensi—who started performing as a hip-hop ensemble in 2000—brought a trenchant critique of Cuban society that integrated Cuba's trans/queer movement with histories of Afrofeminism to mount a vision of the island that transcended its white supremacy, machismo, and trans/homophobia (Saunders 2015, 297–99). The members of Krudxs Cubensi participated in the creation in 2005 of Grupo OREMI, an organization devoted to the social and political aims of lesbian and bisexual women, particularly those who identified as Black (Saunders 2009, 169–70; 2015, 299). OREMI served as a key site for the political organizing of what would eventually become the transformismo masculino movement in Havana, which I discuss in chapter 5. Overwhelmed by the social demands of this group and its reception by the Cuban public, however, CENESEX restricted its support of the group after a few months (Saunders 2009, 170).

As I suggested in the introduction, the year 2008 was something a turning point for official engagement with sexual diversity, one that would have profound implications for transformismo on the island.[18] That year, CENESEX began recognizing and celebrating the International Day Against Homophobia with its own Jornada Contra la Homofobia and rolling out its campaign La Diversidad es Natural (Diversity is Natural). This would form the basis of their sexual-diversity rhetoric for years to come and, among other things, led the Ministerio de Cultura in

2010 to consent to a transformismo show in a state-run establishment, the Cabaret Las Vegas in El Vedado (González González 2014, 10). Literary critic Rubén Gallo has suggested that Cabaret Las Vegas, then, just might be "the only gay bar in the world that was opened by military decree" (2022).

Other shows soon followed, and by the time I started traveling to Cuba in 2015, a sprawling network of state-run and privately owned restaurants and nightclubs featured transformismo in fiestas gay throughout the city and on various nights of the week. Legal problems persisted, in the sense that almost no transformistas had standing as state-affiliated artists, and thus could not be hired legally to perform in state-run venues, but clearly the official attitude toward trans/queer performance had shifted. Unlike in the 1990s, parties were public knowledge, with large placards outside of nightclubs advertising the transformistas who would be performing on any given night.

The same time period witnessed Cuba's economic liberalization in the wake of the fall of the Soviet Union, including the efforts to capture more foreign currency through the expansion of the tourism economy. These transformations, as I discussed in the introduction, have further widened racial, economic, and sexual inequities that were addressed by the Revolution and have been festering since the fall of socialism. If transformismo came aboveground thanks to the successes of grassroots organizations and sympathetic state actors (like the early GNTES workers), it landed in the middle of this tourism economy.[19] In what follows, I discuss how this proximity influences the social, material, and aesthetic contents of transformismo in mainstream spaces in contemporary coastal Havana.

"¡Bienvenidos al Divino Show!"

Yunior had been telling me for weeks that he wanted to go out to a fiesta gay with us, so Kerry and I invited him out one Friday night in the fall of 2017. We told him to come to our place first, and he said he would bring his friend Armando, a connoisseur of transformismo. They arrived around 10 p.m., and we poured them both sips of rum while we sat down to catch up.

"Bueno, ¿adónde vamos a ir esta noche?" ("Well, where are we going tonight?") I asked eventually.

"¿Las Vegas?" Yunior offered, still the go-to gay nightclub for transformismo in Havana, just a couple of blocks from Kerry's and my apartment.

"Well, it's Friday, so we could go to Karabalí," Armando reminded.

"¡Ay, qué bajeza! ¡Vámonos!" ("How filthy! Let's go!") Yunior replied, assenting to the plan.

Armando was referring to the fact that, while Las Vegas featured a fiesta gay with transformismo every night, most other nightclubs only had such parties on certain nights of the week. The parties themselves were actually "proyectos" or "projects," a discrete group of performers, organized by an artistic director, that appeared in different nightclubs each weekend night. So, whereas Proyecto Bravissimo had a fixed place at Cabaret Las Vegas every night of the week, Proyecto Divino would be at Karabalí on Friday night and then on Saturdays at Café Cantante, the nightclub underneath the Teatro Nacional. Certain proyectos were associated with particular transformistas, and each had its own flavor. Proyecto Ibiza, for example, was known for attracting more of a lesbian public than the others, almost all of which attract audiences composed overwhelmingly of gay men, while Divino is known for its "strippers," erotic dancers uncommon in Cuba who do not, despite their title, disrobe completely.

Yunior, meanwhile, was locating Karabalí in the ecosystem of Havana's gay nightlife at the time. Though Las Vegas, just around the corner, was often derided for its rundown appearance, it was Karabalí that was seen as more of an *antro* or dive. This was reflected even in the cost of entrance; it cost 3 CUC (roughly 3 USD) at the time to get in to Las Vegas, but just 1 CUC got you in to Karabalí.[20] If these prices seem low, it is worth recalling that the average state salary for a Cuban person at the time was equivalent to roughly 30 CUC per month. Thus, even state-run establishments like Las Vegas and Karabalí were clearly not geared toward Cubans of typical means, to say nothing of independently owned establishments in El Vedado, which might not have a cover but would charge exorbitant prices for drinks, multiples of those charged by the state and far out of reach for most Cubans.

Around midnight, we decided to start making our way to Karabalí, and I told Yunior that we would be meeting another friend, Gabriel, on the way. Sure enough, when we headed out he was already at the park on the corner outside of our apartment, where he could connect to the internet.

"¡Marica!" ("Faggot!") I shouted at him, and he blew me a kiss. The park was bustling with young people talking, looking at their phones, and selling internet cards. Some of the queer ones eyed me and Kerry hopefully when we approached Gabriel, wondering whether one of us foreigners might be willing to pay their entrance to Las Vegas or Karabalí that evening. With its location in the epicenter of queer nightlife in Havana, the park was a frequent meeting place for queer Cubans and foreigners.

Before anyone could approach us, however, we were off. "¿Y por qué Karabalí?" ("Why Karabalí?"), Gabriel asked. "Because it's Friday, and I want to see Devora and Blankita," Armando replied. Truly a transformismo expert, Armando knew which transformistas could be seen any night of the week in any nightclub. Devora was the host on Fridays at Karabalí, and most weeks she invited Blankita, perhaps the best-known comedic transformista of the younger generation, to join her.

When we arrived, I saw Blankita outside, her suitcase full of drag in tow. She was dressed simply and within the expectations of normative masculinity: tight jeans, a button-up shirt, and sneakers. Many transformistas arrived to work like this, only to transform in the cramped and hot dressing rooms backstage. Others, like Devora, arrived in simple feminine clothing and then put on the accoutrements of their drag persona alongside their co-performers. Much of this has to do with gender subjectivity: many transformistas are trans and thus present in life as the gender they perform on stage, whereas others are cisgender and are sometimes particularly invested in the transformation they make between the street and the stage. It also has to do with respectability, to be sure, and historically there have been *anfitrionas* (hosts of shows, who are often drag performers themselves) and club owners who insist that their invited artists arrive dressed in the "opposite" gender to the one they will perform onstage, a practice that certain transformistas understand to be transphobic and discriminatory.

These dynamics filtered into the treatment of the audience members, who were forming a small crowd near Blankita waiting to enter Karabalí. Most of those in the crowd seemed to be gay men, though some probably identified as travestis or trans women.[21] Some were just finishing one last cigarette before heading in, while others were still waiting to see if they could scrounge together enough money to get in, if the doorman would even allow them. Travestis in particular have experienced considerable discrimination in gay nightclubs, and multiple trans/queer Cubans told me about incidents in which queer establishments turned travestis away when they try to enter. Some gay men I interviewed described travestis as "conflictivas," or difficult, and felt that the state-sanctioned LGBT rights movement had focused too much on their needs. In my experience in Cuba, travestis remained among the most marginalized elements of trans/queer social life, especially when they refused to conform to the expectations of normative transgender femininity.

Yunior, Armando, Gabriel, Kerry, and I eventually handed our cover to the doorman, and he opened the door for us without a problem. Karabalí was, to be frank, nothing to write home about. As you walked in, you were assaulted by the blasting sound system operated by the *sonidista* just to the left of the entrance. You entered along the wall on the right of the club, which looked onto a space with tables for audience members and, in front of it, a sizeable stage. The tables went for a steep 35 CUC or more, but as you continued into the space, there was a bit of a clearing in front of the bar in the back to allow for dancing, standing, and ordering drinks. Behind the bar, a stairwell took you down to a lower floor dedicated to dancing, smoking, and socializing. If the upper floor would be host to the performance itself, this lower space was home to much of the affective linking that made a place like Karabalí feel alive. What's more, if the space for the audience upstairs catered to foreigners, this sweaty, cramped downstairs always seemed to offer a refuge for Cubans.

We all stayed upstairs that night and bought small pours of rum to accompany us as we waited for the show to start. As audience members slowly trickled in, the DJ put on a confusing mix of songs and videos, primarily from abroad. While the music video for Sia's "Chandelier" played, for example, I wondered what this English-language song and its child protagonist dancer meant in this context. Perhaps it made the steady stream of foreigners filling up the expensive tables feel a bit more comfortable. Perhaps it spoke to the ways the Cubans among them imagined life off the island. Before I could finish my thought, however, Sia was immediately followed up by the omnipresent 2015 Cuban reggaetón track "Guachineo" by the once-local Chocolate MC, who had recently relocated to the US. I suppose that this, too, gestured to life abroad, but in a more tangible sense, as evidence of the Cuban who flew from the island. No matter who was playing, the sound was deafening, as usual, and I discreetly slipped my earplugs in. As the DJ continued alternating between these distinct but overlapping opposites, Yunior and the rest of us shouted over the blasting music to catch up and comment on our fellow spectators: Gabriel characteristically knew about half of the Cubans who arrived, and Yunior spotted an old flame from afar.

It was just before 1:30 a.m. that the lights and music signaled the beginning of the show. "Damas y caballeros," the emcee boomed as he made his way to the stage, "¡bienvenidos al Divino Show!" ("Ladies and gentlemen, welcome to the Divino Show!"). The emcee was flanked by scantily clad male dancers, and he wore a tight-fitting outfit that exposed his muscular physique. This presence and his welcome, in the context of a country whose trans/queer movement has developed a broad lexicon of gender-expansive language, reflected the fact that these spaces—just as they are elsewhere—are largely dominated and curated by gay men. Nightclubs with names like XY further drive home the intended audience of these spaces.

As was typical for shows like El Divino, the emcee started off the night by asking where the audience was from. Kerry and I implored our friends not to say anything, mortified that we might be called onstage. Instead, as audience members shouted out their home countries, Gabriel yelled "¡Corea del Norte!" which sent us all belly laughing. To our relief, another US American was outed, and he was called up to the stage as the emcee belted "¡Estados Unidos!" The DJ played a clip of a Pitbull song meant to represent our shared homeland, and the US American flag flashed on the screen behind the stage. "¡Imperialistas! ¡Gusanos!" Gabriel shouted ironically, unable to be heard anyway over the blaring music. Visitors from Italy and Spain followed the one from the US, and likewise danced briefly onstage with the emcee.

The ritual drove home the fact that these shows are indeed put together for a foreign gaze, geared toward capturing the sorely needed *divisas* tourists bring with them. That's what made Gabriel's interjection of "¡Imperialistas! ¡Gusanos!" all the more hilarious: Cubans know well that the state's hardline stance against US imperialism and its attitude toward defectors as "gusanos" ("worms") had long ago thawed in favor of welcoming the capital that tourists and Cubans in the US bring. By shouting "North Korea!" however, Gabriel pointedly disrupted the revelry of this spectacle, recalling North Koreans' and Cubans' shared lack of mobility within global capitalism, the contrast between their isolation and European and US tourists' frictionless movement across borders. Both post-Soviet states in the "axis of evil," this space was clearly not designed with either of them in mind.

The presence of Spanish and Italian tourists, meanwhile, was a testament to the place of European, and especially Spanish, capital in contemporary Cuba. Spanish hotel chains Iberostar and Meliá own the lion's share of Cuba's hotels geared toward tourists, including the all-inclusive resorts that are the only lodging option along Cuba's most sought-after beaches, such as Varadero and the keys off of Villa Clara Province. My abuela once recalled to me seeing Fidel Castro walk into the Havana Hilton during the Revolution, a space that would become the Hotel Habana Libre, which had a beautiful mural outside by the lesbian Cuban artist Amelia Peláez. Visitors to the Habana Libre today are greeted by workers wearing nametags with the Meliá logo, as the hotel has been managed by Spanish corporations since 1993. Cuba, like much of the Caribbean, then, remains subject to the whims of foreign colonial powers and global capital, its fate having passed from their Spanish colonizers from the 16th to the 19th centuries, to US imperialists for the better part of the 20th century, to the USSR for the first thirty years of the Revolution, and now back to European capitalists in the wake of the fall of the Soviet Union.[22]

Once his opening bit was over, the emcee announced Devora, and to the soft sounds of keyboard and strings she emerged wearing a long, gold, form-fitting dress that showed off her formidable breastplate (see figure 3). A high slit on the left exposed her thigh, and she waved her drapey, flowing sleeves with her arms as she lip-synched to the opening of Aretha Franklin's 2014 rendition of Gloria Gaynor's classic "I Will Survive"; her short and slightly textured wig recalled the way Franklin wore her hair later in life. Devora towered on the stage in tall, gold platform heels, easing into the performance with the capacious percussion beat of this arrangement before heating up with the four-on-the-floor boom that dominates after the first chorus. Here, her gestures with her head and arms became freer and grander as she followed along to Franklin's scatted interlude. Two young gay men approached her on stage to plant kisses on her cheek and tips in her bust.[23]

Just after the second chorus, however, the track cut abruptly to Celia Cruz's Spanish-language version of the same song, this time "Yo viviré," with its salsa arrangement full of Afro-Cuban percussion. At first, Devora ambled creakily around the stage, imitating the wobbly walk characteristic of Celia's later years. But then, not unlike James Brown's performative rebirths, Devora exploded into a rumba-inspired dance at the arrival of the faster-paced, more improvisatory concluding montuno section, stretching her hands out to each corner of the audience and spinning around before urging us all to clap along with the musicians. Finally, she made her way shakily to the back of the stage as the song wound down, resting one hand on her hip as though she had transformed back into the aging salsa diva.

Devora's performance, her musical and aesthetic choices, revealed some of the key dynamics that had long informed and continued to shape transformismo. In choosing Franklin and Cruz, Devora, too,

Fig. 3. Devora, a celebrated young transformista from Havana, performs at the gay nightclub XY.

reflected transformismo's investments in music from abroad, in imagining life elsewhere. This was as true in the capitalist nightclubs in the 1950s as it was in the UMAP camps and sanatoria of the 1960s and 1980s or during the harsh scarcity of the 1990s and 2000s. Transformismo's embrace of foreign music not only reinforced these nightclub's focus on foreign capital, it exemplified the ways Cubans more generally imagine life off of the island, "en el exterior." The prominence of diasporic Cubans like Cruz, La Lupe, Mirtha Medina, and Maggie Carlés—which is disproportionate relative to their place in Cuban taste on the island more generally—further articulates transformismo's orientation toward Cubans who go elsewhere.

Moreover, Franklin, Cruz, and—by extension—Gaynor evince the crucial role that Black music and especially Black women's affective and vocal labor play in transformismo. From transformismo's earliest days, racialized performances of gender were central to the performance complex, through Rita Montaner's blackface drag and Musmé's *mujer china*. If transformismo's golden era relied on Spanish-language popular music from abroad, it was also based in Black musical forms like the bolero and heavily featured Afro-Cuban women such as Elena Burke.[24] Now, you are just as likely to hear Beyoncé, Whitney Houston, and Jennifer Hudson as you are non-Black Spanish or Latin American queens like Rocío Dúrcal, Gloria Trevi, or Isabel Pantoja.

Listening to Devora perform Aretha and Celia, I looked out over the audience, which was overwhelmingly dominated by men, including a large number of foreigners. Though her performance was beautiful, I became unsettled as I thought about Argelia, the leader of Havana's transformismo masculino movement, who you met in the introduction and who had struggled for so long to gain a foothold in this mainstream, lucrative scene, facing lack of interest and investment from the gay men who served as the artistic directors and often the hosts of these parties and shows. It seemed that in these mainstream transformismo spaces, the affective labor of Black women was entirely welcome, ready to be capitalized on, while Black women themselves were simply not valued. This was, to be sure, not specific to Cuba, but instead reminded me of dynamics I had encountered in so much queer space in the US, too. As Kemi Adeyemi wrote of Chicago: "Blackness is produced as a disembodied aesthetic to be pleasurably consumed or it is a fully enfleshed terror, a scourge of the landscape" (2022, 7).

As Devora made her way back to the dressing room, a video of Cuban singer Lourdes Torres appeared projected on a screen in front of the back wall of the stage. Over the sound of a melancholic keyboard, seated in front of an ornate tea set, she delivered her message: "Cualquier hombre o mujer, joven, viejo, soltero, o casado, con una conducta sexual determinada que no se proteja en cada acto sexual está dispuesto a contraer el VIH. Protégete siempre. Tú puedes." ("Any man or woman, young, old, single, or married, with a certain sexual behavior who does not protect themselves in every sexual act is exposed to contracting HIV. Protect yourself always. You can."). The message reflected the important role CENESEX has played in the history of parties like these. As you will recall, the approval of CENESEX made it possible for these proyectos to exist, and probably also allowed them to hire performers who were not technically employed as artists by the state. Sexual health campaigns, then, were a common part of state-sponsored shows that featured transformismo, as part of a broader practice in which CENESEX and other public health organizations turn to artists for health promotion efforts.

Though it would be fair to see this sexual health programming as a thin veneer legitimizing the state's capture of foreign capital through queer nightlife—and indeed these messages seemed to pass by with little engagement from performers or audience members—some transformistas take their role as health promoters very seriously. Kiriam, for example, was proud to tell me that she trained more than one hundred sexual-health promoters in her role as the founding coordinator of the Proyecto TransCuba, and health promotion is an important part of the work of Havana's transformistas masculinos, who I will discuss in depth in chapter 5.

"Y seguimos con la reina del humor, ¡Blankita!" ("And we continue with the queen of comedy, Blankita!"), the emcee announced as the video played out. "¡Agua!" Yunior shouted, and he turned to tell me that he was a fan of hers. Armando added that he felt she was one of the most original transformistas in Cuba at the time. Gabriel, meanwhile, made a slightly irritated face, quietly voicing his dislike for her. I wondered if this was because of the racial politics of her coming performance or simply because she wasn't a beauty queen. The club was still dark as Blankita took the stage to diasporic Cuban singer Maggie Carlés's Spanish-language version of "And I Am Telling You . . ." from the musical *Dreamgirls*. As the lights came up, they revealed Blankita's transparent floor-length dress, underneath which were visible her false breasts, her awkwardly and excessively padded buttocks, and a large rubber vulva. She managed the stage gracefully despite her sky-high platform heels, and she set down her iconic bejeweled stiletto purse upstage after carrying it in by its long chain. With her right hand, she removed her bright, cartoonishly oversized glasses to show off her characteristic jumbo eyelashes, crafted from neon-green cardboard.

Immediately, then, it was clear that Blankita's aesthetic had been culled from a telling assemblage of vernacular performance traditions based in racial and sexual impersonation (see figure 4). Her improvised eyelashes were a throwback to the inventive use of materials that characterized the shows of the UMAP camps and the Special Period, while her racy outfit recalled the burlesque elements of the 1950s cabaret shows. The vast majority of her aesthetic choices, however, relied on the 19th-century tradition of teatro bufo in Cuba, especially its deployments of the transnational imagery of blackface performance. Blankita's overstuffed rear end and her lips painted impossibly large depicted a subject who pushed the limits of humanity. Her unkempt Afro wig and the oversize red bow affixed to it gestured toward histories of racist iconography. In addition to blackface, bufo included satirical renderings of contempo-

Fig. 4. Blankita, one of the best-known comedic transformistas in Cuba, performs at Karabalí in Havana.

rary political economy, which Blankita accomplished here through her necklace of fake grapes and her *libreta de abastecimiento* earrings, made of the booklets Cubans use to buy state-subsidized goods at local bodegas. Together, these pointed not only to the need for Cubans to recycle ordinary items for their daily adornment, but also to the decreasing real value of the libretas, which each year yield fewer and fewer subsidized goods to ordinary Cubans.

Blankita's musical choice, too, betrayed multiple registers of complex racial signification. "And I Am Telling You . . ." was one of the songs I heard performed most frequently in the context of transformismo during my fieldwork, underscoring the importance of Black feminine affect to the performance complex, as I suggested above. In performing Maggie Carlés's version, however, recorded by a fair-skinned, diasporic Cuban, Blankita was participating in transformismo's engagement with Cubans abroad while adding another layer of blackface to Carlés's interpretation of this signal piece of Black popular culture. In this number, we witnessed the performance of a song written by a gay Jewish man to be sung by a Black woman, later reinterpreted by a fair-skinned Cuban woman, only to be lip-synched to by a gay Black man in drag and blackface—a palimpsest of racial impersonation that recounts the long hemispheric histories that endure as much in drag as in the music that propels it.[25]

If Devora had mined "I Will Survive" for its drama, Blankita's interpretation of "And I Am Telling You . . ." turned gravitas into an opportunity for parody. From the first verse, Blankita farcically exaggerated her lip-synching, using her massive lips to produce animalistic gestures. The DJ purposefully skipped the track on Carlés's repetitions of "que tú" ("and you"), so Blankita got stuck in a loop, pointing over and over again into the audience. This, too, recalled the bufo tradition, as this built-in joke was merely a reflection of the reality that these shows go on with outdated and improvised audio equipment. To Carlés's moaning melismas at the end of the verse, Blankita crouched down and winced her face as though she were having a difficult bowel movement.

Leaning into these performative incongruities, Blankita broke into a fast-paced dance with rumba-like movements just as the music slowed and softened at the section analogous to "We're part of the same place . . ." in the original, and she lifted her dress to expose her ersatz vulva. She departed from the music entirely when she received an unusually large tip during the second verse, launching into a frantic dance and hurrying to the back wall to support herself so she could twerk in the audience's direction before landing a cartwheel to stage right. Each time Carlés's vocal timbre crossed into a growl, Blankita would contort her face as though she were screaming. Finally, as the song came to an end, Blankita and the sonidista exploited the long fermatas that characterize Holliday's as much as Carlés's coda, making the track skip once more so that Blankita was stuck lip-synching to one interminable vowel. To accompany this, Blankita did a slow, jerky body roll, finally breaking out to close the song with a signature move in which she scoots along the stage on her backside. The audience erupted in cheers and applause as she slowly collected herself and picked up the microphone to do some crowd work.

Though Blankita's performances are on their face offensive and derisive of Black women, and I have no desire to perform a reparative reading here, I do think they help clarify some complicated racial politics that shape transformismo more broadly. On the one hand, Blankita's performances turn Black women into the butt of a joke for profit, in the context of a space that has historically excluded Black women from participation. On the other hand, however, I would suggest that Blankita's performance relies on depictions of Black women as physically excessive in much the same way that Devora's rely on understandings of Black women as psychically so. I don't say this to rescue Blankita's aesthetic choices or to condemn Devora's, but rather to call into question the mainstream scene of transformismo more generally and the racial politics from which the tourism economy profits. In both cases, it seems that Black women are being used to sell Cuba to foreigners, as they were before the Revolution and as they have been since the Special Period. And all the while, Black women are largely excluded from enjoying the economic fruits of their labor in the tourism sector within which the transformismo performance complex circulates.

Moreover, Blankita's performances in many ways reflect the dissonance so many Cubans perceive—as much in transformismo as in popular culture more generally—between blackness and beauty. In my interview with Devora, she described various labels that artists, artistic directors, and audience members alike use to categorize transformistas. Along with the "mejores vestidas" ("best dressed") and the "lindas" ("pretty ones") are the "humoristas" ("comedians"), like Blankita, and the "temperamentales" ("temperamental ones"), like Devora. She likened them to social classes, in that once you are associated with one you cannot escape it. I noticed in my time in Cuba that—though Margot, the most famous and veteran humorista in Cuba, is not Black—dark-skinned Black transformistas were much more likely to perform as humoristas than their light-skinned counterparts. This was true not only for Blankita, but for Blanca Nieves and Blaccucini, who you will learn about in chapters 2 and 4, respectively. The racial politics of transformismo are complex and do not lend themselves neatly to oversimplification, but I can safely say that in the context of mainstream transformismo spaces in coastal Havana, Black skin was often more likely to draw laughter than appreciation of beauty.[26]

As she began her crowd work, Blankita headed upstage to retrieve her purse. "¡Qué tacaños son!" ("You're so cheap!"), she shouted at the audience as they started throwing tips to her. In this recurring bit, the audience would throw coins on the stage, often trying to hit her with them, and she would then go around picking up the money with a magnet affixed to the bottom of the purse. The magnet, however, would only pick up change in foreign currencies, not in *moneda nacional*, the local one. Blankita would make a big show of this, demonstrating that the purse would not accept the local currency, which has no value on the global marketplace. "¡Ella no es bruta!" she shouted, "Sabe que eso no vale nada." ("She's not dumb! She knows this isn't worth anything.")[27]

Once more, the performance fit within Blankita's revitalization of Cuba's teatro bufo tradition. If the act of throwing coins at her colluded in the general debasement of her character as a human being, the distinction between currencies reflected Cuba's contemporary political economy. Cubans experience daily and on a visceral level the divide between those who have access to foreign capital and those who must subsist on local forms of value. At Karabalí, Blankita's purse underscored the fact that this space catered to the former.

After Blankita, a duo of dancers did a short and gently seductive number, and then the third transformista of the night made an appearance that perhaps disrupted some of the racial-sexual dynamics I have been describing thus far. Uma Rojo is a dark-skinned Black transformista who clearly fits within the "linda" category mentioned above, despite its domination by white Cubans. For this number, she appeared in a beautiful short natural wig with caramel highlights and an understated black jumpsuit with flowing legs and a form-fitting, sparkly, translucent top that extended to her wrists. She gave a relaxed performance to "Danza Ñáñiga" by the Black Cuban jazz artist Mayra Caridad Valdés. Ñáñiga in Cuba refers to practitioners of the Afrodiasporic Abakuá religion, and this song has a lineage from the Afrocubanismo of Ernesto Lecuona through the arranging of Valdés's tremendously famous brother Chucho and their foundational band Irakere. That night at Karabalí, Uma Rojo swayed dreamily while she mimed the distinctive syncopated piano part of the song and lip-synched breezily to both Valdés's soulful runs and her subtle scatting.

The performance was unlike anything else that happened that night: Uma's understated and groovy look, her intended place in the aesthetic universe of transformismo, and Valdés's comparatively soft and mellifluous sounds. To be honest, I don't recall the audience being particularly interested. In her act, however, however, I see the possibility of more liberatory performances even in the space of these mainstream nightclubs. Here was a beautiful Black transformista just being beautiful and Black, performing to an Afro-Cuban jazz piece by another beautiful Black artist. If it didn't necessarily fit into the dominant aesthetic universe of the space, it was evidence of the fact that there can be compelling performances here, that we trans and queer people have the capacity to make something affirming even in contexts where we know people and institutions are taking advantage of us.[28] And isn't that just what Uma Rojo's ancestors did two generations ago, when they put on shows in the UMAP camps?

The show continued like this for another forty minutes or so, with each transformista coming out for another number and another group of dancers adding some variety to the performance in between. Finally, a little after 2 a.m., the emcee came on to bring the show to a close and invite the "strippers" to come on stage. Dutifully they did, muscular and scantily clad, gyrating to the rhythm of the newest repartero craze. "¡Ahora gozamos!" ("Now we party!") Gabriel shouted as he smiled and bent over slightly, shaking his behind. He wasn't referring to the strippers, however, who most of the audience ignored. Instead, he was looking forward to the almost two hours of dancing we would be allowed before the club closed at 4 a.m.

Though many young trans/queer Cubans admire transformismo, at least half of those I spoke with saw the shows at these parties as brief distractions from the main event, which for them was this early-morning dancing. As such, queer Cubans often look for parties that last as long as possible, like El Divino's Saturday show at Café Cantante, which goes on until 6 a.m. One transformista told me that they preferred the rural parties in Bauta or Artemisa, which would easily continue until sunrise.

If in many ways the shows in these spaces are merely a convenient backdrop for the accumulation of foreign capital, the party is a welcome opportunity for Cubans themselves to meet the foreigners who bring that capital. The Cuban state's utilization and management of these interactions drives home the linkages between queer nightclubs and the tourism economy. Not unlike in the 1950s, state actors continue to use the specter of sex work as a cover to shut down queer establishments that threaten their control over the mainstream trans/queer nightlife and transformismo scene. Though it is well known that *jineterismo*, or hustling, proliferates in these spaces, accusations of *proxenetismo*, or pimping, can be enough to shutter an independent nightclub or party.[29] This is what happened, for example, with the party at Humboldt, a gay nightclub that was tremendously popular the first time I went to Cuba in 2015. By the time I returned in 2016, however, friends told me that the space had been closed by the state, purportedly for proxenetismo, drugs, and "corruption of minors," a vague legal term in Cuba and elsewhere that carries particularly severe penalties and, in this case, referred to the involvement of people under age eighteen in sex work.

None of these things were on our mind, however, as Yunior, Armando, Gabriel, Kerry, and I danced to a steady stream of club hits. Recent local reggaetón favorites mixed with funk carioca from Brazil and reggaetón from Puerto Rico, as countless bodies conspired to overcome the air conditioning through the heat of our friction. The five of us formed a tight little circle, at intervals copying each other's dance moves and pairing off to make space on the crowded dance floor.

The rousing chorus of "me voooooooooyyyy pa' mi casa" ("I'm going home"), the infectious Afro-Cuban invention of Cimafunk, disrupted our abandon at around 4 a.m. and signaled Karabalí's closing.[30] "¿Pa'l Malecón?" ("To the Malecón?") I asked once we were out in the open air, away from the stifling heat and overwhelming sound of the nightclub. Historically, this had been a well-trodden routine for weekend nights: gather with some friends, make your way to one of the queer parties, dance until the early hours of the morning, and then head to the sea wall to talk until the sun rises, the public transportation starts back up, or everyone falls asleep on one another. We stopped in to a little bar before crossing the Malecón and bought a small bottle of rum and a couple of beers for 8 CUC or so. Kerry and I had noticed that the Malecón was less trafficked by trans and queer people those days, having quieted down in the wake of Hurricane Irma in the summer of 2017. An increased police presence also tamped down the trans/queer revelry. But this night there was a healthy contingent of people enjoying the relatively fresh night air.

We walked for a bit before settling on a small vacant spot where a couple of us could sit while the others stood. Sharing the bottle of rum by the capful, we told jokes and posed topics for conversation, asking each other, for example, where we would live if we could live anywhere in the world. "España," Armando said. "Niño, ¡eso también está en llamas!" ("Boy, that place is also a mess!") Gabriel countered. "Cada lugar tiene lo suyo" ("Each place has its own issues"), Yunior offered. I looked past Kerry to the Florida Straits lapping gently behind her. I love going to the Malecón, being on the coast, close to Yemayá, my mother and yours. It always makes me think about my family: my abuela bringing my mother there to soothe a cough, and then their eventual flight over the blue expanse to Miami and then New York, where my mother would grow up. The Malecón is also a public space, the kind that would be impossible in my hometown of Miami, where similar stretches of coast have been overdeveloped into oblivion and are owned entirely by private developers and residents.

To me, the Malecón exemplifies the ways that we trans/queer people take up space, even in the face of repressive policing, even in the face of economies that profit off of our creativity without investing in our well-being. I struggled to overcome my exhaustion and enjoy the Malecón just a little longer, but as 6 o'clock approached it overtook me, and Kerry and I started our goodbyes. Everyone agreed it was as good a time as any to acknowledge that it was, indeed, tomorrow. "Calabaza, calabaza, cada uno pa' su casa," Yunior said, and we all made our ways to our respective homes.

Staging Transformismo

The contemporary mainstream transformismo scene relies on a long history of social, political, and economic transformations that have shaped everyday life in Cuba since the Republican era. Transformismo emerged out of a host of cross-dressed performative practices that were each tied up with Cuba's histories of racialized coercive migration, its independence movement, and its trans/queer subcultures, and by the 1950s it had become a part of the cabaret scene that reflected Cuba's place as a pleasure island for foreign capitalists. The Revolution sent transformistas underground, where they thrived for decades until the fall of socialism—coupled with shifts in the social imagination of the state—created the conditions of possibility for their incorporation into the official sphere. If these spaces have effectively decriminalized trans/queer performance to some extent, their situation relative to the tourism economy means that their aesthetics, social structure, and political economy rehearse the very same racial, sexual, and economic exclusions that have characterized state liberalization in Cuba since the fall of the Soviet Union. Nevertheless, within and outside of this scene, transformistas manage to stage meaningful performances that affirm the "otherwise" lifeways of trans/queer Cubans.[31]

CHAPTER 2

Apocalipsis

Transformismo at the End of the World

Just before 3 a.m. one warm *madrugada* in July 2017, Esmeralda came on stage to close the show at Apocalipsis, the weekend party she hosted in her neighborhood of Párraga, roughly six miles south of Havana's city center. The tall, elegant Black transformista emerged to sounds of the band from the famous Cabaret Tropicana playing "Bembelequa," best known for its interpretation by Celia Cruz, who was once the lead singer at the nightclub. Esmeralda got her name from her aunt, Esmeralda Caridad Cuervo Pedroso (better known as Caridad Cuervo), who was also once a lead singer at the famous nightclub and whose portrait hung behind Esmeralda as she danced on stage (see figure 5). Just like those of the performers at the Tropicana, Esmeralda's outfit was over the top: A long, frilly red train fell from her hips to the floor, and a tall red headdress reached up to the ceiling. Most of her body was covered by a black bodysuit and sheer black patterned tights.

Esmeralda's train danced along with her as she shook her hips, and—as though she were actually on stage at the Tropicana—she was eventually joined by a substantial *cuerpo de baile*. First, two lithe Black men backed her up, dancing synchronously in bright red outfits. Even Elegguá himself, the African and Afrodiasporic trickster deity, made an appearance, dancing around and squawking at her, also dressed in his black and red. When the body of the song gave way to a faster-paced

Fig. 5. Esmeralda performs at Apocalipsis. A painting of her aunt Caridad Cuervo hangs upstage.

coda featuring the band's horn players, percussionists, and chorus, three beautiful Black women in revealing blue outfits and tall blue headdresses joined, as did one more male dancer, so that six performers danced in tandem behind Esmeralda while Elegguá pranced around them. Over the din, the emcee thanked the audience, the performers, and the crew, bringing the show to an end as the horns blared on.

If this performance mirrored aesthetically the five-nights-a-week spectacle at the Tropicana, its social and economic context could scarcely have been more distinct: While entrance to the Tropicana will set you back at least $75 US, at Apocalipsis the audience had paid roughly $1 US each to enter. If the audience at Tropicana is almost exclusively tourists, Apocalipsis's patrons are predominantly Black Cubans from the surrounding neighborhood of Párraga, on the outskirts of Havana in the Arroyo Naranjo municipality. Never mind the fact that at Apocalipsis, unlike at the Tropicana, the leading lady was actually a gay man in drag.

In this chapter, I consider the work transformismo is doing in these socially, economically, and spatially marginalized contexts, so distant both materially and symbolically from the mainstream *fiestas gay* I narrated in chapter 1. In the latter spaces, state or private capital draws on trans/queer performance to extract foreign currency from tourists, a dynamic reflected in the contours of the shows: their cost, their focus on foreigners, and their familiar reliance on and marginalization of Black women. By contrast, the parties I narrate here provide affirming renderings of Black/queer life that cater to Cubans at prices they can afford. I suggest that this scene, then, offers an example of the kinds of mutual care trans/queer *habaneros* on the social-economic-spatial margins of the city are providing to one another in the face of more mainstream projects that do not address or improve their well-being. In this way, and in concert with other marginalized trans/queer people throughout the hemisphere, trans/queer Cubans are generating life-sustaining alternative systems of value that work beyond the limitations of mainstream LGBT spaces and politics.

To contextualize this scene, I first discuss the formation of *los repartos*, the peripheral neighborhoods in Havana, elaborating on the racial, economic, and spatial distinctions between the Havana that I narrated in chapter 1 and the one I describe here. I briefly situate trans/queer performers' interventions here within ongoing discussions about spatial stratification in trans/queer studies and Cuban studies. I then turn to the parties themselves and describe how they rely on *folklor* (in this case, Afrofolkloric performance), *festival* (a drag competition), and *fiesta* (the party itself) to craft spaces that address the needs, desires, and aspirations of Black Cuban people of typical means in Havana's repartos. In each of these narratives, the parties provide racial, sexual, and economic antidotes to the shortcomings of the tourism economy, LGBT rights politics, and mainstream trans/queer nightlife in Havana.

Los Repartos: Race, Space, and Capital in Contemporary Cuba

"¡Está haciendo un *Mariposas en el andamio* nuevo!" ("She's making a new *Mariposas en el andamio*!") This was how a young transformista at Apocalipsis introduced me to her drag mother, to which I smiled politely and gently protested. *Mariposas* was a cherished documentary portrait of transformismo in the 1990s, and I was writing a dissertation for a PhD in ethnomusicology. In surprising and substantive ways, however, *Mariposas* does dovetail with the contents of this chapter: They both tell stories about the work that trans/queer performance and entertainment have done on the social, economic, and spatial margins of Cuba's capital city. *Mariposas* centered around an informal cabaret established in the cafeteria for the workers constructing public housing in the La Güinera neighborhood in the Arroyo Naranjo municipality of Havana. The parties that animate this chapter take place a stone's throw from La Güinera, and they, too, provide sustenance to Cubans of typical means. Here, I want to provide some context by elaborating on the social and material significance of los repartos, Havana's peripheral neighborhoods, in contemporary Cuba.

Recent events in La Güinera demonstrate the ways that interlocking formations of race, class, and space determine Cubans' life chances in a postsocialist context. On July 11, 2021, Cubans took to the streets in different locales on the island to protest a variety of material, political, and economic difficulties that were taking a toll on their lives during the COVID-19 pandemic. In the wake of the protests, Cuban critics within the Afrodescendant movement noted the racial, spatial, and economic inequalities in the state's punishment of participants in the demonstrations. La Güinera—a predominantly Black and working-class neighborhood—is an epicenter of this inequality, and journalists have pointed out that, despite the neighborhood's small size, 12 percent of all arrests and 60 percent of all sedition charges related to the July 11 protests involved residents of La Güinera (Borrero Batista 2022; Pineda 2022; Amerise 2022).

This disparity speaks to the distance between the coastal Havana that tourists encounter, the one I described in chapter 1, and Havana's repartos. Though the word *reparto* refers to the divisions of Havana into neighborhoods at one greater level of specificity than *municipio* (municipality), when *habaneros* say "los repartos" they are generally referring to the neighborhoods on the outskirts of the city, particularly to the south. Cuban/Dominican historian Haroldo Dilla Alfonso (2008, 62–63) has suggested that these divisions actually point to two Havanas:

- La primera, constituida por los cinco municipios costeros, representa La Habana dinámica, donde residen los poderes políticos y económicos, donde pululan y gastan los turistas, donde se ubican las firmas extranjeras y las industrias biotecnológicas, donde se realizan las mayores inversiones, y finalmente donde vive la población más capaz e insertada (formal e informalmente), que percibe ingresos tres veces superiores a los promediados en los otros diez municipios.
- La segunda, que reúne a la decena restante de municipios capitalinos, es la zona de población más vieja y con una mayor proporción

de obreros, que alberga las industrias tradicionales, muchas de ellas altamente contaminantes, y hacia donde los turistas raras veces van, excepto cuando en sus ómnibus refrigerados visitan el museo de Guanabacoa o acuden a algún *babalaw* prominente en Atarés.

- The first, constituted by the five coastal municipalities, represents the dynamic Havana, where the political and economic powers reside, where the tourists abound and spend, where the foreign firms and biotechnological industries are located, where the biggest investments are made, and finally where the most capable and embedded (formally and informally) population lives, which receives three times more revenue than the average in the other ten municipalities.
- The other, which contains the other ten capital municipalities, is the older population center with a greater proportion of workers, which is home to the traditional industries, many of which are highly contaminating, and to which tourists rarely go, except when they take air-conditioned buses to visit the museum in Guanabacoa or go to a prominent *Babalawo* [priest] in Atarés.

Although Dilla Alfonso doesn't explicitly mention race here, the sectors he describes in the first Havana are dominated by foreigners and white Cubans, while those he mentions in the second are dominated by Black Cubans.[1]

Though spatial stratification has always existed in Cuba, this current dynamic is in many ways a remnant of political economic transformation in the wake of the fall of the Soviet Union. Cuban geographer René González Rego (2018, 2019) explains that, while tourism has been a part of Havana's narrative since colonization, and the historic center of the city has for centuries been favored from the perspective of development, economic changes since the fall of socialism and the development of the tourism economy produced intense social-spatial stratification in Cuba and Havana. González Rego (2019, 67–68) highlights in particular the restoration of Havana's northern coast, the internal migration toward Havana from the provinces, and the need for internal migrants to set up informal and precarious housing on the periphery of the city.

The symbolic and social meanings of "los repartos" in contemporary Havana reflect this historical and material context. In their song "La miki y la repa," for example, the hip-hop duo La Reyna y La Real act out the distinctions between one woman who is "miki"—consumerist, preppy, with an eye to *lo extranjero*—and another who is "repa," or from the repartos. While the miki character brags about the expensive places her boyfriend takes her, her repa counterpart raps about her boyfriend's Abakuá tattoo and his stint in prison. I saw these kinds of distinctions play out when one friend would say, jokingly, of another, "¡No lo dejes escoger la música¡ Es muy repa." ("Don't let him choose the music! He's so repa."). Or when I would tell someone that Kerry and I were going to a fiesta in the repartos, and they would express concern for us, describing the repartos as dangerous or unworthy of attention. This was always balanced, to be fair, by others who saw the repartos as more genuinely Cuban, less hampered by the presence of tourists and able to sustain alternative trans/queer possibilities.

To situate this chapter in a broader trans/queer-of-color context, I see trans/queer performers and spectators in the repartos cultivating a "spatial practice of possibility" (Bailey 2014). As Kemi Adeyemi recently said of neoliberal Chicago, Havana's tourism economy produces a reality in which "people, feeling, and landscapes are knitted together as the value of financial profit is bound to the accumulation of *certain kinds* of good feeling for *certain kinds* of people in *certain kinds* of places" (2022, 8). In the face of exclusion in gay spaces, Black heteronormative spaces, and touristic spaces, the Cubans who populate this chapter are "using performance to carve out—to engender—and transform normative geographies into spaces of communal celebration, affirmation, and support" (Bailey 2014, 490).

Discussions about internal stratification in Havana also complicate existing discourses about space in Cuban studies. People who study Cuba have long known that there is a tremendously disproportionate amount of research on Havana and a paucity on any other part of the country. Perhaps worse, many authors—myself included—primarily examine Havana but make claims about Cuba, as though the capital can stand in for the island as a whole. As Cuban historian Hernán Venegas Delgado has said, "tenemos una ciudad, La Habana, y su región, que se han convertido en el pivote casi absoluto para construir esa explicación que nos ha propuesto machaconamente sobre la historia patria" (2001, 107; "we have a city, Havana, and its region, that has become the almost absolute center for constructing that explanation of national history that has insistently been proposed to us"). In the face of such spatial arrogance, one friend routinely reminded me that "La Habana no es Cuba, y Cuba no es La Habana" ("Havana is not Cuba, and Cuba is not Havana"), a fact that is abundantly clear to anyone who has traveled outside of the capital city.[2]

The heterogeneity of the city of Havana itself or of other cities and provinces in Cuba, however, rarely receives such scrutiny. Venegas goes on to say that "no se explica realmente cuáles son los límites de esa región capitalina por el oeste, en el linde con Pinar del Río, ni por el este, en el límite con Matanzas, ni muchísimo menos cuál es su composición interna" (2001, 107; "it is not really explained what are the limits of that capital region to the west, in the border with Pinar del Río, nor to the east, in the border with Matanzas, nor much less what is its internal composition"). We don't have an understanding of Havana, he says, "como esa especie de microcosmos que es toda urbe" (2001, 107; "like that kind of microcosm that every major city is"). Traveling around Villa Clara Province, which I will discuss in the following chapter, I saw that in many ways the city centers of Santa Clara and Havana had more in common with each other than they did with their respective peripheries. That is to say, if Havana is not Cuba, then Párraga is not El Vedado.

In what follows, then, I offer an account of what transformismo is doing in this other Havana. In particular, I spend time in the repartos of Párraga and Mantilla, both working-class Black neighborhoods in the Arroyo Naranjo municipality. Much more importantly than intervening in trans/queer or Cuban studies, these narratives represent the reality of most Cubans, who do not have the luxury of easy access to the foreign capital that now determines their quality of life in their own country. In the face of a dominant LGBT cultural sphere that confers value based on the possibility to extract foreign capital, the parties I turn to now are instead offering possibilities for racial, sexual, and economic affirmation to Cubans of typical means.

Folklor: *Apocalipsis I*

Kerry and I were first invited to Apocalipsis by Argelia and Ángel Daniel, two transformistas masculinos (drag kings), to see them perform on the same night that opened this chapter. We met up with them in La Palma, a central hub for transportation around the repartos, at around 8:30 p.m. and caught an informal bus for five pesos (roughly US$0.25) that dropped us off right in front of the Iglesia de Santa Bárbara in Párraga.[3] Before long, the distant sound of music led us up a hill and down a small, dark street to the party. What would follow that evening gave us a window into the ways that transformismo in these spaces drew from Afrodiasporic cultural production—especially folkloric and religious performance—not for its potential marketability to tourists and, thus, profitability within the tourism economy, but rather for its meaningfulness to ordinary Cubans who would, in turn, help sustain a local, family-run party in their own community as a reciprocal and mutually beneficial gesture.

Apocalipsis took place in the covered outdoor patio behind the house of Alianys—the dancer behind the transformista Esmeralda, who opened this chapter. Attendees would enter the space through a door on the side of the house, where one of Alianys's relatives would charge them 1 CUC (roughly US$1) for admission. The patio they stepped into was lovingly appointed, with ten or so tables set up with blue tablecloths, a little bar in the back with lights hanging above it, and an open-air space behind for smoking, mingling, and dancing. The accessible prices of the refreshments matched the intended audience of locals: you could get a beer for 15 pesos (roughly US$0.50), a meal for 1 CUC (roughly US$1.00), and a bottle of rum for 5 CUC.

Alianys started hosting Apocalipsis in 2015 in his old house in Mantilla, a neighboring reparto, and its success turned it into a weekly affair. The very name "Apocalipsis" emerges from its grounding in the community and reflects its place in Cuba more broadly: In the party's early days, Alianys told two young girls participating in a community project he ran that provided entertainment and education for neighborhood kids that he needed a name for the weekly event. After considering it, the two girls came back with "Apocalipsis" (Apocalypse). "¿Apocalipsis?" he replied, "¿Cómo le vamos a poner a una discoteca el fin del mundo?" ("Apocalypse? How can we name a party after the end of the world?"). The girls insisted, however, and to appease them Alianys obliged. Trying to make sense of this unlikely name, he went around asking people about the concept of the apocalypse, and he was pleased to learn that "Apocalipsis no es la destrucción solamente. Apocalipsis es la destrucción y el comienzo de algo nuevo, algo que se destruyó y está creciendo nuevamente" ("The apocalypse isn't just the destruction. The apocalypse is the destruction and the beginning of something new, something that was destroyed and is growing again"). Indeed, Apocalipsis symbolizes some of what might come after and in the wake of the failures of tourism economies and mainstream LGBT rights discourses.

Kerry and I accommodated ourselves at a table near the stage alongside other invitees of Argelia and Ángel Daniel, and then we scooted another table next to ours as more poured in. They were all lesbian women, the vast majority of them Afrodescendants. When Kerry and I interviewed him a couple of months later, Alianys suggested that historically the party had attracted a primarily heterosexual audience, though over time a number of gay men started attending. This night, however, Alianys was surprised to see that the audience was overwhelmingly comprised of lesbian women. As I discuss in chapter 5, this was often the case wherever Argelia and Ángel Daniel performed, as they brought their networks with them while also attracting other lesbian women eager to participate in sorely needed lesbian space.

I struck up a conversation with Amalia, who was seated next to me. Amalia was a Black lesbian woman who happened to work at the very Cabaret Tropicana that opened this chapter. She lived in Playa, an upscale coastal neighborhood on the west side of Havana, an eight-mile trek from Apocalipsis, even in a private taxi. She joked that we found ourselves in "el culo del mundo" (the ass of the world), so I asked her what made her travel so far to come to this party when there were several nightclubs in her neighborhood and many more in El Vedado, a much easier journey from her neighborhood. She told me that it was her first time at Apocalipsis and that she was looking for a place to relax and feel comfortable. She was sure, she said, that she would be able to spend significantly less money and have a much better time at Apocalipsis than at any party in a more centrally located neighborhood of the city.

More specifically, of course, Amalia was there to see Alberto and Dany, Argelia and Ángel Daniel's stage personas, perform in the show that began a little before 1 a.m. with a lively number performed by Esmeralda in a floor-length, form-fitting white and red dress, backed up by three beautiful Black women dancers. The show went on for 40 minutes or so, alternating between the dancers, an emcee, two singers, Esmeralda, and—of course—Alberto and Dany (see figure 6). The duo closed this part of the show with what became a participatory performance to the *rumba guaguancó* "La gozadera" by the folkloric ensemble Yoruba Andabo.[4] When the distinctive triplet rhythmic gesture that opens the song sounded, a young Black woman seated near the stage shook her shoulders to the beat and then gave a knowing glance to a friend behind her in the audience. Along with many in the audience, she sang along to the opening lines of the song while Alberto and Dany emerged from backstage lip-synching. As soon as the percussion entered, a full-figured Black woman near stage right stood up to start dancing, and Alberto gestured for her to come closer to the center. She approached Alberto and danced in front of him before turning around to back up into him.

Though she quickly returned to dance closer to her table, the rup-

Fig. 6. Alberto and Dany perform together at Apocalipsis.

ture of the space between audience and stage had opened up a possibility, and soon an older Black woman got up to dance in front of the stage. By the time the faster-paced and more improvisatory *estribillo* (refrain section) approached, Alberto and Dany had been engulfed by Black women dancing the rumba, including two particularly talented performers. One of them backed up into Dany while smiling widely at her friend, shouting "¡Ahí va!" while the other danced virtuosically in front of her as her long, tied-back dreadlocks spun around her shoulders. Rather than let the recording's long decrescendo play out, the DJ cut the music off abruptly, just before one of the many repetitions of the final line ("Mira como te maté" ["look how I killed you"]), and the women filled the silence with their own a cappella rendition. Then the space lit up with shouts and laughter as the two dancers up front hugged each other tightly before returning to their table. One of the women at our table shouted at a friend across the audience, "¡Aquí hay una pila de artistas escondidas!" ("There are a bunch of hidden artists here!").

I had seen Argelia and her fellow performers entice and invite many audiences into such embodied collaborations on countless occasions through the rumba. What was different here was the value placed on Black women's sociality through the rumba, both materially and socially.

Argelia and Ángel Daniel often incorporated the rumba into their performances at afternoon peñas, but these were spaces where they were volunteering their time. It was possible, too, to bring Afrofolkloric music to more mainstream spaces (as you will see in chapter 5), but these were contexts where Black women were routinely sidelined. Here, instead, Black women were the authors and readers, the performers and spectators, of their own narratives.

During the duo's performance, a synchronicity emerged between the sounds of Yoruba Andabo and the conga drums that two young Black men were calmly and deliberately setting up behind Alberto and Dany. As if to not waste an ounce of the feverish energy that was circulating at the end of the song, the musicians started up abruptly, with two vocalists alternating Afroreligious chants and three percussionists playing sacred rhythms off of one another on a cowbell, a woodblock, and three congas. After so much time spent listening over the speakers, the live sounds stirred me. Alianys would tell me later that these performers were all part of the orchestra of the Comparsa de la FEU, a group of university-educated performers that bears the name of the Federación Estudiantil Universitaria (Federation of University Students) of the University of Havana.[5] Alianys is a member of the *comparsa* as a dancer, and he hires his colleagues to lead a conga on Sunday afternoons that starts at the Iglesia de Santa Bárbara and ends at Apocalipsis.

As the musicians played on, a handful of the dancers assembled downstage dressed as various orishas, deities from the Afrocuban religion Regla de Ocha: Oyá stood off to stage right, Yemayá and Ochún were seated in front, and Obbatalá stood behind them.[6] They all stayed still while the musicians played for Elegguá, who was being embodied by Alianys's husband. Elegguá is the conduit between the world of humans and that of the orishas; anything ceremonial begins and ends with him in Ocha. Elegguá ambled around the audience and the musicians dressed in black and red, gesturing toward them with his *garabatos*, the short canes he uses to clear his pathways. Ever a trickster, he stole some popcorn from an audience member as his canto ended and gave way to Oggún—a warrior, orisha of minerals and tools (Bolívar Aróstegui [1990] 2017, 79)—who emerged from backstage dressed in green pants, a green sash, and a straw hat. As Oggún danced around the stage, he moved his arms downward, as though striking an anvil with a hammer, one of the orisha's distinctive gestures. Ochún came next, rising and laughing as she danced around in her bright yellow dress. Despite her beauty, my attention was elsewhere, fixated on Yemayá, portrayed here by Alianys. She caught my eye and bowed her head ever so slightly, raising the hairs on the back of my neck.

As the lead singer offered her canto, Yemayá began screeching out. Her shoulders shook rapidly while she remained seated, eventually bowing her head to the ground and sweeping the floor with her long blue dress. Deliberately, she rose, as one of the percussionists played a slow triplet rumba clave on the cowbell. Along with the melodious metal clang, she spun in slow circles, embraced Elegguá, and then spun increasingly fast with the music. Devotees approached to salute her, touching both shoulders to her and embracing her while offering some money. Not yet knowing exactly why, I gave her an unusually large sum of money. She spun her way through the audience, and once she arrived at a larger opening toward the back, she lifted her dress, exposing a long white underskirt. As she continued twirling, this mixed with the skirt to form undulating patterns of blue and white.

When the *canto* (chant) for Oyá sounded, Yemayá made her way back to the stage and took her seat once more. The performance continued like this for almost half an hour, cycling through Changó—orisha of fire and war (Bolívar Aróstegui [1990] 2017, 257)—and Obbatalá, as audience members danced and sang along, making offerings to the orishas when appropriate. When the performers reached their last canto, each of the orishas rose and did their respective *bailes* in tandem, filling up the space with their colors and divine presences. Elegguá characteristically swiped a sip of one audience member's beer, and Yemayá made her waves toward the back of the crowd. When the musicians returned to the same chant that had opened the set, the orishas lined up in the center of the stage area and continued dancing together, slowly filing out of the space into the yard behind the patio. The musicians punctuated the end of the cycle with a concise hit to one of the congas, which the audience took as a cue to begin applauding and cheering.

In our interview with Alianys, he described the material, social, and spiritual significance of the orishas for himself and his community. He said that this was his first time performing as an orisha in the context of transformismo, and that he enjoyed it immensely. The costumes were all carefully crafted in accordance with religious symbolism. His dress as Yemayá, for example, had seven shells, as Yemayá is associated with the number seven and the sea. The dress was blue, her color and the color of the ocean, and the underskirt was white for the seafoam. While dancing, Alianys spun around so these colors could mix, as though a wave were crashing on a reef. He told me that he was a child of Yemayá himself, and I asked him what it felt like to dance as and for her. He replied:

> Cuando estás bailando para un santo, y más el que tienes coronado, ese santo se siente como que homenajeado, se siente como que alegre, ¿entiende? Porque tú lo estás representando. Y te llegas a erizar y todo; te llegas a sentir una cosa extraña así en el cuerpo, y esa es la vibración del mismo santo.

> When you are dancing for a saint, especially the one you are crowned with, that saint feels you are paying them homage, they are happy, you know? Because you are representing them. And you get goosebumps and everything; you start to feel something strange in your body, and that is the vibration of the very saint.

These feelings, however, are not just for Alianys. Most people in Arroyo Naranjo, he said, are religious, and he provides these experiences because they appreciate and enjoy the presence of religious performance in nightlife. This observation was borne out by the way almost everyone in attendance danced and sang along capably with the hired musicians. Moreover, Alianys said, representing the orishas at Apocalipsis brings good fortune—materially and spiritually—to the space, the house, and the party.[7]

After the religious cycle, the musicians continued with a few secular rumba songs that were also appreciated by the audience, who were happy to continue dancing and singing along to the folkloric music. Then the show closed with one more performance by Alianys and a rendition of Yoruba Andabo's "La cafetera" by Alberto and Dany. The indefatigable dancers in the audience welcomed the return of the rumba, and once again the duo's appearance turned into a collective folkloric performance, a collaboration between Black women on stage and in the audience. When the show ended, we moved our table to the wall and danced together as the DJ put on some music. Around 4 a.m., the handful of us who had come to see Alberto and Dany left together to catch a bus outside of the Iglesia de Santa Bárbara, and a second bus took several of us to El Vedado, where Kerry and I collapsed in our bed a little before 6 a.m.

That first night at Apocalipsis has stayed with me, in particular as an example of what transformismo can look and feel like when it is curated by Cubans for Cubans. The presence of Afrodiasporic folkloric and religious cultural production was certainly not unique to these spaces; rather, what set them apart was the fact that nothing was being packaged for foreign consumption, the performances were not culled for their material value to the tourism economy. Rather, religious performance and the rumba here were summoned for their social and spiritual value to Black Cubans from the repartos, for their capacity to fulfil the needs, desires, and joys of Cubans of typical means.

Festival: *Apocalipsis II*

During our interview with Alianys, he invited us back to Apocalipsis for their next *festival*, or drag competition. Alianys explained that they decided to begin holding *festivales* because they were a prominent feature of the local nightlife scene that both transformistas and audience members enjoy. The minute one festival ends, he said, everyone is asking for another. For the audience, he said, it is an opportunity to see more transformistas at one show, and for the transformistas it is an opportunity improve their craft and gain recognition. Like the performances above, the festival demonstrated how parties like Apocalipsis stage trans/queer performance and sociality not for their profitability but for their value to their neighbors.

Alianys told us to come early so we could spend time with the performers while they got ready, and when we arrived he ushered us into the dressing room near the entrance to the house. Titi, one of the judges, was sitting shirtless on the dressing room floor putting on makeup, and one of the competitors was getting ready with the help of a transformista friend. The atmosphere was focused, and I sensed that Kerry and I were intruding. Alianys had barely introduced us, and here were two non-Black foreigners occupying the space of these three Black/queer transformistas. Over time, however, the environment warmed up, particularly after Titi donned his wig. Bending over to affix it and then snapping back up to let the dirty blonde curls fall all around his shoulders, he explained that he finally felt like Deyanira, his drag persona, once his wig was on.

Kerry and I met several memorable figures backstage, in addition to the unforgettable Deyanira, who you will encounter again in chapter 4. Shakira was the travesti drag queen who had won the last competition at Apocalipsis and would be crowning tonight's queen. She asked me to take a picture with her and told me to show it to RuPaul back in the US. Ariadna was the kind transformista who had been helping out the competitor when we arrived and whose boyfriend Yamila was one of the transformistas on the jury. Javier, a young transformista who was just hanging around, asked us if we, too, were off-duty drag queens. And Adam and Leo were the two young competitors who had earlier compared the book you are reading to *Mariposas en el andamio*. They were just starting out in transformismo and were proud to tell me that their drag mother Sol would be performing that night, too, as an invited guest.

The show finally started a little after midnight with an ensemble performance by the three jurors Alianys, Titi, and Yamila. They brought a witchy aesthetic—complete with teased-out wigs and long, dark dresses—to an arrangement of "De mis recuerdos" (written by famed Cuban bassist Juan Formell and best known for Elena Burke's interpretation) from *Amigas*, a 2011 dance musical produced by choreographer Lizt Alfonso's well-known eponymous company. Then the emcee came on to introduce the competitors, six transformistas relatively new to the practice, and they began to move between various rounds, each with its own challenge. For one, the transformistas had to act as the host of a television show, interviewing another transformista about her career. For another, the competitors were invited to simply show off their best drag and lip-synching. Here, the visual and sonic aesthetics varied considerably: Some queens came out wearing long, elegant dresses that would fit in on the stage of any nightclub in Havana; others showed signs of limited resources, with creatively assembled outfits pieced together from multiple garments. One came on nearly nude, covered in black lace that exposed her sizable breastplate and a long open robe lined with black feathers.

Perhaps because this was a transformismo competition, the music tended toward the classic boleros that characterized the golden age of the performance complex, as well as more recent ballads that followed in that tradition. The transformistas lip-synched, for example, to songs by queens of Spanish-language music from Mexico, Spain, Cuba, and Puerto Rico such as Isabel Pantoja, Yuri, Massiel, and Lucecita Benítez. Aesthetically, then, the competition recalled the shows featured in *Mariposas*, which took place decades ago but not too far away.

Zahara, for example, gave a representative performance that clearly impressed both jury and audience. A thin, light-skinned Black transformista, she emerged in a simple but elegant gold-and-black patterned, form-fitting dress and a straight, burgundy wig that fell to the small of her back. "¡Guao!" someone shouted as she took the stage. Perhaps because of her nerves, her performance to a medley of songs by Isabel Pantoja was understated, her movements slight. Nevertheless, she was intensely focused, with impeccable lip-synching and a stare that fixed on us in the audience. The lyrics of the last number, "Para sobrevivir," seemed particularly self-referential. In the song, Pantoja rejects the various ethical compromises one might feel compelled to make to survive:

> Para sobrevivir dicen que hay que jugar
> Y ponerse del lado de aquel que triunfó
> Y mirar al caído desde un pedestal . . .
> Para sobrevivir dicen que hay que mentir
> Yo digo que no
>
> To survive they say you have to play
> And put yourself next to the one who triumphed
> And look down at the fallen from a pedestal . . .
> To survive they say you have to lie
> I say no

It struck me that this was precisely what Zahara and Alianys were doing, trying to make as honest a living as possible in a political economic context that made even the most basic needs and desires feel forever out of reach.

As the competitors got ready between rounds, the jurors broke up the show by giving performances of their own, some of which—like the performances above—prominently featured Afroreligious elements. Their presence signaled the enduring importance of Afrocuban religions to Apocalipsis, the repartos, and trans/queer performers more generally. For one *salida* (appearance), Alianys came out in a frilly red and white dress, lip-synching to a dreamy pop rendition of a chant to Elegguá. Before long, Alianys's husband appeared from the audience, once again representing the orisha. He pranced around the stage smiling, childlike and impetuous, and then approached the audience, reaching out to several attendees with his garabatos. When he came to our table, Argelia offered him some rum from her cup. He took a sip and then sprayed it back at us in a mist, the same way you would offer rum to Elegguá in a religious context.

The introduction gave way to folkloric ensemble Grupo Abbilona's traditional "Elegguá: Rey del mal y el bien," to which Alianys's husband danced onstage as the orisha. Several audience members approached him to make offerings, and when they did he would remove his hat, invite them to leave some money in it, and then brush them with his garabatos. Abbilona's "Yemayá: Reina del mundo" came next, and Alianys emerged once more as Yemayá, in the same dress I had seen her in my first time at Apocalipsis. Unlike her slow windup then, on this night she wasted no time, quickly launching into a dizzying spin that mixed the blue of her dress with the white of her underskirt. She took a breath to salute and embrace Elegguá and then got back to her dance, spinning so fast at one point that her tall blue headdress fell to the floor. She let it go and continued dancing feverishly for the orisha for several more minutes, letting her wig fall off, too, before heading backstage as the canto played out. Titi finally closed out this segment with Cuban singer Haila Mompié's "Madame Caridad," dedicated to Ochún, representing the orisha in a floor-length yellow dress and tall yellow headdress.

When they returned to the competition, the transformistas came out for a unique round: a transformismo *masculino* number in which the competitors had to dress and perform as men. For many of them, especially those who had effortlessly performed femininity moments earlier, this was an insurmountable challenge. Adam, for example, looked like a young girl dressed in her father's clothes when he came out to lip-synch to Spanish artist Melendi's emotive "Jardín con enanitos." Others, however, leaned more heavily into the masculine swagger of the genres they performed, grabbing their crotches as they swayed to reggaetón beats. None was as successful, however, as Yadira, who had towered in her elegant transformismo femenino just moments earlier. For this number, he appeared with a liberally unbuttoned shirt exposing his chest, a backward flat cap, and a little chinstrap beard penciled on his face. He looked like he could have been one of Argelia's recruits as he floated around the stage, flashing a toothy smile at the audience to Cuban salsa artist Leoni Torres's massively famous "Soledad." The audience ebulliently sang along with the blaring sound system and cheered for Yadira at the chorus.

The challenge no doubt provided some comedic relief to the audience, but it also reflected an expansive approach to gender at Apocalipsis. For one, the entire premise of these performances was based on an understanding that these performers were feminine subjects for whom such a masculine appearance would be difficult. Meanwhile, other feminine subjects who might be sidelined in mainstream spaces—like the travesti performer who won the last festival—here saw themselves celebrated as an important part of the festival. Which is to say nothing of the inclusion of Alberto and Dany above, when their performances were so often elided in mainstream transformismo spaces. It seemed that, at Apocalipsis, a kind of trans/queer gender equity was possible that felt out of reach in the mainstream nightclubs.

If this transformismo masculino detour had offered a bit of comedic relief, the announcement of the winner at the end of the competition was received with deadly seriousness. Nobody was surprised when two impressive but outperformed transformistas were awarded third and fourth place. But the crowd erupted when Reyna, who many had seen as the superior transformista of the night, was named runner up. "Noooooo!" two young women shouted continuously from the back of the audience, while the third- and fourth-place winners stood upstage with their mouths agape. Reyna humbly accepted the prize and shrugged her shoulders in acceptance, but the audience started shouting "Reyna! Reyna! Reyna!" repeatedly as the emcee tried to take control.

In the end, Esmeralda had to take the mic to address the audience: The jury was taking into consideration earlier performances from other nights of the competition, she explained, and they had also factored in the audience's preferences, which were split. "Hay que ser crítico y autocrítico con uno mismo, y reconocer las cosas cuando son" ("You have to be critical and self-critical and see things as they are"), she added. Reyna asked to speak, then, to assuage the audience:

> Quiero agradecer a este maravilloso jurado. . . . Yo me voy satisfecha. He conocido varias amistades aquí; nos llevamos todo el mundo muy bien. La he pasado muy bien. . . . ¡Yo me voy muy contenta! . . . Sea quien sea quien ganó el primer lugar, no me interesa. Todas las que estamos aquí, todas somos reinas.

> I want to thank this wonderful jury. . . . I'm leaving content. I've gotten to know several friends here; we all get along very well. I've had a great time. . . . I'm leaving very happy! Whoever wins, I don't care. All of us here are queens.

The audience cheered for her, and then Titi took the stage to announce that Erika, a young, slight Black transformista, was the winner of the competition. The audience showered her, too, with applause as her friends and supporters surrounded her onstage.

I do not mean to overstate the significance of the drama following the announcement of the winner of a drag competition. Such a reaction would be expected at similar events anywhere. But I am always a little struck when it happens in Cuba, as it does tend to, because there is generally very little at stake materially in the island's *festivales*. The reactions, then, are evidence of an alternative system of value through which audience members and participants understand trans/queer history, sociality, and aesthetics. All of us leave these parties into a world in which we are likely to be called maricón on the street, followed home by a lascivious man, ridiculed by our families. In the *festival*, however, the wig, the gestures, and the wit all count, they matter.

Of course, everyone is also there for the queer party that will go on afterward, making space for us to dance, joke, and talk until the buses start running again in the morning. Mostly, Kerry and I spent our time talking with Javier, who eventually led us to our departure a little before 4 a.m., since the first bus would pass by the Iglesia de Santa Bárbara at 4:20. Titi joined us, too, along with a few dancer friends, mostly young Black/queer femmes. They pranced and joked and laughed all the way to the bus stop, prodding me and Kerry about our relationship, as Cubans often did (Are you in an open relationship? Do you like Black men?). They paused periodically to strike poses, asking me at one point to photograph two of them as they supported each other on one side and executed high leg extensions on the other. Titi asked another man walking with us to hold him so he could show that his extension was even higher. I can still hear the way one of them lovingly described us all as "criaturas de la noche" (creatures of the night), almost eating the last "e" entirely, as was popular in the Havana dialect at that moment.

To me, the way they all carelessly danced their way through the madrugada in Párraga was a spectacular performance of their freedom. Notably, their carriage was a far cry from the body language of, for example, the trans and queer people who hung out all night in the little park off the apartment where Kerry and I lived in El Vedado, around the corner from Cabaret Las Vegas and down the street from Karabalí. There, another hotbed of trans/queer socializing, the tones were hushed, the glances furtive, and throughout the night police officers periodically picked off primarily Black trans/queer Cubans as a way to remind all the others that they are not quite free. Amalia was on to something, then, when she went all the way to Párraga in search of a place to relax and feel comfortable. Here, these creatures owned the night as they walked through it.

Fiesta: *Chalet*

Argelia and Ángel Daniel became involved with Apocalipsis because they, too, were a part of the neighborhood, with Argelia's house also situated in Párraga. Around the corner from Ángel Daniel's house in nearby Mantilla, they would occasionally perform at another weekend party that took place at an outdoor restaurant called Chalet. They told me that I should interview Rafael, the *anfitriona* (host) of that party, who performed as Lara. Our eventual interview with Rafael was perplexing: gracious, honest, and engaging, Rafael was also open about his distaste for effeminate queers, for travestis, for lesbian women, and for unrespectable trans/queer subjects in general. Rafael reflected some of the attitudes that shape mainstream trans/queer spaces and laid bare the ways they do still apply to some extent in the repartos. Notice, for example, that the parties I narrate in this chapter are both run by men in establishments that could not have been acquired and appointed without foreign capital.

Despite these limitations, when Kerry and I went to see Lara perform to a mostly heterosexual audience at Chalet in February 2018, we saw further evidence of the ways transformismo was providing fulfilling entertainment to Black Cubans of typical means at prices they could afford, in a political economic context in which the well-being of Cubans outside of the tourism economy was declining and becoming, it seemed, less and less a concern of the state.[8] In particular, Lara and her co-performer offered affectionate performances of their and their audience members' racialized and spatialized class positions in Havana that affirmed their value in the face of an economic context that disregards their worth.

That evening, Lara had invited the skilled comedic transformista Blanca Nieves as her guest. Not unlike Blankita, the humorista I discussed in chapter 1, Blanca's lip-synch performances relied on various material and affective incongruities, especially ones that dramatized everyday material realities of life in Cuba. For both of them, a chief incongruity is between their names and their appearances: Names like Blanca Nieves (literally Snow White) or Blankita de la Claridad del Sol (Little Whitey of the Sunlight) are meant to conjure extreme whiteness, which, in a Cuban context where beauty is associated with whiteness, sets the audience up to expect a beautiful queen. When the transformistas emerge bedraggled and Black instead, the audience is expected to laugh at the incongruity. When Lara—a lighter-skinned transformista—introduced Blanca, for example, she made a big deal about the beautiful queen named Blanca Nieves, "Snow White," who would be coming out. Then, Blanca, a lanky Black transformista, emerged to Gloria Trevi's "Que bueno que no fui Lady Di" (roughly, "Thank God I'm Not Princess Diana") in a lopsided hot-pink wig and a noticeably haphazard outfit that included a patterned long-sleeve top, a clashing form-fitting black patterned dress, and the cover for an electrical outlet as a pendant tied around her neck.

And yet there were subtle differences between Blanca's performance and that of Blankita that I narrated in chapter 1. Most significantly, Blanca's self-presentation did not rely so heavily on hemispheric tropes of blackface, including the depiction of Black women's bodies as physically excessive. Instead, her humor played primarily with her reluctance to participate in the codes of beauty standards generally accepted in transformismo. Her body unpadded, her movements jerky, she pranced around the stage and lifted up her skirt to expose her underwear while lip-synching to Trevi, who expressed relief at not having to endure the expectations of royal life, at being free to "comer a mis anchas / tacos de suadero y chuparme los dedos" ("eat as many beef tacos as I want and suck my fingers"). Like Trevi in Monterrey, Blanca insists that she is "plebeya pero contenta" ("plebian but happy") in Mantilla.

To me, this difference has to do with audience: whereas Blankita was performing in a space that sidelined Black women and welcomed their caricature, Blanca was performing for an audience that was dominated by Black women. If at nightclubs like Las Vegas gay men laugh at Black women in their absence, at Chalet the show was meant to solicit laughter *from* Black women, not at their expense but rather at a price they could afford. Moreover, her performance affirmed her audience's class position and their decision, too, to spend a night "plebeya pero contenta" in Mantilla.

Even when she was performing an emotive, foreign ballad—in this case Celine Dion's iconic "My Heart Will Go On" from the 1997 film *Titanic*—the incongruity Blanca exploited was not so much between her appearance and the song's beauty as between the frivolous nature of her performative gestures and the song's sappy sincerity. As the intro played, Blanca emerged from backstage standing inside a cardboard replica of the *Titanic* hanging from her shoulders on ropes. She mimed the song's lyrics with farcical precision: when Dion finished the first chorus with the line "My heart will go on and on," Blanca pretended to rip her beating heart out of her chest, toss it up in the air, and knock it out of the nightclub with a baseball bat, which had me and several others screeching with laughter. The performance was subtly different from that of Blankita, narrated in chapter 1, in the ways that—despite her deliberately messy appearance—it refused to settle on tropes of Black femininity as the butt of the joke.

Blanca's crowd work, too, catered to her audience, who she addressed lovingly, using light self-deprecation that flattered them while situating herself in community with them. After her first number, she took the mic and had a lighthearted back and forth with a couple seated near me and Kerry, a Black middle-aged school teacher and her husband:

BLANCA: ¿Cuántos años llevas junto con él?
AUDIENCE MEMBER: Diez.
B:¿Quién aguanta a quién, tú o él?
A: Los dos.
B: Ah, pero tú tienes cara de dar golpes, mi vida. De mandona.
A: Sí.
B:¿A ti dicen la patrona?
A: No, la señora de los cielos.
A: ¡Ay, que dura! ¡Eres una mariconsauria! Me encanta, mi vida.

BLANCA: How long have you been together?
AUDIENCE MEMBER: Ten years.
B: Who puts up with who? You or him?
A: Both of us.
B: Ah, but you look like you hit people, my dear. Like you're bossy.
A: Yes.
B: Do they call you boss?
A: No, lady of the heavens.
B: Ay, how fabulous! You are a fag-o-saurus! I love it, my dear.[9]

The audience laughed as Blanca folded her interlocutor into the Cuban language of queerness through her creative deployment of "mariconsauria."

Then Blanca turned her attention to another table, shouting "Compay Segundo!" as she beheld a Black man wearing a cap and likened him to the famed Cuban singer often pictured with his Panama hat on. "¡Que duro, moderno! Buenas noches." ("How fierce! Modern! Good evening."), she said, before addressing his glasses: "Tienes tremendos lentes, tremendo farol. Estás como la Habana Vieja, patrimonio de la humanidad. Me encantas." ("You have huge glasses, huge lamps. You're like Old Havana, patrimony of humanity. I love it.") Here, she played on the historic streetlamps that dot Old Havana, suggesting that his large, thick glasses looked like a pair of them.

Blanca's jokes at once situated her and her audience in a Cuban context, while perhaps suggesting a distance between them in Mantilla and her references: Old Havana in the epicenter of the tourism economy and Compay Segundo as a beloved figure from Cuba's Oriente. Lara later complemented this by acknowledging Chalet's place in the broader political economy of the island. After a performance of Isabel Pantoja's "Abrázame muy fuerte," she took the mic and sang a reworked version of the chorus: "Abrázame muy fuerte amor que llegó el pan a la bodega, y no quiero comer picadillo de soya porque me sabe a pelleja" ("Hold me tightly, my love, because the bread arrived at the bodega, and I don't want to eat soy *picadillo* because it tastes like leather"). "¡Muchacha!" an audience member shouted approvingly. Lara humorized the quotidian realities of Cubans: waiting hopefully for something (like bread) to return to the corner store or lamenting the repetitiveness of certain widely available foods (like ground soy).

While it would not be uncommon to encounter such humor in more mainstream spaces, other jokes from Chalet emphasized the distance between these two worlds. At one point, for example, a male audience member spanked Blanca playfully while walking from the bar to his table. "¡Ay!" she shouted, "esos son cinco cañas por tocarme" ("that will be five lashes for touching me"). Then she reconsidered: "Cinco pesos, no cinco cañas. Cinco pesos." ("Five dollars, not five lashes. Five dollars.") "¿En qué?" an audience member shouted out, asking to which currency Blanca referred, since five CUC was twenty-five times as valuable as 5 pesos in local money. "No, en cubano, mi vida," Blanca replied, adding, "Yo no soy tacaña; yo cojo cualquier cosa." ("No, in Cuban pesos, my dear. I'm not stingy; I'll take anything.")

Blanca's offhand comment reflected the real difference between the economy of the mainstream nightclubs in coastal Havana and that of places like Chalet. Recall Blankita's purse in chapter 1, for example, which distinguished between foreign currency and the Cuban peso, only picking up the former. Here, by contrast, Blanca would take anything. Indeed, the former spaces move in foreign currencies, from the cover charge to the bar tab to the tips for the performers. Meanwhile, in places like Chalet everything was charged and paid for in moneda nacional, the local currency, a signal at the time that it was an establishment geared toward working Cubans themselves.

Lara's musical and performative choices throughout the night ensured that even at these prices her audience enjoyed themselves, largely through their vocal participation. From Yuridia to Edith Márquez to Olga Tañón to Malú, Lara's spectators belted chorus after chorus along with her lip-synching, so much so that Lara would occasionally ask the DJ to mute the track and let the audience offer a line or two a cappella. If the voices sometimes deviated from normative beauty in their pitch or timbre, they always communicated the intense pleasure of the audience. These sonic collaborations came to a fever pitch in Lara's final salida, when she lip-synched to Tania Pantoja and Los 4's rendition of "Evidencias," the first song she performed by Cuban artists and her only danceable number. As the first verse played, all of the women seated at the table nearest Lara rose and began to dance. Lara—a trained dancer—broke into some subtle salsa steps as the percussion section entered, and one of the women in the front mirrored her. As the chorus approached, the audience's voices started filling the space, until eventually it sounded like all of the women in attendance were belting along at full voice.

Notice, then, how all of these performances were structured around Black women's joy. Still, when I think back to that night I picture the school teacher clapping along to Lara's dancing, the young woman who sang along to every song with a wide smile on her face, the older woman who tried to teach me and Kerry to dance later in the night, encouraging us with chants of "¡Bótalo! ¡Bótalo!," which referred to the jerky motion she wanted us to emulate in our hips. It is not as if singing and dancing don't take place in the mainstream nightclubs; of course they do. They just come at a price most Cubans cannot afford and in a context that is generally unwelcoming to Black women. The whole night at Chalet, by contrast, was a participatory spectacle aimed at providing entertainment, joy, and nourishment to Rafael's primarily Afrodescendent neighbors in Mantilla, of typical Cuban means, on the outskirts of both Havana and the social, political, and economic transformations that have characterized Cuba since the fall of socialism.

Another Havana

Lara closed the show with a beautiful rendition of Juan Gabriel's "Hoy me emborraché por ti." As the intro played, the bartender readied a can of beer and a glass for Lara, who took her wig off while lip-synching to the first verse. Juan Gabriel was one of the only male singers to whom transformistas would perform in drag, and by removing her wig Lara offered a kind of bridge between her semi-transformed appearance and Juan Gabriel's at times androgynous voice. During the first chorus, she turned to the bar, poured some beer into the glass, and held it up over her head, letting some spill down her hand and sleeve as though she were as drunk as the song's narrator. In the instrumental interlude following the first chorus, she chugged the beer that remained and then poured what was left in the can hard and sloppily, so that the beer foamed up wildly and spilled again from the glass onto her hand. As she lip-synched to the second verse, she dipped her fingers in the foam and sprayed it in the audience's direction. Finally, when the instrumental coda played out, Lara downed the rest of the drink, saving the tiniest bit so that she could toss it up above her head with the final band hit and let it shower her, to the audience's delight.

The foam that accumulated on the top of Lara's glass was a far cry from the *espuma* that Alianys represented with her undulating dress, to call to mind the domain of Yemayá, her mother and mine and yours. And yet weren't they doing similar work? With their performative gestures, both sacred and profane, Alianys and Rafael offered possibilities for Cubans of typical means to access affirming entertainment at a reasonable price. Through *folklor*, *festival*, and *fiesta*, they recognized the inherent value of Afrodiasporic cultural production and trans/queer performance not as tools to extract capital from tourism but as nourishing elements of Cuban culture that can provide social benefit to ordinary Cubans. These parties may not be a utopia, but they provide social and material resources in geographic, social, and economic contexts that have been more or less left out of Cuba's turn toward a tourism-centered economy, contexts that do not stand to benefit from the trans/queer parties and nightclubs in coastal Havana that cater to tourists and operate in foreign currencies. In this way, these parties enact a distinctly Cuban trans/queer worldmaking that goes beyond the material and symbolic limitations of mainstream trans/queer nightlife spaces on the island.

CHAPTER 3

El Mejunje

Provincial Transformismo

*This chapter is dedicated to the memory
of Javier "Cinthya"*

November 5, 2017, was an unusual day for the residents of Remate de Ariosa, a small rural town in the central Cuban province of Villa Clara. Early in the afternoon, a school bus arrived from the provincial capital of Santa Clara and came to a stop in front of the park at the center of the town. A handful of people from El Mejunje, Cuba's oldest queer cultural organization, streamed out and quickly got to work. One opened a panel on a lamppost to connect sound and lighting equipment to its electrical wiring; two others hung a large rainbow flag from the pillars of the gazebo in the middle of the park. There would be a show that evening, part of the community-based theater project Proyecto Yo Me Incluyo, and this would be the stage. In a few hours, Zulema—a decorated young transformista from Santa Clara—would fill all of that space with her high heels and her long arms. She would lip-synch to Spanish singer Isabel Pantoja's interpretation of Juan Gabriel's "Perdona si te hago llorar," leaning into Pantoja's flamenco-inspired aesthetics with a floor-length light blue gown and a massive bunch of red flowers affixed to the left side of her low bun. She would gather her skirt in one hand, and—while gesticulating above her head with the other—turn fully around, sweeping the gazebo with one corner of the dress's hem, while seemingly all of the people of Remate looked on in wonder.

In this chapter, I tell a story about the work that transformismo and transformistas are doing in Villa Clara province. Above, Zulema brought the ideological and aesthetic contents of Santa Clara's El Mejunje to rural Remate de Ariosa out of a sense of solidarity with her fellow *villaclareñxs*. Alongside her, I suggest here, Santa Clara's transformistas manage to bring together the provincial center and the periphery, private and public economies, and Revolutionary ideology and trans/queer interests in order to produce a distinct *mejunje*, or mix, that embraces a coalitional politics that exceeds the limitations of mainstream LGBT spaces and politics. Like the parties on the outskirts of Havana I described in chapter 2, then, transformistas in the provinces are finding creative ways to imagine and create beyond the shortcomings of mainstream trans/queer spaces that are caught up with the social and economic exclusions of the tourism economy.

I contextualize this work by first offering some history of El Mejunje and discussing its place in Santa Clara and Villa Clara. I further reflect on the role provincial transformismo might play in discussions about regionalism and space in Cuban studies and trans/queer studies. I then take you to a handful of events in Villa Clara Province: a show at El Mejunje, the performance in Remate that opened the chapter, the debut of a new queer party in the center of Santa Clara, and a night out at a ritzy outdoor nightclub on the outskirts of town. Together, these performances and the accompanying commentary of Santa Clara's transformistas demonstrate how transformismo in the province draws on particular social and ideological commitments to foster solidarities and honor intergenerational affinities between trans/queer people.

Gloriosa Santa Clara

In 2009, the *Miami Herald* published an article describing the celebration of the 25th anniversary of El Mejunje in Santa Clara, Cuba. In it, one participant suggested that there are two sights to see in Santa Clara: the massive monument to Ernesto "Che" Guevara that houses his remains, and El Mejunje. "[P]odríamos decir," they said, "que el que venga a Santa Clara y no visite al 'Che' y no vaya a lo de Silverio nunca estuvo en esta ciudad" (Ríos 2009; "We could say that anyone who goes to Santa Clara without visiting Che and Silverio's place never came to this city").

What a curious pair, then, this city upholds: Historians point to Guevara as the architect of the Revolution's most homophobic policies and practices, including the UMAP camps I discussed in chapter 1. And now, to go to Santa Clara, where Guevara captured *el tren blindado*, you have to pass as well by El Mejunje de Silverio, the cradle of transformismo in Cuba.[1] Here, I tell you a bit about the ideas that undergird El Mejunje as a space, how it fits within the broader context of Villa Clara, and the significance of Villa Clara to discussions about regionalism in Cuba, Cuban studies, and trans/queer studies.

Much of the history of El Mejunje has been documented elsewhere, so I will focus here on the comments of Ramón Silverio Gómez, El Mejunje's founder, on the meanings of the place in an interview with me and Kerry in November 2017.[2] Silverio founded El Mejunje in 1985 as a space that was premised on a holistic and total inclusion of social groups at the time. "A la par de no excluir," Silverio explained to us, "pues empezó a asistir los excluidos de otros lugares, que para mí todos tienen la misma importancia. Así empezaron los gays, las lesbianas, los roqueros, que eran gente muy excluidas también y muy mal vista." ("Since I didn't exclude, groups that had been excluded from other places started to attend, which for me are all equally important. So, the gays came and the lesbians, the rockers, who were also very excluded and looked down upon.")[3]

Silverio understood these groups as among those left out of the Revolutionary imagery of "El Hombre Nuevo," the New Man.[4] At that time, he explained, the country was caught up with this expectation for the New Man who would create Cuba's socialist future, a man who, in Silverio's estimation, did not exist. Instead, for Silverio, the state's rigid insistence itself generated counterproductive social exclusions: "Un Hombre Nuevo no podía ser gay, no podía tener el pelo largo, no podía ser esto ni el otro, y creo que también allí se perdió una oportunidad de darle cabida a toda esta gente que estaban buscando también un lugar en la sociedad para ellos aportar." ("A New Man can't be gay, can't have long hair, can't be this or that, and I think they lost the opportunity to give space to all of those people who were looking for a place for themselves in society.")

In 1991, El Mejunje moved to its fourth and present location, and received its first proposal for a show that would include transformismo in the context of an homage to Freddie Mercury, who had died earlier that year. Before long, El Mejunje became an epicenter of transformismo in Cuba and synonymous with trans/queer activism on the island.

Nevertheless, Silverio has always maintained that El Mejunje has a collective mission, and he ties its successes in cultivating trans/queer space to El Mejunje's activism "a favor de los roqueros, a favor de los músicos, a favor de los negros, de la mujer" ("for the rockers, for musicians, for Black people, for women"). His aim is to be "comprometido con todo, no con una sola causa" ("committed to everything, not just one cause"). This policy of social inclusion underscores the fact that El Mejunje—despite its prominence within the country, its popularity among tourists, and its profitability—is a distinct space from the mainstream queer nightclubs I described in chapter 1, which cater to particular clientele based primarily on their access to capital.

It would be nearly impossible to overstate the tremendous significance of El Mejunje to the transformistas who perform there. Every transformista I interviewed who has a relationship to the space described Silverio as family and El Mejunje as home. Zulema said, simply, "para mí El Mejunje es todo" ("For me, El Mejunje is everything"). "And Silverio?" I asked her in response. "Más todavía. . . . No sé qué sucedería el día que él no existiera" ("Even more. . . . I don't know what will happen when he no longer exists"). Cinthya, one of the more veteran transformistas of El Mejunje at the time, explained that "Cada ladrillo de este lugar cuenta una historia de un marginado" ("Every brick of this place tells the story of a marginalized person"), herself among them. Then she told us, "Lo he dicho muchas veces: Dios, Fidel Castro, Silverio" ("I've said it many times: God, Fidel Castro, Silverio"), using her hand to indicate the respective rank of these three figures. Though her trinity seemed unusual in the face of the historical tensions between religiosity, queerness, and the Cuban Revolution, several others echoed it during my time in Santa Clara. For Santa Clara's transformistas, there did not seem to be a contradiction between trans/queer vitality and the Cuban Revolution. Instead, they drew on their pride in el Che and the Revolution to articulate an otherwise vision for Cuba's future.

This comfort in strange bedfellows perhaps reflects the broader tensions that make up Villa Clara Province's history and present. Revolutionary agrarian reform transformed the agricultural sector, which had been dominant in the province since at least the 19th century. After the fall of the Soviet Union, however, the keys off the northern coast of Villa Clara became home to the most exclusive resorts on the island. Many of the tourists who come to Santa Clara, in fact, are foreigners spending a night in the city after landing at the airport before taking their private transport to the beaches. Villa Clara's borders, then, contain a mix of both the most redistributive reforms of the Revolution and those that have produced the greatest social and material inequity.

The provincial context and content I offer here contribute to existing scholarly attention to regionalism in Cuba while working outside of the tension often documented between eastern and western Cuba. As I discussed in chapter 2, Cubans and Cuban studies scholars often critique the tendency to represent Havana as though it were all of Cuba. More specifically, some Cuban studies scholars have lamented the ways that Havana is called to stand in for the nation, despite the fact that the east has historically been the epicenter of the revolutionary activity that has come to define the national project (see Bodenheimer 2015, 26–43). In this chapter, I mean to draw attention to the cultural significance of central Cuba—not least in the realm of transformismo—while continuing to highlight the internal heterogeneity of Cuba's provinces, especially in the divide between the principal city center and the periphery of the province.

This account of the work and ideas of Santa Clara's transformistas also fits curiously within broader discussions in trans/queer studies about space, geography, and region. Certainly, following Gayatri Gopinath, this chapter looks at "queer regions" in a "subnational sense" (2018, 30), aiming to situate local creativity within transnational discourses about gender and sexuality. As Scott Herring (2010) did with regard to New York City, it balks at the presumptuousness of trans/queer Havana, which too often stands in for Cuba as a whole. And yet all of Cuba sits in an uneasy relationship to trans/queer studies, since most of the interdiscipline imagines that trans/queer life and politics begin and end in English-speaking North America, or at most in some vague "global" sphere. Perhaps most accurately, then, since this chapter offers one look at trans/queer performance in a midsize province in an embattled Caribbean nation, it recalls the kinds of approaches trans/queer studies authors have taken to disregarded populations in underexamined places, like Marlon Bailey (2013) in Detroit and Julio Capó (2017) in Miami.

Regardless, this chapter and the transformistas who populate it invest in creative coalitions that get beyond the failures of mainstream LGBT politics. By invoking this coalitional politics, I refer to Cathy Cohen's pathbreaking Black/queer conception of "a politics where one's relation to power, and not some homogenized identity, is privileged in determining one's political comrades" (1997, 438). I see this "differential coalitional consciousness," to borrow from Sandoval (2000, 79–81), as a Third World feminist/trans/queer strategy for liberation. Throughout the pages that follow, Villa Clara's transformistas link their fortunes as trans/queer people to relations of power in Cuba as they pertain to racialization, geography, and capital. In doing so, they go beyond the limitations of trans/queer spaces that are situated in closer proximity to Cuba's tourism economy.

A Night at El Mejunje

Kerry and I arrived in Santa Clara in November 2017 in the wake of Hurricane Irma and in the company of the crew for *¡Quba!* (2024), a documentary being made by the US American artist Kim Anno. After Silverio and Kim visited Caibarién to see the recovery efforts following the storm, Silverio invited Adela Hernández—the delegate to the Asamblea Municipal del Poder Popular (Municipal Assembly of Popular Power, the local government body) for Caibarién and the first transgender person to hold public office in Cuba—to perform in the small theater at El Mejunje. Like the work to repair Caibarién after Irma, the show at El Mejunje was a community effort: Cinthya, one of El Mejunje's most celebrated transformistas, helped to dress and do makeup for Silverio and Adela, and Blaccucini—El Mejunje's resident *humorista* (comedian)—rounded out the lineup. The show would provide insight into the ideological backbone of El Mejunje and a clear articulation of the relationship these transformistas imagine between the Cuban Revolution, trans/queer liberation, and social and political transformation more generally.

For the performance, Silverio made a rare appearance in drag, emerging as Carmita, an outspoken *campesina*, to diasporic Cuban Carlos Oliva's "You Are Unique," whose bouncy retro energy gave the event the feel of a talk show. Carmita wore an ornate black gown with a gothic aesthetic, complemented by the crucifix that sat on her exposed chest; a longish shock of hair extended from her short, sensible wig to frame the right side of her face. She greeted the public and introduced Adela, who was a sight: A massive, teased out, hot pink wig stood up to make an impressive oval around her face. Her dress combined a sparkling silver bralette with a form-fitting black body and short skirt. Off-white stockings were tucked into leopard-print, high-heeled, lace-up boots (see figure 7).

In many ways, the event felt like any other drag show: A dramatic transformista and a comedic transformista split the bill, and a young singer rounded out the cast. Adela, however, was returning to transformismo, something she had experimented with in the 1990s, after a

Fig. 7. Adela performs at El Mejunje, with Carmita, the drag persona of Silverio, in the background.

long hiatus. "Aquí estoy para demostrarles a ustedes que también tengo talento. Quizás no sea la mejor como hay estrellas aquí, que aquí está Cinthya . . ." ("I am here to show you that I have talent, too. Perhaps I am not the best like the stars here; we have Cinthya here . . ."), she said before her first performance, gesturing toward the veteran transformista in the audience.

Seated in the front, I could see Adela's hand trembling slightly as it grasped a microphone. She had chosen to perform to Los 4 and Tania Pantoja's rendition of "Evidencias," a lively, danceable number that was very popular among transformistas at the time. Early on, she flubbed some of the lip-synching, clearly intimidated by the legendary transformistas all around her. Before long, though, she found her stride, dancing gracefully and deftly, swaying her hips and stepping surely in her considerable and narrow heels.

Blaccucini, by contrast, felt nowhere as comfortable as she did on any stage at El Mejunje. She came out from backstage in a gorgeous chartreuse jumpsuit and massive gold hoop earrings to perform nonagenarian cabaret star Juana Bacallao's eponymous anthem "Yo soy Juana Bacallao." Like Bacallao, Blaccucini mixed grace with humor, interrupting her lithe movements with ridiculous facial expressions that coincided with band hits at the ends of phrases. In an interview a few days later, Blaccucini told me that she used to make herself up in a grotesque way for comedic effect, not unlike Blankita, her comedic counterpart in Havana who I discussed in chapter 1. She learned, however, that she could remove all that and still be funny, so she did. The effect was a performance that explicitly referenced her blackness without ridiculing it, instead offering a loving portrayal of Bacallao distinct from the kinds of performances I narrated in chapter 1.

The show was unlike a typical performance at El Mejunje, however, in the space it offered Adela, Silverio, and Cinthya to reflect on the social and political nature of their work in contemporary Cuba (see figure 8). Through her commentary, Adela united her community-based work with her belief in the strength and power of trans and queer people on the island. Off the bat, she commented on her historic status as a trans public official, explaining, "me he dado la tarea de mostrarle a mi pueblo, a la comunidad gay que puede contar conmigo para lo que sea" ("I've given myself the task of showing to my town, to the gay community that they can count on me for anything"). She mixed, then, her commitment to her constituents and to an imagined "comunidad gay" that stretched throughout the island.

Adela then turned to her own upbringing *en el campo* as a way to complicate dominant understandings about the relationship between trans/queer people, campesinos, and the Cuban Revolution. Growing up, she explained, she did indeed face the kind of homophobic abuse Cubans would expect in the countryside. But, she amended, the very campesinos who were hurling insults at her during the day were waiting for her in the cane fields in the evening "para que Adela moliera tanta caña como el mismo central que lleva mi nombre" ("so that Adela ground as much cane as the very mill that has my name"), referring to the Adela sugar mill and using grinding metaphorically, to be clear. "Así que no eran tan homofóbicos los campesinos" ("So, the country people weren't that homophobic"), she explained:

> Demostraban aquel don de ser hombre, tan hombre, tan cubano como las palmas, pero de noche eran tan maricones como los gays que hay en este país tan revolucionarias como nosotras, como Cinthya, como Silverio, como yo. Y como muchas más que le estamos demostrando al mundo y a este proceso revolucionario que, aunque tengamos preferencias sexuales diferentes, también somos comunistas y somos revolucionarias y damos nuestras vidas para esta Revolución.

Fig. 8. Adela, Carmita, and Cinthya (out of drag) discuss the significance of El Mejunje to Santa Clara and Cuba.

> They showed that talent for being a man, such a man, so Cuban like the palm trees, but at night they were so gay like the gays there are in this country so revolutionary like us, like Cinthya, like Silverio, like me. And like many others who are showing the world and this revolutionary process that, even though we have different sexual preferences, we are also communists, and we are revolutionaries, and we are giving our lives for this Revolution.

In her remarks, the perceived distance between the campesino and the queer, the queer and the Revolution, is collapsed in favor of an articulation of the revolutionary histories and potentials of trans/queer people.

Cinthya's comments perhaps tempered the officialist discourse of Adela, but they evinced a similar steadfastness. "Es que no somos mujeres comunistas" ("It's that we're not communist women"), she countered, "somos maricones patriotas de estos tiempos, y esta es la revolución que nos toca" ("we are patriotic faggots of today, and this is our revolution"). Here, Cinthya distanced herself from the historical imagery of the "mujer comunista," the kind of woman who would have been fighting in the Revolution, who would later participate in the Federación de Mujeres Cubanas. But she also distanced herself from the respectable discourse of LGBT rights, of "hombres gay" and "mujeres trans." Cinthya, instead, is a "maricón patriota."

Kerry and I later asked Cinthya about this complex cluster of terms (i.e., mujer, comunista, maricón, patriota, revolución) in an interview.[5] He, out of drag as Javier, explained that he always had tremendous pride in the Revolution, in the important role Santa Clara played, and in the intimate relationship between his city and Ernesto "Che" Guevara. But it had hurt him deeply when he learned more about the history of homophobia in the Cuban Revolution and the important role Guevara played in its elaboration. Nevertheless, he chooses to understand these as faults of humanity, possibilities for revolutionary evolution that has yet to come, that is perhaps on the horizon.

Maricones, as Javier went on to say, have an important role to play in this (r)evolution:

> Los maricones sí somos patriotas. Somos tan luchador y enfrentamos a tanta gente que somos rebelde, somos patriotas. No hay un sinónimo más grande para un maricón que la palabra patriota, porque es que hacemos revolución. Contra los heterosexuales, contra los decisores, contra los políticos, contra los administradores de trabajo, contra los profesores, estamos constantemente luchando. Entonces, ¿qué somos?

> We faggots are indeed patriots. We are so persistent and we confront so many people that we are rebellious, we are patriots. There is no greater synonym for a faggot than the word patriot, because we revolt. Against heterosexuals, against the powerful, against the politicians, against our bosses, against our teachers, we are always fighting. So, what are we?

Here, Cinthya inverts the historical logic of the Cuban Revolution toward trans/queer people. Where the Cuban state has seen us as a threat to its cohesion for our minoritized subjectivity, our challenges to social norms, Cinthya sees our investments in *rebeldía*, itself a key term in the Revolutionary lexicon.[6]

Cinthya sees revolution in the work of El Mejunje. During our interview, she lamented not having been old enough to fight in the Revolution, to participate in the literacy campaign. But, she explained, "Ahora lo hago, lo hago en Me Incluyo. Voy, hago shows, converso, ayudo." ("Now I do it, I do it through Me Incluyo. I go, I do shows, I talk, I help."), referring to Proyecto Yo Me Incluyo (PYMI), the project I referenced at the beginning of this chapter. Far from being antithetical to Revolutionary aims, then, for Cinthya transformismo is a tool for carrying out Revolutionary work.

Back at the show at El Mejunje, she recounted the first performance of Proyecto Yo Me Incluyo (PYMI) in the rural town of Manicaragua, an hour south of Santa Clara. When they first arrived, she and Blaccucini were nervous, unsure how they would be received in the setting, surrounded by eighty or so of their audience members' horses. Though at first people did keep their distance, Cinthya and Blaccucini were surprised that by the time they left, people were hugging and kissing them, snapping pictures alongside them because they wanted "una foto con una mujer famosa" ("a picture with a famous woman"). "No saben el amor que sentí esa noche," she told us; "me sentí artista por primera vez." ("You have no idea the love I felt that night; I felt like an artista for the first time.") She continued, "Aprendí ese día que el tiempo que la gente pierde en las grandes ciudades en criticar a los gays, en las montañas lo aprovechan en ser felices. Por tanto . . . me encanta ser un maricón de montaña" ("I learned that day that the time that people lose in big cities criticizing gay people, in the mountains they use it to be happy. For that reason . . . I love being a faggot of the mountains").

Here, I see the kind of deep reciprocity that was indeed an important part of early Revolutionary efforts like the literacy campaign. Blaccucini once suggested to me that there is not homophobia in more remote parts of the island, but *desconocimiento*, a lack of awareness. Through PYMI, the transformistas of El Mejunje replace desconocimiento with intimacy and solidarity, forming a coalition between the campesino and the queer.[7]

Blaccucini closed the show that evening at El Mejunje with a spirited collective performance (see figure 9). She came out lip-synching to a live rendition of "¿Qué culpa tengo yo?" by Cuban-American lesbian singer Albita, looking stunning in her tan high-heel shoes, a green velvet bodysuit, and a curly black wig. During the rumba break that comes in the middle of the song, while Albita sings well-known *comparsa* refrains from Cuba's Carnaval tradition, Blaccucini marched across the stage, as though she were heading down the street in a procession, occasionally breaking into a rumba-inspired step or two. Eventually, she invited Silverio and Adela to join her, and they danced around the edges of the stage. When the song eased back into its chorus, Blaccucini extended her hands so that Adela and Silverio could come closer. They each took one of Blaccucini's hands, and the three of them walked downstage

Fig. 9. Blaccucini performs at El Mejunje, holding a young singer's hand while Adela looks on.

slowly to the beat as Albita repeated "¿Qué culpa tengo yo?" As the band played Albita out, they stood together, receiving our applause, but Blaccucini did not miss her mark to lip-synch to the chant of "¡Cuba! ¡Cuba!" that closes the song.

You could be forgiven for reading the performance as a complication of the broader Revolutionary rhetoric: Albita is well known for having left Revolutionary Cuba, and here she rehearses white Cubans' historical and ongoing cooptation of Black popular culture. I might see Blaccucini as reterritorializing the song, making it Black again while exceeding the limitations of both poles that have defined Cuban existence and representation at least since the fall of socialism: the embrace on the one hand of liberal reform by the Cuban state that has exacerbated social and economic inequality, and on the other hand the racial antipathy that has driven Miami Cubans' desire for a return to their pre-Revolutionary world order.

I am more tempted, however, to take the song at its word, to appreciate what it might mean for the four people who made this show to ask, "¿Qué culpa tengo yo de haber nacido en Cuba?" ("What fault is it of mine that I was born in Cuba?"). Yes, of course, the Revolution is deeply unfinished; yes, of course, Cuba struggles with a tremendous lack of resources in the face of insurmountable need. But we are going to do what we can as trans/queer people to carry out "la revolución que nos toca." This committed, communitarian spirit was not unique to El Mejunje, however, but instead radiated outward to influence performances I saw in rural Villa Clara, at an incipient party downtown, and at a shiny new nightclub on the outskirts of the city.

Proyecto Yo Me Incluyo

Our journey to the show in Remate that opened this chapter began, of course, at El Mejunje, where we met up with Kim and her crew before departing Villa Clara's principal city. After the hour-long drive from Santa Clara to Placetas, we turned off the main drag onto a dirt road that followed the train tracks that run between Santa Clara and Camagüey. We gingerly crept along this winding path in our white van for another hour or so—during which the *habaneros* made lighthearted jokes about the remoteness of the town (e.g., "¿Remate? ¿Viene después de jaque mate?" ["Remate? Does that come after checkmate?"])—before finally arriving in Remate de Ariosa. Once there, we would all see a performance that demonstrated just how transformistas santaclareñas deploy their unique mix of Revolutionary and trans/queer liberatory ideas to form solidarities between the city and the campo.

Remate is a small, rural town in Remedios, the municipality best known for its Parrandas, Carnival-like celebrations that take place in the week leading up to Christmas. Remate felt far from this purportedly raucous tradition: the semipaved roads were lined with concrete houses, roosters ambled in the corner of a field where some young boys were playing baseball, and a couple of dogs lazily napped in a patch of grass nearby. We parked the van outside of the Círculo Social, where we were received lovingly by an official from the town, and Silverio and his troupe arrived in their repurposed school bus and began setting up. Before the show, the town feted the visitors with a hearty *almuerzo* of roast pork, rice, and black beans for all of us. Toward the end of the meal, the artists discreetly peeled away to start preparing for their performance.

The show would feature two transformistas who together encompassed the recent history of transformismo in Santa Clara. Laura had been a member of the famed Compañía Futuro, the group of artists who participated in the very beginnings of El Mejunje, its move to its present location, and the Freddie Mercury memorial in 1991, the year she began performing as a transformista. And Zulema—eighteen years Laura's junior—belonged to the younger generation with which, according to Silverio, "terminó lo interesante del transformismo" ("ended what was interesting in transformismo"). There was a familial bond between the two, in fact: Laura was one of the artists who brought Zulema into transformismo in around 2005 along with her friend Lili Martin, who now lives in Miami.

Kim, Kerry, and I followed Laura and Zulema to spend time with them as they prepared for the show, finding them in a building just off the park where they would be performing. When we entered, we quickly learned that the oppressively hot space was a Masonic lodge, with the faces of Grand Masons past looking down on us from framed photographs high up on the walls. The artists helped each other get ready: Laura shared her makeup with Zulema; Maikel, a comedian who would also be performing, secured a tight beige corset around Laura before she draped a glittering black dress over it. As soon as she was dressed, however, Laura escaped to a chair outside of the building's door, avoiding both the heat and—she would tell us later—the stares of the Grand Masons.

The show started a little after 8:30 p.m. with an announcement from the town official, who offered a certificate to Silverio for his work in Remate: "En el nombre del Consejo Popular y de todo el pueblo de Remate, hacemos reconocimiento a Ramón Silverio y el Proyecto Yo Me Incluyo por el aporte sistemático en la vida sociocultural hacia nuestro poblado. 'Honrar, honra,' como dice nuestro José Martí." ("In the name of the People's Council and of all of the people of Remate, we recognize Ramón Silverio and Proyecto Yo Me Incluyo for the systematic support toward the sociocultural life of our town. 'To honor is an honor,' as our José Martí said."). The event had the discursive trappings of state-sanctioned LGBT rights events: the name PYMI dovetailed with the slogan "Me Incluyo" ("I Include Myself," or "Count Me In") from recent Jornadas, and the obligatory Martí quote situated us within the imaginary of the Cuban state.

Nevertheless, the tone of the events that followed seemed to sidestep the political posturing and international image consciousness that permeate such spaces. Silverio took the microphone and went on to thank the official, welcome all those in attendance, and explain the purpose of PYMI:

Este espectáculo . . . está dedicado a lograr que estas comunidades rurales sean comunidades libres de homofobia y de transfobia donde no se discrimine a nadie por el color de la piel, por el pensamiento, y por su preferencia sexual. Comunidades que vivan en paz, vivan en harmonía, en contacto con la naturaleza, que realmente están dentro y rodeado de esa naturaleza. Y eso es nuestro mensaje que creemos y estamos convencidos que ya ustedes lo han aprendido y, bueno, se han hecho personas, por supuesto, más cultas, personas que aceptan a todas y a todos.

This show . . . is dedicated to ensuring that these rural communities are communities free from homophobia and transphobia, where no one discriminates against anyone for their skin color, their thoughts, or their sexual preference. Communities that live in peace, that live in harmony, in contact with nature, which are really inside of and surrounded by that nature. And that is our message that we believe and we are convinced that you have already learned and, well, you have become people of course, more aware, people who accept everyone.

If his depiction of the countryside comes off as a bit patronizing, it is worth noting that Silverio himself is of the *campo*, having grown up in a rural setting and retaining his commitment to social life there (see figure 10). I was more struck in his commentary by the seemingly easy marriage between LGBT rights, regional stratification, and racial inequity in a nation known for its discourses of racelessness and the hard price that Cubans in the provinces have had to pay for the focus on tourism and development in Havana since the fall of socialism.

And yet this marriage makes perfect sense given Silverio's commitments and his orientation with regard to the arts and culture in Revolutionary and trans/queer Cuba. PYMI emerged right out of this intersection: For decades, Silverio had been putting on community theater in the Escambray Mountains, premiering works that would later appear onstage at El Mejunje and following in a tradition of community theater on the island.[8] For one performance in Manicaragua, however, the principal actors were not able to make it, so Silverio had to invent something for the show. Where would Silverio turn, then, except to the transformistas of Santa Clara and El Mejunje? He brought two comedians and two transformistas (Cinthya and Blaccucini) to put together a little variety show for the rural public, they gave the show that Cinthya described above, and its success gave birth to PYMI.

That night in Remate, Laura opened the show, coming out to the vin-

Fig. 10. Silverio introduces the show Proyecto Yo Me Incluyo in rural Remate de Ariosa.

tage sounds of a medley of songs by Spanish singer Massiel, her floor-length, long-sleeved sparkling dress and faux diamond neckpiece sparkling in the stage lights (see figure 11). The improvised sound system blasted the music clear out into the night in Remate, showering us in Massiel's piercing voice. Accordingly, Laura's performance was all drama: sharp lip-synching, an icy stare, and measured hand gestures that frequently mimed the lyrics. The medley started with "Hallelujah" and passed through "Eres" and "Te amo" before closing with "El amor," whose intensely '80s sound (e.g., its rhythmic piano left-hand ostinato that undergirds spacey synthesizers) has perhaps been resurrected now because of the song's prominent place in the 2016 Irish film *Viva*, which centered around transformismo in Cuba.

For this last song, Laura planted herself upstage and fixed her gaze out into the audience as the ostinato bass riff played. She was captivating in her stillness, breaking it only to follow the lyrics with subtle hand gestures. Each time Massiel described the effects of "el amor" in the second person (e.g., "te hace daño"), Laura would point out into the audience, implicating each of us in the narrative. As the song's affect grew more stormy, Laura scrunched up her face and tightened her neck, as though Massiel's just-raspy voice were coming from her mouth and out through the speakers.

Fig. 11. Laura Marlen, one of the most veteran transformistas still active in Santa Clara, performs in Remate.

When the climax approached, Laura gracefully and deliberately took part of her long skirt in her hand and slowly descended to her knees, slapping the floor with her right hand as Massiel sing-shouted "y te deja hecho mierda" ("and it leaves you fucked up"). Laura offered the next few lines on her knees, and then, as Massiel sang the turn-around of the last phrase—"Y de pronto se para y te ve y se apiada" ("And suddenly it stops and sees you and takes pity on you")—Laura slowly rose to her feet again, using the gentlest touch on one of the gazebo's pillars to support herself. She made the sign of the cross with the word "apiada" and blew a kiss to the audience before lip-synching the last few repetitions of "el amor" and making her way offstage to applause.

I didn't know it then, but this performance in many ways dramatized Laura's own path in Santa Clara, the various difficulties she had been through and the way she had navigated them all to remain performing after thirty years. Laura had been one of the main transformistas in the city in the 1990s and 2000s, helping to form Compañía Futuro and El Mejunje and to launch others' careers, like that of Zulema. In 2011, however, she became sick and had to take a year off of transformismo. Though she remains partially paralyzed, she came

Fig. 12. Zulema, a prominent young transgender transformista from Santa Clara, performs in Remate.

back to performing in 2012 and is the only transformista actively performing from the *época de oro*, the golden age of transformismo in the 1990s and early 2000s.

Zulema appeared next, and through her number she closed some of the distance between the santaclareña performers and their rural audience. She ascended the steps of the gazebo to a medley of songs by Selena that opened with the ranchera "Tú, sólo tú." She seemed impossibly tall, with her sky-high red heels, a bright red bodysuit, and frills dancing off the lace bodice and sleeves; it looked as if her arms, dramatically posed above her head, would easily reach the structure's ceiling (see figure 12). By the end of the song, however, she had brought herself down, sitting upstage to perform to an older man at the front of the audience. For "Si una vez"—in this case the live rendition by Mexican singer Alicia Villarreal—Zulema descended further into the crowd, dancing just in front of them as they clapped along with the beat.

The show went on with an entertaining set by the comedian and another round of appearances by Laura and Zulema, and then we all made our way back to the Círculo Social for a little snack, receiving the transformistas with applause when they finally followed out of drag. Eventually, we all made the long trek back to Santa Clara, Kerry and

I arriving at our *hostal* around midnight. Like Blaccucini and Cinthya described above, I felt transformed by the experience, not necessarily because it had destabilized any preconceived notions I had about the campo, but rather because I had seen trans/queer performers give of themselves not for profit, but for the benefit of those who had been left out of Cuba's rush to amass foreign capital through its tourism economy. That evening, provincial transformismo provided community education around gender and sexuality as well as free public entertainment in rural Cuba.

Una Fiesta Nueva

The kinds of intergroup solidarities that were on stage in Remate radiated throughout diverse spaces in the city of Santa Clara. In one new party started by a middle-aged gay santaclareño, for example, the performers and their audience demonstrated their investments in creative and intergenerational coalitions. Kerry and I got there by way of a worker at El Mejunje who we befriended over our two trips to Santa Clara. We sought him out each time we went to El Mejunje, and he would invite us to other places around town, such as El Bosque, perhaps the most popular place for transformismo in Santa Clara beside El Mejunje. The outdoor nightclub was known for its Wednesday-night shows, but the evening we went with David the performance had been canceled because of rain. No matter; we spent the night chatting and dancing with the rest of the trans/queer public happy to brave the weather in order to socialize. Among us were a group of volunteers from the HSH network (for men who have sex with men) of the Centro Provincial de Prevención (Provincial Center for Prevention, CPP) who were there passing out condoms and safer-sex literature. I felt an affinity with them, as I had done similar work as an undergrad, and we struck up a conversation. One of them, who I will call Héctor, told us that he had started trying his hand at transformismo and would be hosting "una fiesta nueva," a new party with a show in a bar off of Parque Vidal the following night.

David, Kerry, and I were all eager to go, so the next evening we met up at El Mejunje and walked over together. When we arrived, we were shocked to hear that all of the tables had been reserved already. Fortunately, David had a friend with an extra seat, and Kerry and I were able to squeeze in at a table with one of the CPP volunteers we had met the night before. The show had its setbacks: The air conditioning was out, so we all sat cramped in this dated locale in the sweltering heat. Throughout the performance, a strobe light flashed from *behind* the performers, which made it almost unbearable to watch them. Finally, because of the surrounding residents, they cut the sound right at midnight, so the artists had to try to close the performance in near silence. Nevertheless, everybody did their best to put on a good show, and it was appreciated by all, especially the glamorous Zulema, who was seated at a table in the back.

Héctor had assembled a particularly heterogeneous lineup. In addition to himself, he had invited a singer, a young transformista masculino, and another older transformista femenina who I had seen several times out of drag around Santa Clara. It was this last transformista who opened the show in a floor-length sparkly blue gown and a long blonde wig, lip-synching to Puerto Rican singer Kany García's pop ballad "Cómo decirle" with a classic transformismo style: an icy expression, measured steps, and baroque hand gestures.

The show was particularly notable, however, for the space it gave to Víctor Víctor, a young Black transmasculine transformista masculino. His first performance was to "¿Por qué no le dices?," an agreeable reggaetón song by the Cuban artist Alex Duvall. Víctor's youth and outfit—a form-fitting white suit with the arms pushed up, an untucked black dress shirt, and a white tie—helped him pull off the soft masculine swagger that characterizes this corner of the genre. With his hair shaved on the sides and slicked back on top and a smattering of facial hair, he convincingly filled the gently erotic role of the young reggaetón star. He grabbed his crotch when Duvall sang about making love, a kind of stock gesture that landed with the gay men in the audience, and he danced effortlessly to the swinging reggaetón beat. His second appearance was a stark contrast, played up by his change into a black suit and white shirt, inverting his earlier combination. Instead of lip-synching to a song, he read a poem for his girlfriend, who was in the audience, that described how their care for one another helps them overcome the lesbophobia they encounter in their everyday lives.[9] Based on my experiences in Havana, I would have expected such a sincere performance in this context to fall flat, but in the environment of Santa Clara it was lovingly received by the audience.

Kerry and I interviewed the HSH volunteers and their director at the CPP the following day, and there Víctor told us about the kinds of support he had found among his fellow volunteers, particularly in the face of the kinds of racial and sexual exclusions he had experienced in other queer social networks. As I discussed in chapter 1, and as I will describe in greater detail in chapter 5, transformistas masculinos have faced difficulty in the overwhelmingly gay male scene of transformismo, with artistic directors uninterested in promoting the causes of lesbian women and transmasculine people, and transformistas femeninas reluctant to give up or share the corner of the market they have cultivated for themselves. Víctor recounted various experiences where, after having been invited to perform at a venue, a transformista femenina there would find a way to prevent him from acting, experiences that resonated with stories I had heard from Argelia, the leader of the transformismo masculino movement in Havana.

Even when people were supportive, it came with its drawbacks. In his early transformismo days, Víctor had a trio with two other young Black transformistas masculinos. Though audiences enjoyed their performances, some would make offensive comments about the makeup of the group. "Había cierta discriminación," Víctor told us, "porque había una más oscurita que yo, otra más gorda, y entonces me dijeron, 'Víctor, usted lo hace fabuloso, pero coño, compadre, ¿por qué no quitas a esa gorda? . . . ¿Tú no puedes buscar un blanquito?'" ("There was some discrimination because there was one who was darker than I am, another who was bigger, and so they would say, 'Víctor, you are so good, but damn, man, can you get rid of the fat one? Can't you find a white one?'")

By contrast, Víctor described feeling unconditionally accepted within the HSH group and supported in his artistic pursuits, as evidenced by his prominent presence in Héctor's show. Though some had questioned why a transmasculine person attracted to women was participating in a group geared toward men who have sex with men, the group's coordinator and Víctor's fellow volunteers were clearly enthusiastic about his presence. "Somos una familia," Víctor said simply about HSH. I see this kind of arrangement and Víctor's role in the show that Thursday night as examples of the kinds of creative coalitions trans/queer people are forming in Santa Clara.

That kind of solidarity was also expressed between Zulema, one of the most successful transformistas in the city, and the novice Héctor that Thursday night. In the middle of the show, Héctor came on stage, as her drag persona Tanya, in a delightfully improvised outfit: Small, color-blocked panels on her top gave her the look of a deconstructed, multi-color disco ball. This extended beyond her waist to meet a short, pleated metallic gold skirt that fell to just above her knees. Fishnets were tucked into her heels, which Kerry noticed had been tied onto her feet to stay on, probably on loan to her and several sizes too large. Her left hand and arm were covered in a long white satin glove, which often reached up to touch her tastefully made-up face and the fashionable straight red wig she wore. She would have fit perfectly in an Almodóvar film.

Her first song was Spanish singer Paloma San Basilio's Spanish-language cover of George Michael's eternal "Careless Whisper." The melancholic nostalgia and the unmistakable saxophone solo punctuated the show's distinct throwback aesthetic. Seated right off the stage, I could tell she was nervous, occasionally losing the words she was meant to be lip-synching. Nevertheless, Tanya bravely worked the audience, embodying the song's affective atmosphere, and by her second number—Mexican singer Kika Edgar's fiery "Ojalá que no puedas"—she had gained a measure of confidence. She milked the song's drama by turning to the mirror behind her to act toward her own image, interrupted only by frequent tips from the audience. As one man approached her to make an offering, she grabbed him by the collar of his shirt, shaking him as Edgar sang "ojalá . . . que no tengas consuelo" ("I hope you don't find solace"), as though he were the song's antagonist. Applause drowned out the end of that chorus, and then, in the lull of the transition to the next verse, I noticed Zulema at the bar getting singles so she could tip Tanya. She made her way over to the stage, planted a dollar and a kiss on the transformista, and whispered "bravo, mi vida" into her ear as Tanya stayed laser focused on her performance.

When Kerry and I interviewed Zulema a couple of days later, I told her that I had noticed her showering Tanya with support that night, both through her tips and her shouts of approval from her table in the back. I asked her what she thought of the performance, and she said, "Yo me quedé fascinada. Yo quedé muerta con el vestido de cuadros." ("I was fascinated. I died with the dress with the squares."), referring to the above outfit. "Es que ese tipo de tela no existe" ("It's that this type of fabric doesn't exist"), she explained, "Es como si fuera algo antiguo. Y entonces la antigüedad, mientras más antiguo, más valor tiene." ("It's like it is something antique. And with that vintage quality, the older it is the more valuable it is.")

Zulema went on to acknowledge how hard it is to get started at Héctor's age, and she applauded and contextualized his aesthetic:

> Lo hizo con mucha dignidad, lo hizo muy bonito, no hizo lo ridículo . . . con un poco falta de recursos, pero bueno, a ver, es su historia, es su onda, y es maravilloso que surjan nuevos talentos, porque es que todas estamos clonadas. Siempre tiene que surgir nuevos tal-

entos, tiene que surgir nuevas cosas, nuevas ideas. . . . Si quieres ver algo retro, hay que verla a ella. Porque es lo retro. Y realmente, lo que ella está haciendo es lo que se hacía en los años 90, con la Compañía Futuro. Es el estilo de ellas, que mucha gente recordaron eso, de aquella época.

He did it with a lot of dignity, he did it beautifully, he didn't make a farce . . . he may have lacked some resources, but, well, that is his story, his vibe, and it is wonderful that new talents come along, because we are all cloned. There have to be new talents, because new things have to come about, new ideas. . . . If you want to see something retro, you have to see her. Because she is retro. And really, what she is doing is what they did in the '90s, with Compañía Futuro. It's their style, and many people recalled that, that era.

Zulema's investment in a heterogeneity of aesthetics and beauty standards alone was refreshing in the often-stifling context of transformismo and trans femininity in Cuba (and anywhere). More immediately, however, her analysis of Tanya's performance showed the importance of genealogy, of an intergenerational affinity, to the transformismo scene in Santa Clara, the enduring presence and example of the renegade artists of Compañía Futuro and the kind of world they were imagining.

The new party ended quietly shortly after Tanya's memorable performance. Since the sound system had to be turned down at midnight, the lovely singer offered a final a cappella number, and then we all made our way home. The small show, however, had offered a living image of the communitarian spirit of so much transformismo in Santa Clara, the ways the performance complex could be used in this setting to invite and maintain the kinds of unlikely and urgent coalitions, of alternative historicities, that are so often just out of reach in trans/queer social and political organizing.

Cubanacán

Tanya's would not be the last show we saw that invoked the importance of ancestrality and forebears to Santa Clara's transformistas. On Saturday, David invited us out once again, this time to Cubanacán, a newer nightclub on the outskirts of town, further past El Bosque toward the beltway that encircles Santa Clara. The show that evening drove home the kinds of violences we trans/queer people endure in Cuba and the Americas and gave insight into the types of intergenerational and ancestral connections transformistas in Santa Clara rely on to survive them. In doing so, it underscored the ways transformistas in Santa Clara draw on the past while imagining their trans/queer struggle as a collective one that will only be overcome communally.

We met up with David at El Mejunje around 10 p.m., and then we squeezed into one of the little carts that park outside of the nightclub to shuffle patrons around town for a couple of CUC. I had no idea what to expect of Cubanacán, and I was caught off guard by the extensive body search that the bouncers performed as we tried to enter. Once inside, I was again surprised by the expansive and well-appointed outdoor space that greeted us: A massive stage to the left was decked out with lighting and audio equipment and looked onto an open area set up with tables and chairs for the audience. There was a bar in the back right, a place upstairs to buy food, and tables set up on the second-floor balcony as well.

We bought a bottle of rum to share and settled into a table, but before long it started to rain. All of us in the audience got into a little dance where we would shield ourselves under the second floor whenever it rained, every thirty minutes or so. Zulema arrived shortly after we did, and Kerry and I went to greet her, having just interviewed her that morning. David told us that the turnout was low due to the weather, but this time the show went on anyway, giving me and Kerry an opportunity to finally see Cinthya perform in earnest.[10]

It was immediately clear why Cinthya was such a fixture in the Santa Clara scene: she was a force, a representation of the aesthetics and performative possibilities of classic transformismo. For one of her appearances, she combined two classic Rocío Jurado songs, "Maniquí" and "¿Quién te crees tú?," evincing both her commitment to golden period transformismo and Spanish popular culture. She wore a knee-length gold and black zebra-print sequined dress, and a large necklace on top of sheer black fabric gave the impression of a plunging neckline. Her long sleeves were made of the same fabric as the body, and cream stockings on her legs met cream platform high heels, so she towered over the audience. A short blonde wig was brushed to one side, framing the right side of her face.

Cinthya started the number upstage, and each time Jurado sang "tú" in the first verse, she pointed out into the audience, implicating each of us in her performance. The fancier sound system and the outdoor setting meant that my senses were not as overcome by the blaring audio as they were in most queer nightlife spaces. By the third phrase, Cinthya was fully downstage, and a tiny flash of footwork between declamations gave some forward motion to the performance. When she approached the chorus, she opened her arms to her sides and faced upward, as though it were her voice delivering Jurado's unforgettable lines:

> Eres tan ingenuo, arrogante, y pretencioso
> Quieres ser dueño de todo, y no eres dueño de nada

> You are so naïve, arrogant, and pretentious
> You want to own everything, but you own nothing

I thought of Cinthya's discussion about the subject position of the maricón. "Yo soy maricón," he told us, "porque soy tan perceptible a tu vista, pero soy tan molesto a tu vida, que tú me estás dando la importancia que yo merezco" ("I am a faggot, because I am so noticeable in your view, I am so disturbing to your life, that you are giving me the importance that I deserve"). Here, I heard her lip-synching back to this "tú," embracing a queer system of value in which the dominant sexual class, despite their considerable power, owns nothing.

As Cinthya began the second half of the chorus, Zulema approached the stage to tip her. Cinthya met her and looked her in the eye as she took the bill, but she didn't miss a word of her lip-synching, and she quickly went to work the crowd on stage right as Zulema went back to her table. When the show was over, the DJ started playing some music for us to dance to, and we all took advantage during the intervals between the bands of rain. A couple of hours later, however, the DJ interrupted our queer revelry to announce that Zulema would be competing in Holguín in eastern Cuba the following weekend. He put on Gloria Trevi's fiery "No querías lastimarme" and handed a microphone to Zulema. She spoke to the audience over the music, thanking everyone for their support and promising to bring them back the crown from Holguín. She saved her last words for a personal thanks: "Gracias a ti, hermana, Omega. Yo sé que estás ahí arriba y sé que me vas a ayudar como siempre" ("Thank you, Omega, my sister. I know that you are up there, and I know you are going to help me like you always do").

Omega was Zulema's counterpart in the young generation of transformistas in Santa Clara until she died unexpectedly two months after winning the 2016 Miss Cuba competition in Santa Clara from complications following unlicensed cosmetic injections.[11] Almost everyone I interviewed in Santa Clara mentioned Omega and her death to me, and Zulema explained that she had lost many friends in their attempts to get clandestine feminizing procedures.[12] Laura described what happened: "Se inyectó en La Habana en los glúteos, un líquido, un colágeno, y la mataron" ("She got injections in Havana in her buttock, a liquid, a collagen, and they killed her.") She died from a pulmonary embolism "por verse mujer" ("to look like a woman"). Silverio further contextualized the trend as he saw it, explaining that Omega died

> en esta historia que se ha metido la gente de ponerse silicona y ponerse cosas que hasta las pone cualquiera. Un muchacho que tenía 24, 25 años se fue a La Habana, le metieron una inyección, y lo mataron. Hace un año. Es el segundo de aquí que se muere.

> as part of this trend in which so many are involved of getting silicone or something, which is given to you by anyone. A boy who was 24, 25 years old went to Havana, they injected him with something, and they killed him. One year ago. He was the second person from here who died that way.

Indeed, Omega was killed the way so many of us trans women are killed, trying to realize ourselves. Santa Clara's transformistas were still processing their loss, and Zulema's performance was a living example of that kindred work.

After her remarks, Zulema handed the microphone back to the *sonidista* and gave a lip-synch performance for those of us standing near her as the song played on. The weight of her hair, wet from the rain, made it toss dramatically as she moved along to Trevi's singing. Once the song was over, the sonidista, having seen the commotion around Zulema, invited her to repeat the performance on stage. He introduced her more thoroughly, telling the audience about her various accomplishments and assuring them that she would return from Holguín victorious. He dedicated the following song to Omega, and then handed his microphone to Zulema, who sweetly asked "¿Qué hago?" ("What do I do?")" in the pause before the music started. Then the reprise of Trevi's anthem began, and Zulema asked us to turn on the lights of our cellphones and wave them like digital lighters.

Through the mic, Zulema's brassy, direct voice mixed with Trevi's sultry alto. In our interview that morning, Zulema had told us that she feels she has a terrible voice and that she gets to realize her self-image as a singer through lip-synching.[13] Through that practice, she said, "me siento una diva, una reina, dueña absoluta del escenario y la pista.... Es mi momento de yo poder lucirme.... Me siento maravillada ... espectacular" ("I feel like a diva, a queen, the absolute mistress of the stage and the dance floor.... It's my moment to shine.... I feel marvelous ... spectacular"). That night, however, she offered a kind of spoken and sung duet with Trevi into the live microphone that redirected the song toward her sister Omega's memory.

Zulema spoke over most of the first verse, listing off Omega's many accomplishments in the world of transformismo. She joined Trevi for the prechorus, however, her throat straining along with the Mexican diva. Zulema was simply dazzling, dressed as she came in blue jeans, a white blouse, and a short black sequined blazer. The audience shouted affirmations at her (e.g., the omnipresent "¡Dura!") and started filling her cleavage with Cuban pesos. As the titular lyric arrived, Zulema steadied herself close to the audience center stage. She jumped up, fell to her knees, and audibly slapped the stage as Trevi sang "No querías lastimarme; me querías matar" ("You didn't want to hurt me; you wanted to kill me"). She stayed on her knees for the first half of the chorus, her voice cracking from both emotion and tessitura. Her performance rerouted the song from its intimate address between former lovers to a more collective statement about the experiences of Zulema, Omega, and we trans women more broadly: indeed, they don't want to hurt us; they want to kill us.

As the chorus came to a close, Zulema rose, singing along with Trevi in full voice. Then Zulema broke again from the song during the second verse to tell us more about Omega with Trevi's singing in the background. Talking about Omega's work as a transformista, Zulema said, "Yo sé que [para] ella siempre ... fue lo que le gustó.... Se fue de este país bella. Se fue de esta tierra bella. Y siempre va a estar bella." ("I know that for her ... it was always what she loved. She left this country beautiful. She left this land beautiful. And she will always be beautiful.") Zulema then turned to herself and the upcoming competition:

> No me hace falta los premios, porque yo estoy segura de lo que yo soy. Yo sé lo que yo soy.... Pero sí algo de respeto porque Santa Clara, y El Mejunje, es la ciudad cuna del transformismo, gracias a Silverio y esa Compañía Futuro. Y ella no está, pero estoy yo para poder por ella.

> I don't need any prizes, because I am sure of what I am. I know what I am.... But we do need a little bit of respect because Santa Clara, and El Mejunje, is the cradle city of transformismo, thanks to Silverio and Compañía Futuro. And she isn't here anymore, but I am here to be able to do it for her.

As she had done at the new party above, then, she situated her work as a transformista as a collective labor with her elders, both on earth and in the afterlife, expressing love and respect for those who came before her.

Zulema finished her remarks just in time to join Trevi for the second chorus, and then she pointed the mic to the audience so we could sing the climax. Rather than finish the chorus, however, she returned to Omega. "A ella la mataron, pero vive in nuestros corazones," she said, and then she repeated herself: "A ella la mataron, pero vive in nuestros corazones. Es muy importante." ("They killed her, but she lives in our hearts. It's very important."). She rejoined Trevi for the coda, in which Trevi adds a beat of silence between each of the last three words of the song ("me querías matar"), which left just the right amount of time for an audience member to approach the stage, open a beer ("me"), and offer it to Zulema ("querías"). As Zulema and Trevi sang "matar" together, Zulema circled herself with the beer, pouring it out around her for her departed sister Omega. "Gracias, gracias, gracias," she said as we showered her in tearful applause, and then she handed the microphone to a stagehand and melted back into the crowd.

Zulema's performative offering to her sister Omega for me encapsulated the communitarian spirit Kerry and I had witnessed throughout our time in Santa Clara. Though it had been Cinthya's show, the venue gave space to Zulema in anticipation of her trip to Holguín. Far from using her platform in a competitive manner to upstage her elder, Zulema chose to honor her ancestors and forebears: Omega, Silverio, and the queens of Compañía Futuro and Santa Clara. She cast an intergenerational net of sisterly solidarity that the transformistas of the city, la cuna del transformismo, have built in the face of hemispheric and global femme-phobic violence.

The Promise of Provincial Drag

Santa Clara's transformistas offer a potent *mejunje* of Revolutionary and trans/queer liberatory ideas and deeds that accomplish a kind of coalitional politics that exceeds mainstream LGBT rights discourses in Cuba. At El Mejunje, they spoke explicitly about the histories and concepts that undergird this work, their unique translations of Revolutionary imagery to trans/queer contexts. These commitments radiated outward to the *fiesta nueva*, Cubanacán, and Remate, charting intergroup solidarities and intergenerational affinities that foster trans/queer liberatory collaboration. Like the parties in Havana's repartos I described in chapter 2, then, transformismo in Villa Clara Province offers vital and viable lifeways to trans/queer Cubans despite the shortcomings of social and economic reform on the island since the fall of socialism. In doing so, it offers insight into how we might craft a more coalitional, intergenerational, and ancestral trans/queer politics that will carry us through the present.

CHAPTER 4

Transformista, Travesti, Transgénero
Performing Trans/Queer Subjectivity

When the nightclubs close in Santa Clara, Cuba, at around 3 a.m., you can hear a collective cry of "¡Pa'l parque!" ("To the park!"), referring to Parque Vidal, the main square in the center of the city. There, trans and queer folks gather in the early hours of the morning to stretch the boundaries of the night. One Saturday in November 2017—the same one that closed chapter 3—my wife Kerry and I arrived at the park after an evening spent watching a drag show and dancing with friends at Cubanacán, a newer, upscale nightclub on the outskirts of the city. When we arrived, a crowd had already formed on the steps of the Teatro La Caridad, the grand colonial-era theater built in 1885 that looks out onto the park. We secured a bottle of rum and settled in to the improvised outdoor queer space. Zulema, the dazzling transformista who had been with us at Cubanacán, had already installed herself as the center of the gathering's attention. Blaccucini, Santa Clara's premier comedic transformista, was standing near her, dressed simply but elegantly in a short black dress with a beige purse and scarf. Her long hair was casually tied up and held back by a black headband.

Someone had placed a large speaker in the corner of the space and connected their phone to it, so this improvised queer party had a sound system. Zulema used the patio as a stage and performed to Spanish singer Isabel Pantoja's version of "Abrázame muy fuerte" by the late

Mexican star Juan Gabriel. Zulema turned her scarf into a prop, flinging it around her neck as she gestured in the air with her free hand, emulating the Spanish diva. It had been raining all night, and her wet hair spun as she turned around with each phrase in the first verse to perform to each corner of the crowd. As the performance went on, Blaccucini mostly avoided Zulema's advances to join her, preferring to socialize with her friends and largely stay out of the fray. Her body betrayed her, however, when Beyoncé's "Single Ladies" came on, and she could not help but dance. She bounced up and down, bending each of her knees as though jogging in place without letting her feet leave the ground. She held either end of her long scarf in her hands, pressing it against her back as she shimmied her shoulders underneath it. Nearby, Zulema casually mimed the distinctive turning-hand gesture from the music video. Before long, however, the performance was over, the music dampened to avoid the attention of a passing police patrol car. All of us trans/queer folks dutifully averted our eyes as if to suggest that nothing had been going on there at all.

Almost two years earlier, on one of my first research trips to Cuba, I was sitting with a sexual diversity worker—affiliated with CENESEX and invested in trans issues—talking about my interest in transformismo, when he interrupted me to assert, "'Transformista' no es 'transgénero'" ("'Transformista' is not 'transgender'"). I understood what he meant to be a variation on the well-rehearsed slogan that trans women are not drag queens. This performative distancing has been an important tool for trans women and advocates as much in Cuba as anywhere else in the Americas. And yet, where does such a formulation leave women like Blaccucini and Zulema, women who are most definitely trans women *and* drag queens?

In this chapter, I tell the stories of three Black transgender or gender-nonconforming transformistas: Blaccucini, Ángel Daniel, and Titi. I pay particular attention to the ways they articulate the relationship between their work as transformistas and their sexual subjectivities as trans people. Before I do so, I discuss some of the ways that the relationship between categories of trans/queer subjectivity has been narrated in the arts and everyday life in Cuba and in trans/queer criticism on and off the island, so you can read the stories against this backdrop. I suggest that, in comparison to the scholarly renderings available regarding Cuba thus far, the transformistas in this chapter describe a more complex and rich relationship between their trans subjectivities and their work, their performances, their desires, their politics, their racialization, their economic position, and their faith.

In this way, their stories also intervene more broadly in the liberal LGBT rights notion that "trans women aren't drag queens." I am not interested here in whether this statement is true (sometimes it is; sometimes it is not), or in whether we as trans women have good reasons for saying it (sometimes we do; sometimes we do not). I am more concerned about what work such a statement is doing. Thinking through Blaccucini's, Ángel Daniel's, and Titi's stories, I see this statement as serving to create a trans subject who is respectable, one who is removed from labor, from doing her subjectivity—through sex work, through drag performance—for money, to survive, as if any of us do it for any other reason. It certainly serves to create a queer subject unsullied by gender transgression, as though there has ever been a category of "homosexual" not marked by gender inversion.[1] This is as much the case in Cuba as it is throughout the hemisphere, where trans women who conform to respectable notions of white femininity enjoy a level of acceptance measures away from that of their travesti sisters who work the streets. The stories here offer a messier account of sexual subjectivity, and in doing so they open up sorely needed possibilities for more explicitly political and historically grounded trans/queer subjectivities, ones that account for the role of racial formations and political economy in shaping gender and sexuality, that encourage survival for and potent coalition between trans and queer people.

Rendering Trans and Queer within and beyond Cuba

In telling these stories, I aim to contribute to cultural and scholarly production that has attempted to apprehend the language and meaning of trans/queer subjectivity within and beyond Cuba. Here, I want to briefly consider some trends in the ways the categories of sexual subjectivity that animate this chapter—in particular transformista, travesti, and transgénero—have been used in everyday life in Cuba and represented in artistic and intellectual production from on and off the island. I suggest that approaches that differentiate starkly between categories of queerness and those of transness tend to overstate actual distinctions, both historically and in contemporary everyday life. Meanwhile, approaches that embrace more complex renderings of the relationship between gender and sexuality tend to make room for more holistic analyses of race, sex, and political economy that might—as I will offer later—encourage more creative and necessary coalitions.

The taxonomical messiness I refer to above reflects the reality that trans/queer as well as more cisgender or heterosexual Cubans alike often conflate terms of gender with terms of sexuality. For example, in one sentence someone might refer to a gender-nonconforming person assigned male at birth as "un gay," "una trans," and "un travesti," all terms that have historically coalesced around effeminacy. Similarly, though terms like "lesbiana" or "tortillera" putatively reference one's sexual orientation, they are just as likely to be used to describe a gender-nonconforming person assigned female at birth. I don't mean to suggest, then, that this imprecision is inherently liberatory, as it also indexes the general public's antipathy toward sexual dissidents.

By contrast, Cubans in certain activist circles today are more likely to uphold some distinctions between categories of gender and those of sexuality. Someone can be "gay" but not be effeminate, "afeminado"—which is almost always used pejoratively by cis-heterosexual Cubans—but not trans. As the sexual diversity worker suggested above, "transformista no es transgénero." Members of Cuba's Afrofeminist/trans/queer movement, however, have been more likely to offer frames of trans/queer subjectivity that, through their foundation in racial formations, blur the boundaries between gender and sexuality. As I discuss in chapter 5, for example, Black lesbian feminists in Cuba critique the ways Black women in general and Black lesbian women in particular are associated with masculinity and sexual depravity.[2]

I do not mean to suggest that paradigms that distinguish between gender and sexuality are wholly harmful or inaccurate. Distinctions like "transformista no es transgénero" do reflect the fact that different kinds people have achieved different levels of social acceptance in contemporary Cuba. For example, a typically masculine gay man will probably be received more favorably in everyday social life than un maricón afeminado. Similarly, una mujer transgénero or transexual with fair skin who presents normatively feminine and has enough means to appear typically respectable is likely to be received more favorably than a Black travesti who wears a revealing dress and a poorly fitting wig to walk Calle 23—the main drag in the gay part of downtown Havana—at night.

Travesti is a critical term here: In Cuba, travesti has been used to describe feminine-presenting people assigned male at birth, and as elsewhere in Latin America, the term is "classed and raced" (Machuca Rose 2019, 242). Though the lines between "travesti" and "trans" in Cuba can be blurry, it is safe to say that people who describe themselves as travesti find themselves outside of the trans/queer politics of respectability that characterizes mainstream LGBT rights discourses on the island. As I discussed in chapter 1, travestis face discrimination even in trans/queer spaces in Cuba, as certain trans/queer people associate travestis with the street or sex work or feel that the state has done too much for them. "Travesti" can also have a political valence, however, and travesti activists have been responsible for transforming the Cuban state's approach to trans people, as I also described in chapter 1. Though Cuba's travesti movement has yet to produce a written record as robust as that of Argentina, for example, I see alliances between the movements in the challenges they pose to normative, respectable parameters of transness in mainstream LGBT politics.[3]

Transformistas occupy in a strange place in relation to these dynamics and interlocking terms. Part of what I am suggesting in this chapter is that through their often-queer identification, performances of gender, and engagement with aspects of trans subjectivity, transformistas trouble the divides often made between these categories. Though CENESEX includes transformistas under the trans umbrella imagined by their trans network, many transformistas discursively and materially distance themselves from transness or gender nonconformity. Some transformistas I spoke with understood themselves as masculine gay men who merely dress up as women for work. These were most likely to speak disparagingly of trans or, especially, travesti transformistas, suggesting that they would not work alongside them or that they are not real transformistas. Others presented as more feminine even in their daily lives but distanced themselves from transness rhetorically for one reason or another. Still others—like those who animate the bulk of this chapter—at one time or another have understood themselves as travestis or transgender people whether or not they see this as conflicting with their work as transformistas.

Cuban literature and film have tended to embrace these slippages in their renderings of trans/queer subjects. Take, for example, the classic poem "Vestido de novia" by playwright and theorist Norge Espinosa ([1987] 2006), from which a notable 2014 film took its name. Hailed as an important poem for its homoerotic themes, the piece actually dwells on the gendered interiority of a nonconforming boy:

> cómo va a poder así vestido de novia
> si vacío de senos está su corazón
> si no tiene las uñas pintadas si tiene sólo un abanico de libélulas
> cómo va a poder abrir la puerta sin afectación
> para saludar a la amiga que le esperó bajo el almendro

...
Con qué espejos
con qué ojos
va a retocarse las pupilas este muchacho que alguna vez quiso
    llamarse Alicia

how can he like that dressed as a girlfriend
if his heart is free of breasts
if he doesn't have painted nails if he only has a dragonfly fan
how can he open the door without affectation
to greet his girlfriend who waited for him under the almond tree
...
With what mirrors
with what eyes
will he touch up his pupils, this boy who once wanted to call himself
    Alicia

Notice how the main character here passes between signifiers that gesture toward queerness, toward transformismo, toward travesti and trans subjectivity, always with an eye toward the incongruities of a feminine body assigned male at birth.

In the film of the same name, director Marilyn Solaya explores the story of Rosa—a forty-year-old transgender woman who works as a nurse—and Ernesto, her husband, who is unaware that Rosa is transgender. The story charts the fallout from Ernesto's discovery of Rosa's past. To flesh out the context of Rosa's narrative, however, the film passes through various elements of trans and queer social life in Cuba that include the home, the street, and the nightclub, and also the maricón, the travesti, the transformista, and the mujer transgénero. Like Espinosa's poem, then, *Vestido de novia* betrays the meaningful linkages between queerness and transness and between various categories of transgender subjectivity in Cuba. Both the poem and the film build on a long history of Cuban literature and cinema on trans and queer topics that includes works by José Lezama Lima, Virgilio Piñera, Severo Sarduy, and Miguel Barnet and films such as *Fresa y chocolate* (1993), *Chamaco* (2010), and *Fátima o el Parque de la Fraternidad* (2014).[4]

Over time, scholars—both on and off the island—writing about gender and sexuality in Cuba have displayed varying levels of interest in pinning down the distinct meanings of these categories and where they overlap. Earlier approaches tended to conflate various categories of sexual subjectivity. Ian Lumsden (1996, 195–96), for example, uses the term "travesti"—which he describes as a type of gay person—to describe female impersonators in the 1990s. Emilio Bejel (2001, 196–210) uses the English word "transvestite" to describe the same groups of people as represented in the documentary *Mariposas en el andamio*. Despite their lack of specificity, in many ways this language captures the reality that many transformistas—trans or not—use or have used both the terms "gay" and "travesti" to describe themselves.

As language around sexual subjectivity in Cuba developed and evolved, so too did scholarly apprehensions of it. Ethnographers from the last fifteen years have been more likely to make or document distinctions between various categories of gender and sexuality that hinged on where, when, and why Cuban people were engaging in gender transformations. These certainly emerge from popular understandings of sexual categories, too. An interlocutor of Cuban historian Abel Sierra Madero, for example, distinguishes between travesti and transformista by suggesting that "el travesti—a diferencia del transformista que lo hace por diversión o por dinero y casi siempre de noche—es aquel individuo que desde que se levanta hasta que se acuesta, se afeita, se maquilla, y se viste con ropajes femeninos todo el tiempo, sin temor a nada" (2006, 166–69; "the travesti—unlike the transformista who does it for fun or for money and almost always at night—is that person who from the time they wake up to the time they go to bed, they shave, they put on makeup, they dress themselves in feminine clothing all the time, without fearing anything").

More rigid distinctions between categories of sexual subjectivity became further codified in later ethnographic work on gender and sexuality in Cuba. As Noelle Stout (2014, 26) explains:

> *Travestis* very rarely used the Spanish word "transgender" (transgénero), and when they did, they were referring to women who had sex change operations. *Travestis* saw themselves as distinct from these women and used the term to mark that difference.... Many *travestis* took estrogen acquired from tourists to develop breasts, but none that I met desired the surgical removal of male genitalia. Moreover, they distinguished themselves from *transformistas* (drag queens), who were often men, gay or straight, that dressed in drag for entertainment.

Notice how in both of these works, categories of performance are separated out from those of subjectivity: Travestis live as women all day "without any fear," while transformistas merely dress up as women at night for "fun," "money," or "entertainment." Doing something "for entertainment" forecloses its possible connections to subjectivity, which is located more firmly in medical or surgical intervention on the body, never mind that many drag performers seek surgery and many trans women and travestis do not or cannot. The categorical slipperiness of the earlier texts has been resolved, but authors still neglect to engage with the meanings of the boundaries and limitations of each of these terms. Instead, they hold up an older understanding from certain corners of trans/queer studies that gender performance is something you *do*, while transgender is something you *are*.[5]

Here, too, Black/queer thinkers have tended to offer more complex elaborations of sexual subjectivity. Reflecting on the particularities of being a Black gay man, essayist Alberto Abreu Arcia (2020) has explained that

> El imaginario occidental-colonial construyó un mito sobre la supuesta virilidad del hombre africano y su descendencia: las proporciones descomunales de su miembro y su ardor sexual, casi primitivo, capaz de transgredir los límites de toda moral y prohibición y que históricamente ha estimulado la ansiedad sexual del hombre y la mujer blanca. . . . Dicha percepción forma parte de los mitos fundacionales de la nación cubana. Muchos homosexuales que conozco han construido sus gustos sexuales a partir de estos estereotipos.

> The occidental-colonial imaginary constructed a myth about the supposed virility of the African man and his descendants: the disproportionate size of his member and his sexual appetite, almost primitive, capable of transgressing the limits of all morality and prohibition and which has historically stimulated sexual anxiety in men and white women. This perception forms part of the foundational myths of the Cuban nation. Many gay people that I know have constructed their sexual preferences around these stereotypes.

Notice here how performances of racialized gender, the construction of the Cuban nation, and the legacy of slavery are all fundamentally constitutive of contemporary sexuality on the island.

Meanwhile, another study of race/sex in contemporary Cuba, this one from a North American academic, introduces a figure who begins to get at the kinds of sexual complexities I consider in the rest of this chapter. Jafari Allen (2011, 75) tells the story of Octavio/Lili, a "transgender transformista" who decides one day to walk down the street dressed as a woman rather than waiting to arrive at a show to get dressed:

> Instead of cowering in the darkened doorways of streets where she would be less likely to be recognized, or quickly getting into a tourist taxi, Lili slowly sauntered down Calle Romay to the Malecón—Havana's famous sea-walled boulevard—where she flagged a *colectivo* (collective taxi) for the ride to Playa. Lili was traveling to attend a party for a friend, La India, who had returned home from Montreal to visit Cuba. The moment Lili turned from her doorway, she was greeted by stunned silence, grumblings of disdain, then laughter. One of the men around me commented that Octavio was a "sick faggot who ought to be put away" for the disgrace.

Walking confidently through her neighborhood, Lili collapses the boundaries between a host of supposedly separate social categories: transformista, transgénero, travesti; race, sex, class; work and play; stage and street.

There are so many women like Lili in Havana, in Cuba, in the Caribbean, and in the Americas. Their narratives trouble investments in a distinction between performance and subjectivity that persists not only in Cuban studies but in trans/queer studies in the US as well. Trans/queer social scientists especially have cast doubt on the kinds of separations dominant queer theory has tried to make between, for example, drag performance and trans/queer subjectivity. Viviane Namaste has noted that drag in this arena is often dismissed as "just" performance, while the homoerotic is cast as more solid identity, so that gender and sexuality as categories are made to "work against each other, even as they are syntagmatically aligned" (2000, 11).[6]

Against this grain, others have relied on the labor of Lili's hemispheric sisters and brothers to imagine more nuanced renderings of gender and sexuality. Reflecting on drag performers in Trinidad, Jasbir Puar has suggested that distinctions between categories of gender performance and transgender subjectivity "are intrinsically determined as much through racial and class distinctions as they are through distinctions of sexual and gendered practices and subjects" (2005, 409). Rosamond King has offered a "Caribbean trans continuum" (2014, 20–62) to contain these multitudes, who, as Lawrence La Fountain-Stokes said of Puerto Rican *translocas*, trouble the "the exhaustion and/or limitations of widely circulating English-language terms such as 'gay,' 'queer,' and 'trans,' which have acquired certain global homo- and transnormative acceptance" (2021, 228). In the US, Black trans/queer critics have offered analyses of Black queer and femme genders that also get beyond the limitations of dominant renderings of categories of gender and sexuality (e.g., Tinsley 2018; Ellison 2019).[7]

In the context of such creative coalitions, I offer these stories about Black transgender transformistas, artists who are so often rendered out of existence in dominant discourse on gender and sexuality within and beyond Cuba. What do they have to say about the intimacies between categories of sexual subjectivity in Cuba and the Americas?

"Gracias a Blaccucini"

Like Octavio/Lili, Blaccucini is a transformista who walks through the world dressed as a woman. Perhaps unlike Octavio/Lili at the time they met Allen, Blaccucini tends to refer to herself as a travesti or a persona trans. Here, I draw on Blaccucini's own reflections about herself in a November 2017 interview with me and Kerry to consider how her work as a transformista contributed to this self-perception.

Blaccucini was born in Camajuaní, a small town in Villa Clara province roughly halfway between Santa Clara and Remedios on the road that connects the former to Caibarién and the ritzy keys off the northern coast of Cuba between Matanzas and Camagüey. When Blaccucini was six years old, her family moved to Santa Clara to be closer to her grandmother, who was working in public health in the city. She described her childhood in Santa Clara as *provechoso* (fruitful), and though she maintained positive feelings toward Camajuaní, once she became accustomed to life in the city she could not imagine going back.

At the age of eighteen, Blaccucini went to El Mejunje for the first time.[8] Her experience with queer nightlife and transformismo had a profound impact on her subjectivity. "Fue cuando descubrí . . . yo misma como gay" ("It was when I found myself as a gay person"), she told me in our interview, referring to her experiences at El Mejunje. "Esperaba siempre que llegara el sábado porque era el día en que yo podía expresar mi sexualidad, en el sentido más amplio de la palabra" ("I would always look forward to Saturday, because that was the day that I could express my sexuality, in the broadest sense of the word"). Before long, the person she was on the weekends began to spill over into the rest of the week: "Después fui descubriendo que no solamente el sábado, que también todos los días de la semana tú podías expresarlo con bastante cautela con límites y fui criando mi personalidad, mi personaje" ("Later I discovered that it wasn't only Saturday, that also every day of the week I could express this, with caution and limits, and I went about cultivating my personality, my character"). Already, then, Blaccucini was contemplating the relationship between her *personalidad* (her self) and her *personaje*, the character she would one day play on stage.

It would be several years, however, before she began performing as a transformista. In 2005, a friend who was an artistic director suggested she try her hand at transformismo and began putting her on stage at a weekly house party in Santa Clara. She began attracting attention as a transformista, and within a couple of years she had secured a regular spot in a weekly show at El Mejunje hosted by Cinthya, a prominent transformista in the Santa Clara scene. Her success in the world of transformismo presented her with a problem: Should she continue her studies at the university, where she was well on her way to becoming a doctor, or should she try to make a living as a transformista? She framed the decision in economic, personal, and social terms:

> La medicina va y viene; la escuela va y viene. Eso se puede retomar quizás en otro momento; voy a concentrarme en mi economía para lograr salir a flote y que mi familia no pase tanto trabajo. Y fue lo que hice. . . . Me gustaba, me gusta de hecho, [la medicina]. [Es] que esto me encanta también. Y puse en una balanza,¿qué pesa más? O la medicina, o ser artista. Y bueno me voy a dedicar a ser artista porque médicos hay muchos, artistas transformistas comediantes y de color negro hay pocos.
>
> Medicine comes and goes; school comes and goes. You can pick that back up at another moment; I'm going to focus on my finances in order to stay afloat and so my family doesn't go through so much difficulty. And that's what I did. . . . I liked, in fact I still like, [medicine]. It's just that I love this, too. And I put it in a balance: What weighs more, medicine or being an artist? And, well, I'm going to dedicate myself to being an artist, because there are many good doctors but few comedic and Black transformistas.

First, Blaccucini addresses the postsocialist economic reality in which it is certainly possible to earn more as a transformista than as a doctor. While doctors earn a state salary on which it can be hard to afford basic needs, transformistas' proximity to the dollar economy places little limit on what it is possible to bring in. This presented attractive opportunities to Blaccucini, who wanted to help support her family. But there was also a social calculus to her decision. Her work as a transformista is tied up with her estimation that while there is no lack of good doctors in Cuba, there is a paucity of Black and comedic transformistas on the island.[9]

Blaccucini's racial analysis is notable given the prominence of post-racial discourses in Cuba, and she has used transformismo in many ways as a space to articulate blackness in Cuba. In fact, Blaccucini's self-conception as a Black person is written into her name. The same artistic director who got her into transformismo came up with her name when he was taking an Italian class. Blaccucini explained to me that -cucini is meant to sound like *cugini* or "cousins" in Italian, and Blac- refers to the word "Black" in English. So, Blaccucini explained, her name means "Black cousin." Blaccucini has also addressed racial formations through her programming and performance. Noticing a lack of representation of Black transformistas in Santa Clara, she organized in 2011 a performance called Noche de Ébano (Night of Ebony), which featured an all-Black cast of transformistas. As I mentioned in chapter 3, over time she has also removed various aesthetic features common to Black comedic transformistas in Cuba—lips painted large, oversized chest and buttocks—which she feels did not add anything to her performance and, as I discussed in chapter 1, emerge out of Cuban and hemispheric histories of blackface performance.

If racial formations and economic considerations shaped Blaccucini's path toward transformismo, her work as a transformista was critical to the development of her subjectivity as a trans person. At first, Blaccucini crafted a character who reflected daily realities of Santa Clara but did not necessarily resonate with her own subjectivity:

> Me gusta crear mi propio personaje que no tenga nada que ver con mi vida diario, o sea recrearme en otro ámbito para creerme y darme cuenta de que no estoy sola en el mundo. Que como ese personaje que voy a hacer hay muchos en la calle.

> I like to create my own character that has nothing to do with my daily life, to recreate myself in another realm in order to believe in myself and realize that I'm not alone in the world. That there are many people on the street like the person I am performing.

Just as her weekend self eventually spilled over into her everyday life, however, over time her character increasingly inflected her everyday self:

> De cierta forma me ha ayudado también a vencer un poco los miedos. De hecho, yo hoy soy travesti gracias a Blaccucini. Porque tenía mucho miedo escénico, o sea salir para la calle, encontrarme . . . estar en un lugar público me daba temor que las personas reaccionaran de una manera negativa. . . . Y Blaccucini en la escena me dio esa posibilidad de decir, 'Bueno, si Blaccucini lo puede hacer, ¿por qué [yo] no lo pued[o] hacer? Vamos a probar.' De todas maneras, si soy capaz de enfrentarme a un público heterogéneo,¿por qué no voy a ser capaz de entregarme a la sociedad que también es heterogénea? Y como hay personas que les gusta mi trabajo hay quien no le gusta, pues entonces hay personas que les gusta mi forma de ser y otros que no les va a gustar.

> In a certain way it has helped me overcome my fears a bit. In fact, I am a travesti today thanks to Blaccucini. Because I had a lot of stage fright, I mean to go out on the street, to find myself . . . being in a public place, it scared me that people might react negatively. . . . And Blaccucini on stage gave me the possibility to say, "Well, if Blaccucini can do this, why can't [I]? Let's try it." In any case, if I am capable of facing a heterogenous audience, why can't I give myself to society, which is also heterogeneous? And just like there are some people who like my work and others who don't, there are people who like my way of being and others who will not.

"Soy travesti gracias a Blaccucini" (I am a travesti thanks to Blaccucini). In this remarkable self-reflection, Blaccucini gives credit to her stage persona for helping her to encounter the person she is now in her everyday life. Over the course of this explanation, the discursive and material divides between the stage and the street, the *personaje* and the *personalidad*, the transformista and the travesti collapse, and we are left with a Blaccucini who encapsulates all of these complexities and contradictions.

Given that this kind of self-conception challenged conventional wisdom in Cuba and Cuban studies, Kerry asked Blaccucini directly what she thought of the differences between the categories transformista, travesti, and transgénero. Her characteristically insightful and complex answer deserves to be quoted at length. First, Blaccucini elaborated a conception of difference as inherent in social beings and suggested that categorization is primarily useful insofar as it improves people's experience of social life:

> Esos son categorías sociológicas . . . que por supuesto yo las respeto. . . . Pero para mí no existen diferencias. Diferencias no existen. Porque ya el solo hecho de ser un ser social nos hace diferente porque todos no nacemos con las mismas condiciones, con las mismas características. Ya las diferencias ya es algo que nosotros tenemos incorporado como seres sociales. A partir de allí entonces empezamos entonces a clasificar quizás [para] levantarle un poco la autoestima o su estima baja que tiene. Y entonces darles categorías para que se vayan ubicando ellos donde ellos quieran.

> Those are sociological categories, which I of course respect. But for me differences do not exist. Differences do not exist. Because already the mere fact of being a social being makes us different, because we aren't all born in the same conditions with the same characteristics. Difference is already something that we have incorporated as social beings. From there, then, we begin to classify perhaps in order to . . . raise people's self-esteem. And so we give them categories so they can go about placing themselves where they want.

She suggested, then, that these various categories really could be eliminated, since they are redundant with other existing social categories:

> Para mí el transformista es sinónimo de artista. El transformismo lo elimino; yo lo eliminaría. Travesti es sinónimo de una mujer; yo quiero ser mujer. Lo eliminaría. O como hicieron los sociólogos después que se dieron cuenta de que hicieron todas esas categorías o esas . . . bueno categorías ahora son subcategorías y las trataron de incluir todas en la categoría "trans."

> For me, transformista is synonymous with artist. I would eliminate "transformismo." Travesti is synonymous with woman; I want to be a woman. I would eliminate it. Or as sociologists did when they realized that they had made all of these categories . . . well, categories are now subcategories, and they tried to include all of them in the category "trans."

Finally, she disidentified with dominant conceptions of the fixity of transgender subjectivity, opting instead for a self-conception that embraces lightness and joy:

> En mi caso, por ejemplo, yo no me siento como una persona trans. Yo soy una persona, gracias a genderqueer, una queer. Porque yo vivo cada día como mi mente amanezca. Hay días que quiero sentirme una mujer muy fina, que soy una mujer fina, pero mañana quiero ser un varón y soy un varón. Psicológicamente lo soy, aunque me guste usar atuendos de mujer. Yo me puedo vestir así, pero mi mente no está enfrascada en que todos los días quiero ser mujer y quiero ser mujer y quiero ser mujer. No, yo quiero ser un ser que disfruta la sexualidad, la vida de una forma así. Light, como llegue. Y creo entonces que para mí no existen diferencias. La diferencia es ese, que somos diferentes como seres sociales, pero no transformista, travesti, transexuales, imagínate.

> In my case, for example, I don't feel like a trans person. I am, thanks to genderqueer, a queer person. Because I live every day how my mind wakes up. There are days when I want to feel like a very classy woman, like I am a classy woman, but tomorrow I want to be a male, and I am a male. Psychologically I am, although I like to wear women's clothes. And I can dress this way, but my mind is not wrapped up in every day I want to be a woman, I want to be a woman, I want to be a woman. No, I want to be a person who enjoys sexuality, life in such a way. Light, as it comes. And I think then for me differences don't exist. That is the difference, that we are different as social beings, but not transformista, travesti, transexual, imagine.

I understand Blaccucini here deploying categories of sexual subjectivity more for what they *do* than for any essential understanding of what they *mean*.[10] For example, while she distances herself from transness above, elsewhere in the interview she said that when people identify her as "una maricón que [se viste] de mujer" (a fag who dresses as a woman), she protests: "¡No! Yo soy una mujer trans, yo soy una persona trans, yo soy una queer" (No! I am a trans woman, I am a trans person, I am a queer).

Here, I see Blaccucini participating in a Black/queer practice of creativity in the face of limiting categories of sexual subjectivity. When we asked her where she encountered all of these terms and ideas, she said it was a mix of reading on the internet and attending CENESEX events.

Her use of these categories, however, seemed to me to rely on a tactical fluidity that exceeds what one might typically find online or at a CENESEX workshop. I see Blaccucini engaging, then, in a "Black femme praxis . . . a lived politics of double-crossing, or making queer use of, racialized and gendered labor constructs" (Ellison 2019, 14).

Blaccucini's narrative underscores some possibilities that emerge from curiosity about the intimacies between transformismo and trans subjectivity. The social and economic realities of a postsocialist Cuba led Blaccucini to transformismo, and her character as a transformista opened the pathway toward her understanding of herself as a travesti. This is to say, her sexual subjectivity as a trans person has depended on her queerness, her blackness, her job, her performance practice, her class position, her geographical location, and various related social and economic calculations she has had to make. The distinctions often enforced between categories of trans subjectivity, then, don't seem to serve her; rather, she tends to occupy a multitude of categories of sexual subjectivity as she navigates everyday life in Cuba and strives to enjoy herself and her sexuality "*light*, como llegue."

Blaccucini has plenty of company here, within and beyond Cuba. Do her comments not recall Marlon Bailey's deployment of "queer" in order to "examine what members of the Ballroom community *do* as opposed to who they *are*" (2013, 23)? Her theorizing of trans subjectivity certainly bears a resemblance to David Valentine's (2007) consideration of the racial and economic dynamics that led to the adoption of transgender as a category among social service agencies in New York City at the end of the 20th century. And the intimacy between her character and her personality recalls drag queens' complex negotiations of trans/queer subjectivities in Key West at the turn of the 21st century (Rupp and Taylor 2003, 36–38). Finally, to be sure, Blaccucini is one of many transgender transformistas in Cuba who—not unlike their US ancestors in Esther Newton's iconic *Mother Camp* ([1972] 1979)—complicate the divide between the home, the stage, and the street.

"Una imagen creada": Ángel Daniel

In March 2018, a Black trans man named Ángel Daniel got on stage to perform as his drag persona Dany at a monthly transformismo masculino event at the Cine Acapulco in Havana. He took the mic to announce that he would be doing a different sort of performance, and he signaled to the *sonidista* to start the music. The sounds of Spanish diva Pastora Soler's desperate and pleading "La mala costumbre" filled the space, its melancholic and sentimental introduction heavy with moody piano, synthesized winds and strings, and understated guitar riffing. Dany lip-synched to Soler's soaring soprano as though it were coming from the man we saw in front of us, in his distressed jeans and tweed blazer. Dany's downtrodden facial expression matches the song's melancholic, regretful opening lyrics:

> Tenemos la mala costumbre de querer a medias
> De no mostrar lo que sentimos a los que están cerca
> Tenemos la mala costumbre de echar en falta lo que amamos
> Sólo cuando lo perdemos es cuando añoramos
>
> We have the bad habit of loving halfway
> Of not showing the feelings for those nearby
> We have the bad habit of blaming those we love
> It's only when we lose them that we miss them

As many of us in the audience knew, the lyrics aptly reflected Ángel Daniel's feelings toward Argelia, the host of this monthly performance, whose romantic relationship with Ángel Daniel had just faltered.

When his performance was over, as the audience applauded, Dany handed the microphone back to Argelia, walked to the dressing room to collect his things, and Ángel Daniel walked out of the large glass doors adjacent to the performance space and stepped into the night air. I ran after him to say goodbye, and he asked if I had listened carefully to the lyrics of the song. I said that I had indeed understood the lyrics, and he said, "He aguantado suficiente" (I've put up with enough) before heading off to catch a bus, dressed in the same outfit he had worn while performing as Dany.

Like Blaccucini, then, Ángel Daniel's story troubles the divide between stage and street, transformista and transgénero, performance and subjectivity. In other ways, however, Ángel Daniel offers a kind of counterpoint to several elements of Blaccucini's narrative. First, Ángel Daniel is among a growing number of people on the island who are beginning to understand themselves in relation to emerging discourses of transgender masculinity. Furthermore, though he performed as a drag king before transitioning, Ángel Daniel understands the relationship between his character and his subjectivity differently than Blaccucini, both in the role it played in his perception of himself and that which he expects it to play as he continues to transition. Nevertheless, like Blaccucini's, Ángel Daniel's trajectory points to the intimacies between performance and the self and the ways that sexual subjectivity depends on a complex web of social formations.

Ángel Daniel grew up in a wooden house in Mantilla, a *reparto* of Havana roughly six miles south of the city center.[11] A tumultuous relationship with his family—not unrelated to his being a lesbian—led to many years living in the homes of lovers and friends. By the time I met him, however, when he was in his late forties, he was once again living in his childhood home, having moved back in a few years before to care for his ailing father, who passed away in 2017.

In early 2016, Ángel Daniel met Argelia serendipitously in La Palma, a centrally located area through which many bus routes pass as they travel between the city center and the *repartos*. Argelia was selling food at the time, and Ángel Daniel stopped to buy something for his father. The flirtation began instantly, and before long the two were dating. In February 2016, Ángel Daniel accompanied Argelia to one of the rehearsals of her drag king ensemble. Watching them rehearse Son by 4's "A puro dolor," Ángel Daniel had a suggestion, and he got up to demonstrate his idea for the performance. Though he thought that would be the extent of his involvement in Argelia's drag king troupe, at the next peña at the Cine Acapulco, Argelia surprised him by pulling out a set of clothes for him and announcing that *he* would be performing "A puro dolor" that day. Ángel Daniel rose to the occasion, and before long he was Argelia's artistic partner, performing alongside her all over Havana (see figure 13).

In late 2017, Ángel Daniel began describing himself as a transgender man. In an interview in March 2018, I asked him about this transition and its relationship to his work as a transformista masculino. Recalling my conversation with Blaccucini, I asked Ángel Daniel whether the character he performed helped him encounter the person he was becoming. At first, he was resistant to this interpretation:

> No. Dany no me ayuda para encontrar a Ángel Daniel. No, no, no, no. No, quien [me ayuda] encontrar a Ángel Daniel fue yo haber entrado en el CENESEX y encontrar a otras personas . . . y eso favoreció de que en círculos de amistades contactara con personas que se han operado y otros que están en el proceso y me puedan comunicar.

> No, Dany does not help me find Ángel Daniel. No, no, no, no. No,

Fig. 13. Dany performs in the Peña de Olga Navarro at Cabaret Las Vegas in Havana.

what helps me find Ángel Daniel is having entered CENESEX and finding other people . . . and that made it possible that in certain circles of friends I found people who had undergone surgery and others who are in the process who I can talk to.

Trans community, then, rather than transformismo, paved the way for Ángel Daniel's transition.

As his answer went on, however, a more complicated relationship between Dany and Ángel Daniel began to unfold:

Dany lo que fue es una imagen creada, es una imagen creada, es un futuro. Porque yo hoy por hoy yo lo enseño donde quiera, y yo lo que digo es, "Miren mi futuro. Esta foto que ven aquí es como van a ver a Ángel Daniel. . . . Esa imagen de Dany Roberts va a ser Ángel Daniel." Y Dany lo que me sirvió es que como yo quiero ser tanto un hombre, y me siento realizado en que ya esa idea la tengo ya. . . . Ya yo estoy ya preparadito ya como si yo fuera ya con todos mis órganos y todo completo. . . . Dany lo que ayudó fue que esa imagen que yo tanto quiero la sacara a luz, disfrutara, interactuara con el público. Era un momento de sentirse realizado como varón.

Dany was a created image, a created image, a future. Because right now I can show him anywhere and what I say is, "Look at my future. This photo you see here is how you are going to see Ángel Daniel. . . . This image of Dany Roberts is going to be Ángel Daniel." And Dany helped me in that since I want to be a man so badly, and I feel actualized in that I already have this idea. . . . I am already ready as though I already had all of my organs and all complete. . . . Dany helped me by taking that image that I want so badly and bringing it to light, enjoying it, interacting with the audience. It was a moment in which I could feel fulfilled (*realizado*) as a man.

To be sure, this is a self-conception distinct from that of Blaccucini, who suggested she was a travesti "thanks to" her character. Nevertheless, Ángel Daniel still elaborates an important connection between his character and his subjectivity as a trans person. Dany was "una imagen creada" (a created image), a literal photograph Ángel Daniel could demonstrate and hold on to and also a social persona he could experiment with out in public, in relation with others. Dany provided an opportunity for Ángel Daniel to visualize himself, to feel actualized as a man in the earliest stages of transition.[12]

As this intricate explanation suggests, Ángel Daniel's transition included meaningful ruptures and continuities with his work as a transformista. Whereas Blaccucini saw no conflict in being *both* a transformista and a travesti, Ángel Daniel was more likely to separate these elements:

> Esa etapa artística ya varía. Dany, sinceramente, después que Ángel Daniel termina todo su proceso, Dany se retira y entra artísticamente convertido en hombre Ángel Daniel. Esos son mis ideas que tengo. . . . Ya Dany Roberts después más adelante no va a existir; voy a poner artísticamente Ángel Daniel. Ya no es un transformista. Es un transgénero que está actuando.
>
> That artistic phase will now change. . . . Dany, sincerely, after Ángel Daniel finishes his whole process, Dany will retire and artistically Ángel Daniel will enter as a man. . . . Later, Dany Roberts will not exist; I will use Ángel Daniel artistically. Now he is not a transformista; he is a transgender [person] who is acting.

For Ángel Daniel, then, it did not make sense to continue thinking of himself as a transformista after his transition, since a process of transformation would no longer be at the core of his artistic practice.

At the same time, Ángel Daniel retains social and political investments from before his transition that are tied to his work as a transformista:

> Tienes que pensar como hombre, y no tampoco porque te conviertas en hombre vas a ser un hombre egoísta, un hombre sin sentimiento, un hombre violento. Porque yo podré cambiar a lo que me guste, pero nunca voy a dejar de darles el lugar de esas otras mujeres que se quedan caminando en la vida y que necesitan apoyo, que no sean violentadas, que no sean maltratadas, ni psicológicamente, ni biológicamente. Por eso hay que seguir luchando.

> You have to think as a man, which is not to say that because you become a man you will be a selfish man, a man without feelings, a violent man. Because I can change into what I want, but I will never stop giving space to those other women who remain walking in life and need help so that they are not violated, not mistreated, neither psychologically nor biologically. That's why we must continue fighting.

The way Ángel Daniel articulates himself within a feminist politics on the island syncs up with emergent discourses of transgender masculinity in Cuba, especially those that come out of the Cuba's Afroqueer movement. In a recent letter to Audre Lorde, for example, the Afrocuban transmasculine scholar Tito Mitjans Alayón (2020) discusses the ways that Black feminism accompanied and sustained him through various elements of his transition:

> I have read your work periodically, as a political and emotional survival drive, mainly in my transition processes, from a Cuban "citizen" to a migrant student on the southeast Mexican border; from woman to queer person to nonbinary transmasculine boy . . .

Similarly, Ángel Daniel's persisting commitment to feminist activism on the island resonates with the political possibilities of transformismo masculino he elaborated before transitioning, a practice he carries out, as you will see in chapter 5, in defense of Black lesbian women.

Though Ángel Daniel's story differs from Blaccucini's in a number of meaningful ways, it still illuminates some of the salient intimacies between transformismo and trans subjectivity. If Ángel Daniel does not feel that he is a transgender man "thanks to" Dany, he still considers Dany "una imagen creada" (a created image) that he could hold on to in his transition. If he does not understand himself as a transgender transformista, he still articulates an Afrofeminist political project that is continuous with the one he advanced as part of the transformismo masculino movement.[13] Ángel Daniel's work as a transformista masculino, work that emerged out of his subject position as a Black lesbian woman from the repartos and his participation in Afrofeminist/trans/queer circles, had a profound impact on his trajectory and self-conception as a transgender man. Like Blaccucini, then, race, space, class, and sexuality are all constitutive elements of Ángel Daniel's gendered subjectivity.

"El bichito me lo quito": Titi

"Sé de una linda mujer," the powerful but sweet voice of Cuban *son* and *timba* singer Haila Mompié told us over the nightclub speakers, "que regaló a la miel todo el hechizo y encanto de su piel" ("I know of a beautiful woman who imparted all of the charm and beauty of her skin to honey"). These words and the moody arpeggiated chords of the keyboard that accompanied them wafted through the dark and hot basement that is Club Tropical in Havana's El Vedado neighborhood late one night in January 2018. Haila, originally from Las Tunas province, between central and eastern Cuba, was referring to the orisha, the African and Afrodiasporic divinity, Ochún, "[d]ueña de la femineidad y del río . . . el símbolo de la coquetería, la gracia, y la sexualidad femenina" (Bolívar Aróstegui [1990] 2017, 219; "[m]istress of femininity and the river . . . the symbol of flirtation, grace, and feminine sexuality"). Fittingly, then, Deyanira—the transformista performing to this song, who you met in chapter 2 and who goes by Titi out of drag—emerged dressed in yellow, the color of Ochún. She wore a large curly blonde wig, yellow gloves that went up to her biceps, thigh-high yellow boots, and a tight yellow bikini with black fringe that had a yellow tulle train attached at the waist.

Deyanira danced sensually to the slow opening, her hands flowing seductively above her head, easily reaching the basement's low ceiling. As the *son* moved into its faster *montuno* section, Deyanira left the stage for the dance floor, swishing her hips among the tables of the seated audience members. Eventually, she flung off her train, giving herself more freedom to dance as the song moved into its *rumba* section. The horns dropped out and the percussion section took over, with congas mimicking the sounds of the sacred batá of Regla de Ocha. As Haila led her band in a religious chant to Ochún in Lukumí (the ritual language

Transformista, Travesti, Transgénero • 127

Fig. 14. Deyanira performs at Apocalipsis in Havana.

of Regla de Ocha), Deyanira—an initiate of Regla de Ocha—twirled in circles on the dance floor to applause from the audience. Before long, the horns reentered, leading the band back to the montuno section. Deyanira fell dramatically to the floor as the audience began clapping along to the *clave*. She rose to offer some salsa steps during the song's closing section, and then she collected the various parts of her outfit she had dropped along the way as she headed to the dressing room, accompanied by our appreciative applause.

I begin Deyanira's story here because it begins to allude to the dynamics of gender, religion, and economics that inform her work as a transformista and its relationship to her sexual subjectivity (see figure 14). Unlike Blaccucini and Ángel Daniel, Titi does not necessarily describe himself as a trans person. Nevertheless, his sexual subjectivity is explicitly caught up with his work as a transformista, and his narrative adds further complexity to the connections between *transformista, travesti,* and *transgénero* as categories. Always flirting with the lexicon of transness, Titi relies on transformismo as a way to navigate sexual subjectivity within the social and economic constraints of a postsocialist Cuba. His creative negotiations of gender demonstrate some other ways that transformismo is perhaps not so removed from gendered subjectivity after all.[14]

Months before the above performance, Kerry and I had interviewed Titi in his family home in Centro Havana. When we arrived at Titi's house, we were greeted by his sister and the sound of a sacred song of the orisha Yemayá spilling out of the window. "Una tarde de folklor" ("an afternoon of folklore"), Titi quipped as he emerged to greet us. The front door opened into the living room, which had comfortable if dated furniture, plenty of religious relics, and the stereo producing the music. Titi showed us around the rest of the house, leading us down a long hallway past a bedroom and a bathroom to the back of the home, where there was a kitchen and two more bedrooms. The walls of the each of the rooms didn't quite reach the very high ceilings of the Spanish colonial house, so the sound from the stereo spilled all around.

Titi was born and raised in this house in Centro Habana. "Siempre fui muy niña" ("I was always very girly"), he said to me when I asked him about his childhood. At seventeen, he was at a party with a friend when she suggested he try his hand at transformismo. She put a mop on his head, tied it in a bun, dressed him in her clothes and shoes, and put a song on for him to perform to. Before long, he was competing in festivals, and in 2010 he won a competition in Sancti Spiritus in central Cuba.

"Era travesti" ("I was a travesti") in those days, Titi said to me. He and his *madrina* would walk the streets together dressed as women.[15] It was more difficult in those days, he suggested; travestis suffered more abuse at the hands of both the police and the general public, and they could be sent to prison for six months to a year just for dressing as a woman in public, Titi said. One time, he was walking down the street in Centro Havana with his madrina when a group of people started throwing bottles and plastic cups—the refuse from a *quinceañera* or some other party—at them, and they had to run to escape the mess. Nevertheless, Titi withstood it and held his place as "la estrella de la noche" (the star of the night).

In 2011, however, Titi injured one of his eyes, and his family suggested he turn to Regla de Ocha for help recuperating. When he was initiated,

Obbatalá forbade going out as a travesti any longer, since Titi was to become a godparent to other initiates, and being a travesti could impede this path in the context of Cuban social life. Titi explained:

> Ya después que me hice santo empecé a tener ahijados y eso me di cuenta, porque no es lo mismo. Hay gente que no tiene prejuicio, pero hay otra gente sí. Y yo tengo que ir con mis ahijados a la casa a hacer una ceremonia, tengo que ir a la iglesia, tengo que ir a la casa para conocer a su familia. No se ve igual. No es lo mismo llevar una gente que tú sepas que sea gay a un travesti.

> Once I was initiated, I started to have godchildren, and I understood why, because it is not the same. There are some people who are not prejudiced, but there are others who are. And I have to go with my godchildren to someone's house to do a ceremony, I have to go to the church, I have to go to their house to meet their family. And it looks different. It's not the same to bring someone who you know is gay as a travesti.

Moreover, Obbatalá suggested to Titi that it would be dangerous for him to continue to walk the streets as a travesti, that he might encounter even more abuse than before.

Admittedly, I was a little disturbed by Titi's story. I had heard of babalawo's, or priests, insisting that their *ahijadxs* (godchildren) dress throughout their year-long *iyaworaje* (initiation) in clothing that corresponded to their gender assigned at birth. As a trans practitioner of Regla de Ocha, I cannot imagine countenancing such a demand. It is entirely possible, of course, that Titi's religious elders were projecting their own transphobia onto their interpretation of Obbatalá's demands. Roberto Strongman (2019, 121–25), for example, has discussed related histories of misogyny, homophobia, and heterosexism in Regla de Ocha.

At the same time, who am I to say that Obbatalá was not truly protecting Titi from a fate he might indeed been at risk of suffering? It would be easy to indict Regla de Ocha for being trans/homophobic here,[16] but indeed these religious edicts merely coincided with the economic and material calculations Titi was already making about his life as a travesti. "Se pasaba mucho trabajo" ("it was very hard") to get the resources necessary to "andar digna" ("go out dignified") as a travesti. "Uno tiene que estar bien vestida, que salga por la mañana en tacón" ("One has to be well-dressed, to leave the house in the morning in heels"), he noted. Since he didn't have the possibility of doing that, he preferred not to go out dressed as a woman at all.

Transformismo offered a kind of compromise in both the social and material respects. In performing as a transformista, Titi could curate a handful of outfits, wigs, and shoes for shows on the weekends. He could accumulate enough to be happy with how he presented himself on stage in a way that was not possible on the street. "El bichito me lo quito cuando trabajo de mujer" ("I scratch that itch when I work as a woman"), Titi told me. "Yo me siento realizada" ("I feel fulfilled"), he said, using a word I had heard from so many trans transformistas. Through transformismo, he said, "[s]aco toda la mujer que tengo por dentro, y después vuelvo" ("I take out all of the woman I have inside, and then I return").

Though Obbatalá may have taken away Titi's self-expression as a travesti, Titi turns to transformismo as a space to perform his devotion to the orishas. As with the performance of "Madame Caridad" above, Titi often embraces the opportunity to perform as various orishas. One friend hires him every year to perform as both Ochún and Yemayá at his *cumpleaños de santo*, the anniversary of his initiation. These performances give Titi an opportunity to deploy his expertise as a dancer and to enjoy his relationship with the orishas:

> A mí me gusta, me emociona. Lo siento lo que estoy haciendo. Aparte como conozco, porque en mi primer papel como bailarín estudié con el Conjunto Folklórico Nacional. Y entonces yo conozco de lo que significa la canción y le doy el objetivo que va. La gente entiende . . . porque yo sé lo que estoy bailando. . . . Porque los cantos de Yoruba tienen sus significados. Y el santo manifiesta según lo que está cantando el cantante.
>
> I like it; it excites me. I feel what I am doing. Also, because I know . . . because as a dancer I studied with the Conjunto Folklórico Nacional. And so, I know what the song means, and I give it the appropriate aim. People understand because I know what I am dancing. . . . Because Yoruba songs have their meanings, and the saint manifests according to what the singer is singing.

Beyond their personal significance, these religious performances are also economically advantageous. "El cubano es folklórico" (Cubans are folkloric), Titi explained to me, so religious songs are some of the ones that bring her the most tips. "Entonces estoy con una canción de Malú y nadie se paga, pero salgo con Ochún y ya tú sabes la cola y el pecho lleno" ("When I perform [Spanish singer] Malú nobody pays, but when I come out with Ochún you already know there will be a line [of people] and a chest full [of money]"). It's as if the orisha bestows on her the very reward whose lack conspired to cut short her days as a travesti.

Titi also feels that a different economic situation might yield a different future, even considering Obbatalá's warnings. Reflecting on the material constraints that hindered her presentation in public, Titi said she would consider going out as a travesti again: "el día que yo me encuentre algo . . . mejor, otro modo de vida, yo lo hago" ("the day that I encounter something . . . better, another way of living"). In this way, Titi's negotiations of gender performance and subjectivity, like Blaccucini's above, resist fixity or neat resolution. At various points occupying positions as a gay man, a transformista, a travesti, Titi described himself to me simply as "una mujer equivocada" ("a mistaken woman").

Transformismo, then, has been a way for Titi to negotiate his sexual subjectivity within the social and material limitations of a postsocialist Cuba. If for Blaccucini and Ángel Daniel transformismo served as a kind of pathway toward other forms of trans subjectivity, for Titi transformismo is the venue within which he can "scratch the itch" and "feel realized" as a woman in a way that he cannot on the street. Titi is not a frustrated trans woman, as he might be understood in liberal LGBT-rights discourses. Instead, he participates in a long history of "Black femme flight, or the re/appearances of queer femininity that disorganize and confound the categories we often use to make sense of the world" (Ellison 2019, 8). Rather than being distinct from his sexual subjectivity, then, transformismo is a central site within which Titi expresses and embodies it.

"Disfruta[r] la sexualidad"

Taken together, Blaccucini's, Ángel Daniel's, and Titi's narratives demonstrate the interconnectedness between transformismo and trans subjectivities, between categories of sexuality and those of gender, between sexual subjectivity and a broader social and political economic realm more generally. In doing so, they invite not only more ways for trans/queer people to perform our own freedom but also new ways of imagining the shared histories, struggles, and fates of trans and queer people.

These three performers also participate in a hemispheric conversation about the role of categories of gender and sexuality in efforts toward better trans/queer futures. Earlier, I linked transgender Cuban transformistas' performances to the work and imaginaries of other Black/Latinx/Caribbean trans and queer people, and their narratives also recall Black/trans Brazilian scholar Dora Silva Santana's observation of "a political distinction but also an overlap" (2019, 213) between categories of travesti and trans subjectivity in Brazil. Like Santana, they encourage a "constant and precarious translation" (2019, 213–14) that demands attention to the historical and social situatedness of categories of sexual subjectivity, refusing overly simplistic recursions to neatly defined terms that tend to exclude the very trans/queer people who have done the most to secure our freedom. Otherwise, "when we remember through presumed and bounded categories," Treva Ellison has cautioned, "we often dis-member Black queer and trans geographies, jettisoning them from their spatial and historical contexts" (2019, 7).

In embracing this messier rendering of trans/queer subjectivity in Cuba and the hemisphere, I do not mean to endorse the kinds of lexical fogginess that characterize much everyday speech and scholarship about trans and queer people, nor, much less, to suggest that we are all trans now. Instead, I mean to encourage curiosity about whether, how, and why these categories get smashed together or pulled apart and what work these discursive maneuvers are doing for whom. Gender and sexuality may not be the same thing (in all places at all times), but (in most places at most times) they are caught up with each other in ways that contemporary discourses threaten to miss. Perhaps by questioning the historical and social transformations that led to the tidy distinctions between gender and sexuality in LGBT-rights discourses, more of us trans/queer people can realize Blaccucini's desire to be "un ser quien disfruta la sexualidad."

CHAPTER 5

Transformismo masculino
The Social Project of Havana's Drag Kings

If you walk by the Cine Acapulco in the Nuevo Vedado neighborhood on the last Friday of the month, you will probably see, through the large glass walls that look onto the lobby, a gathering of people watching a show that includes singers, dancers, transformistas femeninas (drag queens), and—most prominently—transformistas masculinos (drag kings). Had you walked by in October 2017, you would have seen a Cuban-American violinist sheepishly take the stage while the dapper transformista masculino Dany introduced them. The violinist offered a tentative rendition of "Estrellita," the popular Mexican song by Manuel Ponce arranged for violin by the famous virtuoso Jascha Heifetz. The sweet tune gave the drag show the feeling of a religious gathering, where the violin's sound is sometimes offered to the orishas, and when it ended, Alberto—the transformista masculino who hosts the event—approached, shook the violinist's hand, and took the stage.

Alberto was arranged handsomely. His hair was shaved around the ears and pulled back on top. He had a thin moustache and beard that framed his jaw and his full lips. His deep brown skin was complemented by the earth tones of his outfit: a striped brown shirt, a fitted brown blazer, and light khaki pants. Everything was tied together with a pair of stylish almost-black leather shoes. He couldn't have looked more like a typical, sharp Black *habanero* out and about in the city. Alberto interacted with the crowd for a bit, calling out by name those who he recognized. Then he introduced Miguel, one of his transformista masculino collaborators, who told a short joke before Alberto performed his first song.

Trumpets and bass climbed up and down the major scale, accompanied by percussion, in the introduction to "Yo sí como candela," a classic *son* performed by Chappottín y sus Estrellas. Alberto gave a little shake of the shoulders as the intro came to a close, and he began lip-synching to the first verse. During an instrumental break, one of Alberto's friends from the audience rose to give him a tip, and they danced together briefly, Alberto instructing her in the slow-ish steps of the *son*.[1] Alberto's footwork sped up once he was by himself onstage again, the music intensifying before the nonchalant coda, after which Alberto encouraged us, "Un aplauso!"

The night went on like this for a few hours. Had you turned up a bit later, you would have seen Dany dedicate a song to a fellow performer who had recently been incarcerated and to her mother. He strode into Marc Antony's rendition of "Te lo pido por favor" by Juan Gabriel, the original version of which a fellow transformista masculino had recently performed to her mother on the eve of her incarceration. It was a heartbreaking performance, Dany in a black tuxedo, fixing the audience—many of whom were familiar with the recently incarcerated transformista—with an icy, longing stare as he extended his right hand toward us. As the somber string outro played, he stepped slowly downstage and acknowledged our applause.

Later still you would have seen Alberto introduce a transformista femenina over the soulful piano opening of the famous fusion band Síntesis's "Iyaoromi." "Viene ahora otra invitada" ("Here comes another guest"), he said, "Awoyó Yemayá, aché." And in she came, in a blue dress with white accents and a sparkling blue veil covering her head. She faced away from the audience until the vocalists entered, singing about her, then she turned around and let the veil fall to her shoulders, revealing a blue crown on her head. She danced along to the popular song with movements inspired by ritual dances from Regla de Ocha, undulating the hem of her skirt and spinning around so that it's white and blue emulated the sea and its whitecaps, the domain of Yemayá. "Aché," Alberto shouted again from the audience. Yemayá fell into a blue pile of sea on the ground just in time for the chant "Omolode omo ti tiyó," which got her back up and spinning again. As the songs abrupt ending approached, she danced away the same way she had come.

Had you stuck around until the end, you would have seen the show close the way so many of Alberto's performances do, with a collective performance of the rumba.² In this case, it was once again Yoruba Andabo's "La cafetera," for which all three transformistas masculinos and both transformistas femeninas who had performed alongside Alberto joined him onstage. The six of them danced the rumba's steps and shoulder movements together in a line on stage while the explosive percussion and voices of Yoruba Andabo filled the room. Over the course of the song, various audience members approached to dance with the ensemble. First, a beautiful four-year-old Black child with shoulder-length dreadlocks who had been watching the show with his mother and her partner leapt onto the stage, dancing and smiling for the audience. A muscular middle-aged dark-skinned Black man briefly chimed in with angular movements across one-half of the stage, and one of the transformistas masculinos approached a transformista femenina with an erotic charge. Finally, Alberto cajoled the young boy's mother into joining him, and the gorgeous, lithe Black woman with closely cropped hair capably danced the *guaguancó* with him.³ Her young child jumped in at one point, and Dany scooped him up and danced with him on his hip. The joyous ending of the song gave way to a swell of applause from the audience before Alberto signed off the event and went to change in the dressing room, emerging before long as Argelia, ready to greet her friends and grab some much-deserved refreshments at a nearby café.

Let's take stock of some of the work Argelia's *peña*, or gathering, was doing, especially in the context I have elaborated in the preceding chapters of this book: First of all, this peña is a space that is hosted and curated by and for Black lesbian women, a rarity in Cuban social life, including in trans/queer circles. There, the kinds of intimacies and violences that characterize Black lesbian life—especially working-class life in the repartos on the margins of Havana—are the main event, whether that involves a new love, conflict in a relationship, or the state-sanctioned curtailing of someone's life through the carceral system. Unlike the queer nightclubs and informal parties that dot Havana, Argelia's peña takes place in the street-level lobby of a theater, so its Black/queer revelry is on full display for passersby. It also transpires in the early evening, at a time that facilitates the participation of a diverse range of coconspirators.⁴ From this position, Argelia forms curious and creative coalitions and is just as likely to invite a transformista femenina, a diasporic violinist, or a friend's young child to share the stage with her. Throughout, the soundtrack is dominated by Afrocuban music with working-class origins: son, salsa, and—more than anything—the rumba.

In this chapter, I want to reflect on the work Havana's transformismo masculino movement is doing in contemporary Cuba. There are many ways I could tell this story. I could dwell on the plentiful moments in which this movement has been frustrated by the limitations of life in contemporary Cuba, by the prejudices of Cuban people, or by the lack of resources afforded to Black lesbian women. Or I could focus on the movement's shortcomings, the moments in which it failed to live up to its articulated aims. Instead, I focus on the social vision of transformistas masculinos, not to paint a rosy picture of their work, but to appreciate how they create viable lifeways for Black trans/queer people while elaborating a liberatory politics for Cuba and its future.

First, I introduce Argelia and her co-performers and describe their pathways into transformismo, situating their efforts within the currents of Afrofeminist artivism I elaborated in the introduction and related trans/queer-of-color thought from North America. I then discuss how transformistas masculinos are promoting Black lesbian women's visibility in Cuba, cultivating space for Black lesbian women, and articulating a coalitional trans/queer politics that goes beyond dominant understandings of LGBT rights on the island. In doing so, they elaborate a social vision that carries out the kinds of symbolic, material, and ideological transformations that have long been demanded by Black feminists as much in Cuba as throughout the hemisphere. The transformismo masculino movement, then, offers an example of not only the intersection between Afrofeminist/trans/queer critique and transformismo but also the kinds of social worlds that are made possible by a trans/queer liberatory vision.

Argelia, Afrofeminism, and Artivism

I met Argelia the very first time I went to Cuba, in June 2015.[5] A friend of a friend invited me to join him as he went to offer English classes to the workers of the Centro Nacional de Prevención de las ITS-VIH/sida (National Center for STI-HIV/AIDS Prevention, CNP). In attendance that day was the psychologist and prominent Afrofeminist intellectual Norma Guillard Limonta. When I told her about my research interests after the class, she told me I had to meet a woman named Argelia who was fomenting a drag king movement in Havana. She would be at a CENESEX event for Grupo OREMI, the center's network for lesbian

Fig. 15. Alberto performs with his quartet at a house party in Havana.

and bisexual women, the following day at the now-defunct gay bar Humboldt, Guillard told me, and I should make sure to be there.

I arrived dutifully at Humboldt the following day to learn that the speaker had had to cancel. I met Argelia and several of her fellow OREMI participants, however, and they encouraged me to come back for the second installment of the workshop the following day. The following afternoon, a worker from CENESEX spoke with the women about labor and the law, and about their rights in the face of police intervention on the streets. At the end of the workshop, Argelia told me to return once more the following day for the closing of the three-day event.

That was the first time I met Alberto (see figure 15). Out he came from the dingy bathroom in the back of the club, dressed like a middle-aged Cuban everyman in maroon trousers, a pale-yellow shirt, brown tie and jacket, and a Panama hat. Lip-synching to Spanish singer Davíd Bisbal's sappy ballad "Dígale," he winced his face as though in pain, using the folds of his cheeks to match the song's affect and working each bit of the stage for the dozen or so of us in attendance. Despite the smallish crowd, the club's sound system blared out the song as though it were a Saturday night.

The first of us who approached to tip Alberto did so tentatively, looking back at the audience before she went up to the stage, planting a kiss on his cheek as she stuffed a bill into his belt, and then smiling back at us as she turned to take her seat. If the repertoire for transformistas femeninas is well-rehearsed—hand the tip to her, or if you dare, stuff it in her cleavage—how do you tip a transformista masculino? It was as if the tip had opened up a gasket: another woman approached with more gusto and confidently placed a bill in Alberto's crotch, laughing back at the audience. A third woman circled around Alberto to stuff her tip in the back of his pants.

When the number came to a close, we showered him with applause, and he made his way back to the improvised dressing room. Before long, Argelia emerged in his place, joining the rest of us to share sweets and soda and reflect on the workshop. Then, OREMI handed out certificates of participation out to all the participants. To my great surprise, Argelia had discreetly scribbled down my name when I introduced myself to her two days prior, so amidst the crowd of OREMI members I was called up to the stage. I have held on to that certificate ever since and proudly display it as my certificate of lesbianism.[6]

That was just the beginning. I have checked in with Argelia every time I have returned to Cuba since, and she has certainly been one of the primary interlocutors for this book.[7] In a way, following Argelia has been a central methodology in the elaboration of this study. In *Mobile Subjects*, Aren Aizura describes his methodology as "following the actors," referring to "archaeological labors of tracing, discovering footprints, or as an act of tuning in or listening" (2018, 15). This could certainly describe my relationship to Argelia and the ways that serious attention to her political genealogy and artistic world shaped my research: Argelia's performances anchored my participant observation in the transformismo scene in Havana, and she introduced me to countless interlocutors, friends, and chosen family members, of whom she is one.

Just as the ethnographic enterprise is a fine line removed from the touristic adventure, my reliance as a non-Black, fair-skinned Cuban on Argelia, a Black Cuban woman, is not entirely unlike that of the tourists who come to the island in search of *la mulata*. It is certainly not unlike the dozen or so other researchers and writers who have come to speak with Argelia and document her work since I met her. The story of a Black lesbian woman transformista in Cuba is in demand in the media and higher education, but, as with the narration of the Cuban nation more generally, the transformista herself cannot be the primary author.

This book, for example, will list me as its creator, even as multiple Black women served as critical architects for the ideas that scaffold it.

I foreground our relationship here, then, as a way to recognize my own place in this glaring inequity. I do not do so, however, as an apologia or, worse, an aside about my positionality that serves to distance me from blackness and Black women. Just as gay white masculinity in the US is inherently filtered through Black femininity, there is no way to be a trans diasporic Cuban that does not rely on the knowledge, labor, and expressivity of Black women. The work of Black women is in the way we move, the way we sing, the phrases we rely on and the way we pronounce them. I write this instead to underscore the fact that without women like Argelia, I would not be who I am today, so my freedom is inextricably bound to hers. So, too, is yours.

Argelia's pathways to and within transformismo reflect her involvement in broader currents of Afrofeminist artist-activism that I discussed in the introduction to the book. I will focus on Argelia here as the leader of the transformismo masculino movement in Havana and a clear advocate for Black lesbian women in both state and independent spaces. But what follows is not specific only to Argelia, as her subject position and social-political outlook are shared with her co-performers, as you will see below, as well as transformistas masculinos elsewhere in Cuba, like Víctor Víctor in Santa Clara, who you met in chapter 3.

Argelia was born in 1967 and describes her upbringing as "humilde" ("humble") in the context of Altahabana, "un barrio de los que llaman marginales" (de Jesús Fernández et al. 2020, 44–45; "one of the so-called marginal neighborhoods"). In a recent interview, she describes a childhood surrounded by sexual and spiritual violence and an early awareness of her sexual subjectivity (de Jesús Fernández et al. 2020, 45–46). Argelia still articulates her social and material place in contemporary Cuba in four staccato parts: "mujer, negra, pobre, lesbiana" (woman, Black, poor, lesbian), and if she adds a fifth it has to do with her geographical marginality in Havana's repartos.[8]

In that same interview, Argelia credits CENESEX for helping her find her voice and speak openly about early traumas (de Jesús Fernández, Más, and Piña 2020, 45). Like many of her transformista counterparts, Argelia collaborates with state-sanctioned elements of the LGBT rights movements while advocating for a trans/queer politics that—to my ears, at least—goes beyond the limitations of mainstream discourses. She engages in a delicate dance, cultivating her own projects while collaborating with official channels. In this way, I see her making moves not unlike the Afrodescendant movement throughout Latin America and the Caribbean, which has tethered its centuries-long struggle to the UN's International Decade for People of African Descent as a means to get mainstream support for causes for which they have long been advocating.

CENESEX was, after all, the place where Argelia entered the world of transformismo. While participating in events alongside transformistas femeninas, Argelia started experimenting with a transformismo masculino character. Those transformistas gave her the name Alberto, which she has used ever since. It is a name that gives Argelia's character a kind of everyday-life weightiness, a name you might encounter on the street, which perhaps aids Alberto when he takes up public space. In any case, Alberto's transformismo persona lay dormant for a time until the opportunity presented itself to host the monthly gathering at the Cine Acapulco for the women of Grupo OREMI. Argelia began performing there, gradually recruiting others to join her. Before long, there was a critical mass of women ready to perform as men, and they began performing as an ensemble.

During my long-term research in Cuba, in 2017 and 2018, Argelia performed on her own, as a duo with Ángel Daniel (who was her partner at the time), and as part of a group called Cuarteto Habana, which involved several of the women Argelia had brought into the practice (see figure 16). All of these co-performers were either lesbian women or—in the case of Ángel Daniel—transgender men. Most were Afrodescendants, shared Argelia's economic marginality, and were connected to Havana's repartos. The cast of the quartet changed around considerably while I was in Cuba, for reasons connected to the social, economic, and political difficulties of being a lesbian woman on the island today. As I mentioned above, one member was snatched away by the state when she was sent to prison for a term that was inflated by the state's approach to so-called sex crimes.[9] Two others started a competing outfit in hopes of negotiating better pay, while another struggled with personal problems that led to unruly behavior at more than a few performances before Argelia asked her to leave to ensemble. Each time, Argelia was understandably crestfallen, but also swift and resolute in her recruitment of a new transformista masculino committed to the cause.

That cause was the very same Afrofeminist/trans/queer movement I described in the introduction. Argelia has long participated in the Afrofeminist movement in Cuba and is active in Afrotrans/queer organizing on the island. Much of her work takes place under the banner

Fig. 16. One instantiation of El Cuarteto Habana performs at La Cecilia in Havana.

of her community-based social project Afrodiverso, which is specifically directed toward Black lesbian women. Argelia has described Afrodiverso explicitly as "[u]n proyecto para empoderarlas desde su propia historia y su origen. Reidentificando sus esencias como mujer desde el arte inclusivo del transformismo masculino." (Jiménez Enoa 2019; "A project to empower [Black lesbian women] through their own history and origin. Reidentifying their essences as women through the inclusive art of transformismo masculino.")

In this way, Argelia's project engages with Cuba's long history of artist-activism and of arts-based civil society. In one of our interviews, she explicitly linked her state-based activist work with her transformismo masculino performance practice: "Somos activistas de la Red de Mujeres Lesbianas y Bisexuales del CENESEX, y donde quiera hay que hacer activismo. . . . Y si lo hacemos desde el arte, como lo estamos haciendo, impacta más." ("We are activists from the Network of Lesbian and Bisexual Women of CENESEX, and we have to do activism everywhere. . . . And if we do it through art, as we are doing, it has a greater impact.") As Alberto, Argelia collaborates with fellow Afrofeminist/trans/queer artivists like Krudxs Cubensi, as she did when she and Ángel Daniel appeared in drag in their 2017 video "Exkiusmi Yusmi."

These collaborations underscore the ways that Black music is central to transformistas masculinos' Afrofeminist/trans/queer artivism in Havana. As you have already seen above and in chapters 2 and 4, and as you will continue to see below, Argelia and her co-performers routinely staged loving performances of the rumba, Afrocuban religious music, and other Afrodiasporic cultural production, not for cheap touristic thrills but for the substantive nourishment of their own communities. This emerges from their political orientation: as Ángel Daniel put it to me once in an interview, "defendemos lo que es la mujer lesbiana, y defendemos también lo que es la música y cultura también de la rumba cubana" ("we defend what is the lesbian woman, and we also defend what is the music and culture, as well, of the Cuban rumba").[10] For Havana's transformistas masculinos, these are interlocking commitments that arise from their social, material, and aesthetic analyses of Cuba's past, their cultivation of affirming spaces in the present, and their vision for the island's future.

In this way, the moves of Havana's transformistas masculinos link up with affirming Black and Latinx trans/queer efforts throughout the hemisphere to transform trans/queer life and space. Their engagements with visibility participate, as I will describe below, in a Cuban and hemispheric conversation about the tensions between hypervisibility and invisibility for Black women. Their demands for space recall Kemi Adeyemi's (2022, 7) articulation of Black queer women's sense of a "right to the city" in the context of contemporary Chicago. And their coalitional politics engages with broader articulations, as I have discussed already and will continue to below, of Black and Third World feminist and queer critiques of mainstream LGBT politics (see Cohen 1997; Sandoval 2000). Taken together, their politics and aesthetics contain "blueprints and schemata of a forward-dawning futurity" (Muñoz 2009, 1), one that envisions material transformation in Cuba that, finally, centers and addresses Black women's histories, labor, and desire.

"Visibilizar" Black Lesbian Women

If you recall, Argelia's transformismo masculino performance in the 2016 Jornada was unofficial, embedded in the broader Conga. In 2017, however, Argelia and her fellow transformistas masculinos were invited to perform at the nationally televised Gala during the Jornada. The performance that year took place at the sprawling Teatro Karl Marx, the largest theater in Cuba, located in the ritzy Miramar neighborhood of Havana. After a ritual opening that honored Elegguá, the orisha who opens all pathways, with *batá* players, singers, and folkloric dancers, the curtains closed, and as the applause faded away the sound of the barbershop intro of "Hermosa Habana" by 1960s and '70s Cuban *filin* group Los Zafiros filled the immense hall.[11] As the curtains peeled back, they revealed the four members of Cuarteto Habana, dressed in black tuxedos with their hair slicked back and facial hair pasted on their jaws and upper lips. They were flanked by two tall, beautiful women in floor-length white skirts with white bustiers and headdresses that made them look like human streetlights reminiscent of the colonial-era ones that dot Old Havana.

El Cuarteto lip-synched to the doo-wop introduction, swaying in unison, and turned so their right shoulders faced the audience. As the first verse started, Diego fell out of formation to take the lead, moving one pace downstage. At the B section, the other three turned as well to face the audience, and as the heavy triplet groove took over the performers slowed their bopping and gently swayed their upper bodies, arms outstretched toward the audience and mouths open for the expansive vowels. The audience applauded here before the four gathered for a short doo-wop moment at the end of this section, snapping their fingers to the beat. Diego then stayed facing the audience while the other three fell back into formation for the instrumental interlude between iterations of the B section. At the last repetition of the song's chorus, the four stretched their arms wide, embracing the audience as the voice of Ignacio Elejalde, Los Zafiros' distinctive counter-tenor, soared. "*Habana!*" the drag kings mouthed as their public erupted in applause.

The performance—which was televised nationally—was a huge step forward for the ensemble, for drag kings in Cuba, and for lesbian women in the context of Cuba's so-called "sexual revolution." In particular, it worked toward realizing a central goal of the Cuarteto: generating visibility for Black lesbian women. Black women's visibility, to be sure, has been a central theme of Afrofeminism in Cuba and a key term in Black feminism more broadly. Norma Guillard has suggested that, in Cuba, "women who are Black, lesbian, and feminist are almost invisible" (2016, 84). In her rumination on this invisibility, she turns to the work of Audre Lorde, who has considered the fear Black women experience in the face of "the visibility without which we cannot truly live" (in Guillard 2016, 90). Black feminists in the US have also discussed the tensions between invisibility and hypervisibility in Black women's experiences and representation. As Nicole Fleetwood has suggested of Black women's performance, Argelia and her co-performers engage critically with this hypervisibility that renders blackness "as simultaneously invisible and always visible, as underexposed and always exposed" (2011, 111).[12] In what follows, I want to consider transformistas masculinos' own thoughts on the project of visibility and reflect on the ways their performances push back against the "social isolation" Black lesbian women experience in Cuba (Saunders 2009, 168).

Shortly after the Gala performance, I asked the quartet what they hoped drag king performance might be able to accomplish. Ángel Daniel said: "De hacernos notados, visibilizarnos, porque realmente [en el] transformismo masculino partimos de una mujer, una mujer que se está haciendo notar de que realmente ella también puede, que también tiene sus valores, que también una mujer también es independiente realizar lo que desee" ("To get us noticed, bring us visibility, because really transformismo masculino comes from a woman, a woman who is making it known that she can, too; that she also has values; and that a woman, too, is independent to bring to fruition what she wants"). This verb tense, *visibilizar*, to make visible, was the word of choice for these transformistas masculinos as they described their work. This making visible reinserted Black women not only in the space of the drag show, that space where their aesthetic force is so necessary and their presence so occluded, but also in the very history of Cuba, where Black women's contributions are also glossed over in favor of a white masculinist rendering of the nation.

One of the ways that the quartet carries out this making visible is through explicit, performative announcements of their subjectivities as lesbian women. Though heterosexual audiences in Cuba often miss entirely that they are seeing transformismo (femenino or masculino), this problem is particularly acute with transformistas masculinos thanks to their novelty on the Cuban stage. After the Gala, Argelia had to explain to friends who had watched the performance that it was her and her troupe that had interpreted Los Zafiros. Nothing in the program or the emceeing suggested they were transformistas masculinos, a fact that frustrated the performers.

In the face of this, the quartet would often insist that emcees say something about the nature of their performance. At an August 2017 performance at Club Amanecer, a smaller nightclub on the margins of the mainstream scene, Alberto and Dany's performances were bracketed by a dutiful *animador*. At the beginning of the show, he explained that the audience would not just be seeing transformismo from man to woman but also that from woman to man. It didn't hurt that they were performing as part of Proyecto Ibiza, known for attracting a lesbian public. Alberto performed first, offering another particularly smoky performance of Bisbal's "Dígale," the same song I had seen him perform to when we first met. At the chorus, the audience sang along with Bisbal at full voice. If their sonic participation was wholehearted, their physical interaction with Alberto was more hesitant. Men and women alike approached the stage to stuff tips into his collar in appreciation, evincing a mixture of attraction and insecurity regarding how to interact with this figure. One man lingered awkwardly so a friend could photograph him with the new spectacle.

When Alberto was done, the emcee returned to the stage to further clarify. Numerous people had approached him with questions during the performance, he said, so he wanted to leave no doubt:

> Esto es transformismo de mujer a hombre. Él no es un hombre; ¡es una mujer! Lo que pasa es que en el mundo del transformismo—acá por lo menos en Cuba—se ve tan inusual, se ve tan poco, ver una mujer haciendo transformismo de hombre, pero existe en el mundo entero. Y esto es un ejemplo de bien hecho, de calidad y, por supuesto, con un glamour como él se merece. Así qué para Alberto, fuerte aplauso.

> This is transformismo from woman to man. He is not a man; he is a woman! The problem is that in the world of transformismo—at least here in Cuba—it is so rare that you see a woman doing transformismo as a man, but it exists all over the world, and this is an excellent example of it being done well, with quality, and, of course, with the appropriate glamour. So, a big round of applause for Alberto.

The emcee turned to a kind of pedagogical address—one with no small dose of exoticism ("¡Es una mujer!")—to explain to the audience what they were seeing.

It is a somewhat peculiar gesture, no? Isn't transformismo, like drag anywhere, about the believable transformation between gender presentations, the convincing illusion? Argelia clarified that her vision for transformismo masculino goes beyond this aim. "[Q]ueremos que el impacto social que tenga el Cuarteto Habana no sea solamente transformismo" ("We don't want the social impact of the Cuarteto Habana to be just transformismo"), she explained; "no nos formamos para transformistas de hacer un doblaje de números artísticos que imparten a la población o la comunidad desde del punto de vista del doblaje sino del punto de vista de la mujer" ("we don't train to be transformistas who lip-synch to artistic numbers that reach the public or the community from the point of view of the lip-synch but rather from the point of view of the woman"). She went on to describe a feminist style of transformismo: "Yo, como mujer, doy la posibilidad de hacer un tránsito a la masculinidad sin perder mi feminidad. . . . Quién está actuando es una mujer que presta su cuerpo a un hombre para que haga artísticamente llegar un mensaje a la población o la comunidad." ("I, as a woman, create the possibility of making the transition to masculinity without losing my femininity. . . . The one who is acting is a woman who lends her body to a man in order to make a message arrive artistically to the public or the community.") This, she explained, is why they like the emcees to clarify that they are women.

When the emcee at Amanecer did so above, he perhaps overstated the prevalence of drag king performance elsewhere, as though Argelia's counterparts throughout the hemisphere were not working against the same histories of misogyny and lesbophobia. Indeed, I see Argelia and her coperformers engaged in a hemispheric effort for Black women to be seen on their own terms. It reminds me of Omise'eke Tinsley's question about the drag king performances of MilDred "Dréd" Gerestant in 1990s New York City: "How could Dréd make visible that she performs *in the tradition*—in a black tradition of finding healing in expressing multiple ways of performance gender, desire, soul, music, me?" (2018, 37). In Havana today, the transformismo masculino movement is carefully crafting complex renderings of Black femininity and masculinity that trouble Black hypervisibility while combating Black women's invisibility on the island.

"Un espacio de nosotras"

Beyond its capacity to "visibilizar," Argelia and her co-performers were hoping that the Gala performance would bring more stable and better-paying work for the Cuarteto. And, for a time, it seemed that this would be the case. By the end of May, El Cuarteto had been invited to audition for a weekly gig at XY, one of the mainstream gay nightclubs in coastal Havana. For that first Sunday night show, they split the bill with the beloved transformista Devora, and as the show went on they traded numbers in which Devora's tempestuous drag was tempered by the quartet's soft expressions of masculinity.

That is, until the electric closing number. As Devora introduced the ensemble one last time, she heard the sounds of Yoruba Andabo's "La cafetera"—clearly a Cuarteto Habana favorite—filter in through the speakers. Her face lit up, and she signaled to Argelia that she would be staying on stage for the festivity. As Diego took the vocal lead, Devora swayed in tandem with the rest of the quartet upstage. Just as the quartet was breaking into some more elaborate and energetic steps, as the full complement of percussionists entered, a couple rose from the audience to accompany them with a virtuosic rumba performance. The audience clapped along and followed the number with rapt attention, bursting into applause at the end of the song. After they changed out of their suits, Argelia told me that they had secured the gig and would become a regular part of the Sunday night show at XY. The quartet was ecstatic, and the gig would be their best-paying one yet, a balm in the precarious economy of the island.

A few weeks later, Kerry and I called Argelia to tell her we would be returning to XY to see them, and, dismayed, she told us that they had stopped inviting them back after a couple of weeks. In an interview later that month, the members speculated about why this pattern kept repeating—they would be offered a lucrative gig only for it to evaporate after a few iterations. "Son las anfitrionas" ("It's the hosts"), one suggested, implying that the transformistas femeninas who host the shows are not interested in sharing space and resources with lesbian women. "Y los dueños" ("And the managers"), another offered, referring both to the owners of independent clubs like XY and the artistic directors of the shows that circulate in the state-run establishments. They were identifying, then, a lack of coalitional politics, of solidarity between gay men and lesbian women.

In the face of this exclusion, the women were in agreement about the solution, and Katia put it clearly: "buscar un espacio, aunque sea pequeño, de *nosotras*" ("to look for a space, even if it is small, for us"). There was no other option, she said, that would "consolidar esto para que esto nos dé el fruto que lleva" ("formalize this so it brings us the fruits that it generates"). If visibility captures the symbolic work of Havana's transformistas masculinos, their focus on cultivating Black lesbian space points to their investment in the material transformation necessary for trans/queer liberation. It would not be enough for Black women to take up their rightful place in critical re-narrations of the Cuban state; resources need to be redistributed to account for the historical lack of public and private space that has been afforded Black women, especially lesbian women, in Cuba.

Space has long been a key term for trans/queer people in Cuba. The 1994 US documentary *Looking for a Space: Lesbians and Gay Men in Cuba* highlights trans/queer people's quest for social space in Special Period Cuba. Sociologist Tanya Saunders has detailed the ways that Grupo OREMI emerged out of Black lesbian women's quest for a space that fostered "antiracist social critique, lesbian empowerment, and socialization" (2009, 170). Here, I want to discuss both the quartet's articulation of a need for lesbian space as well as some of the ways that transformistas masculinos take up space even as a physical home base remains economically out of reach for Argelia and her co-performers.

The members of the quartet were not overplaying the apathetic or lesbophobic attitudes of the transformista femenina anfitrionas alongside whom they worked. I regularly saw the quartet have their performances canceled last minute or have their fee withheld after performing, which lined up with a broader lack of value placed on Black women's work and on the importance of lesbian sociality in trans/queer space in Cuba. In interviews, I would ask transformistas femeninas what they thought about Argelia and about transformismo masculino more generally. If many had complimentary words, plenty also expressed a lack of enthusiasm about the idea, or outright contempt for lesbian women. One transformista femenina, who also hosts a party where he has in the past hired Argelia to perform, plainly shared his feelings on transformismo masculino: "No tiene auge; no es muy fuerte. Y realmente las que más siguen eso son las lesbianas. Pero las lesbianas no . . . la comunidad que más fiestea es el gay masculino. Las lesbianas . . . son bien conflictivas también, demasiado." ("It doesn't have an impact; it's not very strong. And really it is lesbians who follow that most. But lesbians don't . . . the community that parties most is gay men. Lesbians . . . are also very difficult, too much.") He went on to lament moments when he had a critical mass of lesbians in his space, expressing discomfort with their displays of affection toward one another. And he claimed that his audience didn't enjoy the performances of transformistas masculinos.

To be sure, such sentiments coincide with a broader (and global) front of lesbophobia, which swells even within trans/queer communities and spaces. Ángel Daniel elaborated some of the discrimination the quartet had weathered within these arenas: "[S]omos muy rechazados, somos muy discriminados, tenemos . . . mucha lesbofobia por parte de hasta nuestra propia comunidad LGBTI también, porque nos impiden trabajar juntos con ellos, no comparten" ("[W]e are very rejected; we are very discriminated against; we have . . . a lot of lesbophobia even from our own LGBTI community, as well, because they prevent us from working with them, they don't share").

Ángel Daniel went on to say that he is hesitant to perform alongside transformistas femeninas, since he has come to expect "maltrato verbal, maltrato físico, rechazo" ("verbal abuse, physical abuse, rejection"). Combating this lesbophobia is a central part of their work, as Ángel Daniel explained: "[R]ealmente estamos como decir caminando por un campo lleno de espinas, portando gajo a gajo, poco a poco. Nos hincamos, nos arrancamos, pero estamos allí, avanzando. Lento, poco a poco, pero allí. Rompiendo fronteras y obstáculos" ("[W]e are really so to speak walking in a field full of thorns, carrying bit by bit, little by little. We kneel down, we pull ourselves up, but there we are, moving forward. Slowly, little by little, but there. Breaking down borders and barriers"). Notice how here the language of social struggle becomes material, a story about the real moves transformistas masculinos are making to bring about actual transformation.

Toward that end, the quartet dreamed constantly about a space of their own. They recalled a proliferation of lesbian parties in the 1990s and lamented that while the formalized nightclubs have made things easier for many trans/queer people, they have not improved the experiences of lesbian women.[13] They wanted to provide a space for this kind of lesbian sociality. In physical terms, they imagined taking ownership of a small space that they could fix up and use to host shows. Socially, they envisioned a heterogeneous space that emerged from their Black lesbian feminism ideology and their combination of artivism and health promotion. They articulated this space in musical terms, too, wishing "que la música no sea la música que invita agresión" ("that the music doesn't invite aggression"), referring to the mainstream reggaetón that was in vogue at the time, with its explicitly sexist messages.[14]

Even as they elaborated these dreams, the quartet recognized that such a space was out of reach for them economically. The cost of property in Havana had skyrocketed after US sanctions were relaxed during the Obama presidency, and those with access to the foreign capital necessary to acquire such property were overwhelmingly white Cubans with family abroad. The profit model guided the queer spaces that did exist, and those with the means seemed not to feel that lesbian social life was worth the cost.

As they continued to plan and strategize in their quest for a physical space, the quartet claimed space throughout the city through their performances. In chapter 2, I discussed how Argelia and Ángel Daniel turned Apocalipsis into a veritable lesbian party through their performance, transforming the typical demographic who showed up to the party. I saw the quartet do this time and again at mainstream nightclubs like XY and Amanecer, at afternoon peñas throughout the city, and at private house parties. In the absence of political economic investments in their social well-being from both the public and private sectors, they took up space on their own.

The social impact of those actions was immediately apparent on the occasions when their presence was seen as a threat, and thus repressed. This happened, for example, when they were invited to perform at an afternoon event at the sprawling La Cecilia complex in the Playa neighborhood on the west side of Havana's coast. The quartet was already suspicious and frustrated when the host of the event insisted that they arrive in skirts, performing her version of respectable femininity. It was far too much for her, then, when they started interacting with the audience as they emerged from the dressing room in their handsome drag. "No las quiero hablando con el público *así*" ("I don't want you talking to the audience *like that*"), she told Diego as the rest of the quartet was playfully flirting with the women in attendance and handing out materials promoting sexual health and future quartet appearances.

That event ended explosively, with the host interrupting a very well-received rumba performance by the quartet to take the microphone and launch into a tirade about their appearance and their performative choices. In the end, she refused even to pay the quartet for their lengthy appearance, and a friend of the ensemble shouted down the host for her racism and homophobia. If indeed these kinds of heightened reactions were unusual, they were only indicative of popular attitudes toward Black lesbian women, toward the more subtle social exclusion and isolation they face, and the broader policing of their racial and sexual selves.

Despite all of this, the quartet continued to dream of a space of their own while taking up space in the meantime wherever they found themselves. In doing so, to be sure, they participate in a Black lesbian hemispheric practice. As Kemi Adeyemi said of the dance floor in Chicago, Havana's transformistas masculinos see the stage as one of the "highly contested zones where black queer women directly implicate their bodies as they assert their physical rights within and over the neoliberal city" (2022, 11). They do so in the face of "barriers to building ownership," of spaces "serving queer and lesbian women" (Adeyemi 2022, 11), of public space more generally (Saunders 2008). They make a material intervention into mainstream LGBT spaces that insists that the rightful place of Black women in Cuba is everywhere.

"Juntos con ellos": Performing Black Lesbian Feminist Coalition

Argelia's monthly peña at the Cine Acapulco that opened this chapter offers a window into the kind of social world these transformistas masculinos wish to cultivate. Recall Dany's performance that I narrated in the previous chapter, in which he lip-synched to Pastora Soler's "La mala costumbre" as a way to speak to Argelia during their breakup. This was not an isolated performance; rather, that evening Alberto and Dany traded performances that placed their relationship struggles on stage. Dany opened with Cuban-Mexican artist Francisco Céspedes's heartbreaking "Vida loca," with its soulful guitar and lyric that spoke directly to his situation with Argelia:

Esta lejanía duele cada día	This distance hurts every day
Porque no te tengo	Because I don't have you
No tengo tu boca	I don't have your mouth
No tengo tus ganas	I don't have your desires
Y por más que intento	And as much as I try
Ya no entiendo nada	I don't understand anything
De esta vida loca, loca, loca	About this crazy life
Con su loca realidad	With its crazy reality

As if responding directly, Alberto followed with the frivolous reggaetón song "No te enamores de mí" ("Don't Fall in Love with Me") by Cuban artist El Chacal.

For me—and, I presume, the many in attendance who knew what was transpiring between the two—it was heart wrenching, unusual, and sad to see their complicated breakup play out on stage. At the same time, these performances were also broadly representative of the ways that the transformistas masculinos used the peña as a space to stage lesbian intimacy in a social context in which, as you've seen, lesbian sociality is undervalued and policed. You've seen them do this, too, every time they eschew the stage for the audience, dancing among their spectators. In the peña, they carry out this aim in concert with particular fellow travelers, mostly working-class Black transformistas femeninas from the repartos, who Argelia would help in their pursuit of success in transformismo. In doing so, Argelia and her co-performers modeled and curated the kinds of meaningful trans/queer coalitions they seek to form in the face of an increasingly balkanized LGBT rights movement.

Here, I want to reflect on the peña as an example of trans/queer coalitional praxis. These kinds of coalitions have been, to be sure, a prominent concern of Black feminists transnationally.[15] Just as the members of NOSOTRXS envision an Afrofeminist/trans/queer movement that unites lesbian and trans women in ways that are so often foreclosed in LGBT organizing, Cathy Cohen (1997) elaborated a radical coalitional politics in the 1990s from her own position in relation to the possibilities and pitfalls of activism in the face of the global HIV/AIDS epidemic. Kemi Adeyemi recently described the ways that black queer women in Chicago are striving, in ways that recall transformistas masculinos' work in Havana, to "form sustainable coalitions that are perhaps not grounded in capitalist exchange, but in intimacy itself" (2022, 133). I want to describe some of that intimacy at the Acapulco and the history and ideology out of which it emerges.

Just as Ángel Daniel lamented the shifts in lesbian space since the 1990s, he noted a diminishing solidarity between lesbian women, gay men, and trans people in the intervening decades. In our interview with the quartet, he recalled the kinds of community lesbians forged with gay men and trans women:

El grupo gays, trans, no quito que de verdad pasaron mucho trabajo. . . . Pero sí les quito una cosa. . . . Que cuando ellos tuvieron, pasaron muchísimo trabajo, y tenían problemas en las calles, y eran avasallados por problemas de la justicia, quien estaban juntos con ellos y a veces terminaban hasta en el mismo lugar encerrados juntos con ellos eran las lesbianas. Y se han olvidado que les dio mucho apoyo. Y antes había mucha unión entre las lesbianas con los gays con los trans. . . . Y así se andaban juntos, y había antes más comunicación entre las lesbianas y los gays, y se ha perdido.

I won't take away from gay and trans people that they suffered a lot. . . . But I will take away one thing. . . . That when they went through a lot of trouble, and they had problems in the streets, those who were with them and sometimes wound up locked up in the same place with them were the lesbians. And they have forgotten that we helped them a lot. And there used to be a much stronger relationship between lesbians and gay and trans people. . . . And so we walked together, and there was more dialogue between lesbians and gay people, and that has been lost.

As he went on, he explicitly described the ways that lesbian women would support transformistas femeninas in the complicated days of the underground queer parties:

> No porque tú has llegado a la cima el de abajo no es menos que tú. Han llegado a la cima, y los que están hoy en la cima estaban ayer como nosotros arrastrando una maletica, con taconcitos rotos, se les partió un tacón en pleno espectáculo, y de cuatro plumas se le cayeron tres, pero así mismo las lesbianas estaban. Eran en casas fiestas de lesbianas, y las lesbianas les hacían, "¡Ey! ¡No importa! ¡Ay, qué bien, qué bien, qué bien!" y aplaudían el número. Ahora, ¿por qué tú no me apoyes a mí? Porque es así. Se olvidó de momento, y se olvida de que somos iguales.

> Just because you have arrived at the top doesn't mean that those below are worth less than you are. They have arrived at the top, and those who are at the top now were yesterday just like us, dragging a suitcase, with broken heels, because a heel broke in the middle of the show, and out of four feathers three fell off but even still the lesbians were there. They were in lesbian house parties, and the lesbians shouted "Hey! It doesn't matter! That was wonderful!" and applauded the number. Now why won't you help me? Because that's how it is. They forgot for a moment, and they forget that we are equal.

If indeed transformistas masculinos have so infrequently enjoyed this kind of support from their transformista femenina counterparts, it is precisely the sort of coalition they cultivate in the peña.

The rest of that evening at the Cine Acapulco, as with so many others, Argelia and her co-performers offered creative, expansive performances of gender and race that situated Black lesbian women in relation to trans/queer social life more generally. One of the transformistas femeninas who Argelia had invited made an appearance that recalled those of the 1990s that Ángel Daniel narrated above.

Chantal was a beautiful and slight Black transformista femenina from Argelia's neighborhood who was trying to break in to the transformismo scene. For one of her *salidas*, she performed to Puerto Rican singer Kany García's polished pop ballad "Alguien." In contrast to the highly produced sound of García's song, Chantal's was a beautifully if unintentionally messy interpretation. Her outfit appeared somewhat haphazard and improvised: She was wearing a gold sequined bodice that barely covered her chest, and she had wrapped a black piece of fabric around her waist as a skirt that did not quite make it all around her body, leaving a considerable gap in the front. This was finished off with thigh-high black stockings, very high heels, a brown straight wig, and a bejeweled choker. Rather than wearing a breastplate—an expensive and hard-to-come-by accessory in Cuba—she had shaped the bodice to give the illusion of a full chest.

Throughout Chantal's performance of "Alguien," however, she struggled with the top, which kept slipping down, exposing her flat chest and nipples and breaking what was meant to be a faithful impersonation of a woman. As the song ended, she stepped upstage and turned away from the audience to adjust her outfit. Mexican singer Natalia Sosa's fiery, rock-inspired version of "Fuera de mi vida" came on, and as Chantal gave her more athletic performance of the song, she surrendered to the betrayal of her outfit, incorporating it into the song's desperate affect. To complement the disarray, she tore her choker off in the middle of the first chorus and chucked it to the ground. As the first chorus rose to its climax, she squatted down low to the ground and then leaped up into the air, landing firmly on her considerable heels. Then she fell to her knees, parting her thighs so she could bend from her waist, bringing her face all the way down to the floor. We spectators were entranced by her visceral interpretation, and numerous participants stuffed tips into the openings left by her outfit. At the song's dramatic coda—Sosa sustains a soaring note through a number of sharp band hits—Chantal threw herself to the ground, lying limp and still through the beginning of our adoring applause.

These are the kinds of performances Argelia promotes through the curation of her peña. With an awareness of transformistas' starkly differing access to material resources, Argelia extends her hand to her trans and queer sisters in need of a platform. She is selective, elevating people from the repartos, fellow Afrodescendants, and working-class people. Despite all that has transpired, these performances are able to conjure the social, aesthetic, and material contents of the 1990s shows, reclaiming the solidarity that these transformistas masculinos feel has been left behind.

Other performances that evening further leaned into creative gendered renderings. Once Chantal gathered herself up from the stage, Miguel came on and announced Argelia, telling us that she would be offering a unique kind of performance. Argelia walked out of the dressing room in a long straight black wig, a short and tight lightblue dress, and sensible heels, and began lip-synching to Beyoncé's Spanish-language rendition of her song "Listen" from *Dreamgirls*. We all applauded, cheered, and whistled as we realized she would be giving a transformismo femenino performance. If in chapter 2 I discussed the comedy inherent in transformistas femeninas performances of masculinity during the competition at Apocalipsis, here Argelia gave a sincere performance that leaned into the tropes of transformismo femenino, offering us a beautiful interpretation of Beyoncé's song and of Black femininity more generally. In a move that punctuated the otherwise understated *salida*, and one she would be unlikely to deploy in her transformismo masculino performances, she dramatically fell to her knees as Beyoncé held the last note of the song, burying her head in her hands as the music trailed off.

Here, I see Argelia intervening meaningfully in popular conceptions of Black femininity in ways that would be hard to do in masculine drag. I don't mean to suggest that so-called "bio-drag" is inherently liberatory, or that Argelia's performance offered a kind of gendered freedom that is wholly distinct from the more mainstream transformismo femenino performances of the dominant nightclubs. Instead, I am mindful of the impact of a Black lesbian woman's performance of femininity that is meant to be read as beautiful by the audience. In Cuba, as throughout the rest of the hemisphere, Black women are always already read as masculine, as failing to conform to the normative expectations of femininity. If, as Omise'eke Tinsley has suggested, "the persistent masculinization of black lesbians continues a long, violent history of colonial fictions that categorized black females as inherently, irretrievably mannish" (2018, 36), here Argelia disturbed this shared colonial legacy, moving in unpredictable ways to offer heterogenous accounts of Black lesbian personhood.[16]

Of course, it wouldn't be Argelia's peña if it didn't end with the rumba. Once again Yoruba Andabo's "La gozadera" served as a culmination of the performances that had preceded it. Alberto and Miguel took center stage, lip-synching to the lyrics while Chantal and another transformista femenina danced in tandem on either side of them. As by now you know is customary, by the time they reached the *estribillo*, all of us in attendance were up dancing with them, having collapsed whatever divide between performer and audience the Acapulco allowed. There we were, brought together by the persistent organizing of a Black lesbian feminist from the repartos, an unlikely assemblage of Black and non-Black Cubans and foreigners; trans, queer, lesbian, and gay people; lovers, friends, and acquaintances; all of us wanting a form of trans/queer socialization and politics that eclipses the shortcomings of our present moment. There, however fleetingly, I felt like I was witnessing and participating in the kind of coalitional politics of which so many of us dream.

Transformismo Otherwise

The transformismo masculino movement in Havana is an example of one way that vital Afrofeminist/trans/queer critique and the transformismo performance complex can and do collide in contemporary Cuba, in terms of both their participants and their vision for Cuba's future. As with transformismo in the repartos or the provinces or the work of transgender transformistas, I do not want to suggest that transformismo masculino is perfect, magical, or unfailing. Nor is it Argelia's or any other Black woman's job to save the world, even if that is indeed what they wind up doing. Argelia herself is not afraid of or unfamiliar with failure: I have seen co-performers frustrated by the tacit acceptance of a lack of material support for such tireless work, and I have heard others express concern that, in her desire to promote the needs of Black lesbian women wherever she can, Argelia sometimes finds herself performing for people who do not have her or her communities' best interests at heart. Even in inspired coalitions, people get disappointed.

Nevertheless, Argelia and her fellow transformistas masculinos keep on working, providing sorely needed resources for their communities. Through their performative labor, Havana's transformistas masculinos promote visibility and cultivate space for Black lesbian women. They do so with a vision toward a coalitional politics that recognizes the codependence of various trans/queer people's fates and strives for a future that overcomes the limitations of LGBT rights discourses on and beyond the island. In doing so, they collaborate archipelagically with Black lesbian feminists throughout history and across the hemisphere who complicate Black women's invisibility and hypervisibility, who take up space, and who lead with a coalitional politics.

Coda

The Future of Transformismo

On May 11, 2019, more than 200 trans and queer Cubans assembled in the Parque Central on the border between La Habana Vieja and Centro Habana and marched down the iconic Paseo del Prado boulevard toward the Malecón (Espinosa 2019). Aside from the change in location from Calle 23 in El Vedado, the gathering looked a lot like the Congas Contra la Homofobia that had taken place each year since 2008. Unlike those previous eleven Congas, however, this one was unique in not being sanctioned by the Cuban state; it was instead staged in direct response to the last-minute cancellation of the official Conga, ostensibly due to the economic crisis provoked by the sanctions imposed by US President Donald Trump. As the trans/queer Cubans arrived at the Malecón, they were stopped by plainclothes officials who said they were from the Ministerio del Interior and prohibited them from passing to the seawall, detaining several of those in attendance by force.[1]

Afibola Sifunola, one of the cofounders of the Afrofeminist/trans/queer project NOSOTRXS, described the day as "un nuevo comienzo para la comunidad LGTBQA" ("a new beginning for the LGTBQA community").[2] "Lo hicimos," she explained, "porque quisimos, lo hicimos porque aquí estamos, lo hicimos porque tenemos el derecho de hacer visible, escandaloso, colorido, nuestra manera de amarnos" ("We did it because we wanted to, we did it because we are here, we did it because we have the right to make our way of loving each other visible, scandalous, colorful"). Cuban poet, playwright, and cultural critic Norge Espinosa proclaimed that "El 11 de mayo del 2019 para la comunidad LGTBIQ de Cuba no fue una simple salida del closet ni una toma por asalto a la calle, sino una ganancia en términos de liberación" ("May 11, 2019 for the LGTBIQ community of Cuba was not just a simple coming out of the closet nor a taking by storm of the street, but a gain in terms of liberation").

In the wake of the event, Dr. Mariela Castro Espín, the director of CENESEX (which hosts the Jornada), took to Facebook to denounce the marchers as a "masa de ignorantes" (Espinosa 2019; "a mass of ignorant people"). Predictably, the state quickly claimed that the participants were funded and led by counterrevolutionary elements in the US, the lowest hanging fruit of available explanations for any unruly behavior on the part of Cuban citizens.

The episode highlights the tensions that trans/queer Cubans have to navigate between various groups, institutions, and movements on the island. Certain state elements are supportive of LGBT rights and causes, even if the imaginative horizon of their ideology does not extend as far as many would like. Other factions within the state are resistant to the LGBT rights movement or see it as an uncomfortable political reality in contemporary Cuba. When things go awry, as they did in 2019, the state has to recur to its available explanations for such behavior, which do index the reality that the US government has financed and undertaken many projects to infiltrate Cuban groups and destabilize the Cuban state. This is not the only foreign power at play, however, and some observers of the 2019 march felt that the state was bowing to pressure from evangelicals on the island who were pushing against the proposed reforms to the Family Code, which eventually passed in September 2022. These groups were indeed financed by foreign money through evangelical churches in the US, though their foreign influence was not nearly as roundly criticized as other forms of US imperialism have been throughout the tenure of the Revolutionary government.

Meanwhile, trans and queer Cubans simply want the better futures they have been cultivating for decades. These tensions between foreign capital, official discourses, and trans/queer vitality have animated *Transformismo* throughout: In chapter 1, I offered a genealogy and an overview of the contemporary transformismo scene that demonstrated how mainstream trans/queer nightlife in Havana—which emerged out of state support for the LGBT rights movement in Cuba—is tied up with the incentives and imagery of the tourism economy. As such, it reproduces harmful stereotypes about Black women while shutting Black women themselves out of its most lucrative corners. Throughout the rest of *Transformismo*, I discussed some of the ways that trans/queer culture workers are thinking beyond the limitations of these spaces while creating livable possibilities for trans/queer people in the present.

In chapter 2, I described informal parties in Havana's repartos that are providing social and material sustenance to ordinary Cubans left out of postsocialist reform projects on the island. Chapter 3 offered insight into the ways transformistas in Villa Clara province are acting out a coalitional politics that imagines a more effective marriage between Revolutionary discourses and trans/queer needs. In chapter 4, I considered the ways that transgender transformistas are articulating understandings of trans subjectivity that go beyond dominant notions about gender and sexuality in Cuba and Cuban studies. Finally, chapter 5 narrated the work of Havana's transformistas masculinos as they lived out and performed a Black lesbian feminist vision that redresses some of the signal social and economic challenges Cuba has faced since the fall of socialism.

In what remains, I want to fast-forward and zoom out to consider some of what has transpired since I conducted the primary research for this book, and to situate the lives, work, and ideas of trans/queer cultural workers in Cuba within a broader hemispheric context. I suggest that, if trans/queer people in Cuba have been hit ever harder by crisis after crisis, they nevertheless continue to build better futures in the harsh light of the here and now. They do so not in isolation but rather in concert with trans/queer people throughout the Americas who have been left behind by mainstream LGBT rights discourses. I conclude *Transformismo*, then, by reflecting on what Cuba's transformistas are teaching us as we work to foment a hemispheric trans/queer liberation.

Transformismo since 2018

In a way, the preceding chapters are a snapshot of a world that no longer exists. If many of the spaces, scenes, and performers I discuss are still active on the island, just as many parties have been shuttered and transformistas have left Cuba. During my long-term research, Cuba was just beginning to feel the effects of President Trump's tightened sanctions on the island. Since then, Cubans have witnessed the devastation wrought by the COVID-19 pandemic, the swelling of and response to the July 11 protest movement in 2021, and the ensuing hemorrhage of immigration, the largest since the Revolution. Unsurprisingly, the communities I describe in the majority of *Transformismo* were among those hit hardest by these transformations. And yet they continue to produce life-affirming and life-saving care for one another and for their fellow Cubans.

Though the US blockade of Cuba remained intact under President Obama, the easing of US sanctions had a palpable effect on industry and everyday life. If, as I discuss in the introduction, inequities continued to expand on the island, so too did a vibrant groundswell of new institutions and projects, contributing to a sense of hopefulness among Cubans of diverse means. President Trump's vicious measures against Cuba, which have been extended by President Biden, harshly tamped down that growth and excitement: material scarcity and a lack of economic possibilities led to a growing sense of hopelessness that paved the way for the immigration explosion that has followed.

The COVID-19 pandemic surely did not help things, and Cubans suffered tremendously in the face of not only the health emergency but the dire lack of material resources that dwindling tourism brought. Many Cubans instinctively compared the era to the Special Period, while some suggested that this moment was worse, since this time the necessary goods were present on the island, but they were simply out of reach for Cubans of typical means. Moreover, many of the trans/queer scenes I describe in this book, like so many art worlds globally, could not go on during the pandemic as they once did.

In the midst of this scarcity and the government repression that accompanied it, Cubans mounted one of the most robust expressions of disaffection since the Revolution. On July 11, 2021, Cubans took to the streets en masse to protest harsh living conditions, material scarcity, and punishing inequity. If this, too, was represented as so much reactionary politics by the Cuban state, radical elements on the island and in the diaspora quickly explained that they were in no way seeking to embrace the US's imperial desires or the horrors of global racial capitalism. Instead, they were looking to redress the Cuban state's very real practices of silencing dissent, including the vital racial and sexual dissidence that is so urgently needed, as much in Cuba as anywhere else in this hemisphere.[3]

Together, all of these events have led to the most significant outflow of Cubans from the island since the Revolution. Anyone familiar with Cuba will already know that seemingly every Cuban is considering their options for leaving the island, and in each family and social network at least a handful have already gone. So many of the artists who populate the preceding chapters find themselves in the diaspora: Deyanira made her way to Russia, Zulema became part of the Cuban queer nightlife scene in Miami for a moment, and Uma Rojo has brought her beautiful brand of Cuban transformismo to Spain. What they and so many others have left behind is an increasing sense of hopelessness and isolation on the island and *en la lucha* (in the struggle).

And yet, you can still find many of this book's protagonists in Cuba, continuing to create possibilities for themselves and their communities, to craft desirable futures for the island. NOSOTRXS remained active throughout the pandemic, providing mutual aid to their fellow citizens through the difficult circumstances brought by the pandemic (see *Cubadebate* 2021). Kiriam, Blaccucini, Margot, and many other transformistas continue to grace the stages of Cuba's nightclubs, informal parties, and social projects.

Argelia is one of them, and she continues to work arduously to support her communities. Through her project Afrodiverso, she provides programming for children in the repartos and for trans/queer Cubans throughout Havana. In February 2023, I saw Argelia put on a stunning Festival de Afrotransformismo in which no fewer than ten Black transformistas (four masculino and six femenina) walked the hallways and patio of the Asociación Cubana de las Naciones Unidas, demonstrating, as Argelia's partner said, "que el transformismo afrodescendiente existe y es de calidad" ("that Afrodescendent transformismo exists and is high quality"). In a presentation that followed, Argelia and her partner elaborated their work "empoderando a nosotrxs lxs trans [con] arte, salud, y comunidad" ("empowering we trans people through art, health, and community"). In the wake of COVID, Argelia and her transformista masculino co-performers have even been invited more often to the shows in Havana's more mainstream nightclubs, including El Divino's night at Café Cantante, an accomplishment that was out of reach during my primary research. These advances are, to be sure, evidence of the determined advocacy of people like Argelia.

Grassroots work like Argelia's has led to advances for trans/queer people in the political realm, too, as evidenced most recently by the passage of Cuba's new Family Code in September 2022. This finally delivered long-promised state support for same-sex marriage and adoption on the island. Critics were quick to point out, however, that the new code stops short of making any comment on the lives of transgender Cubans, and in many ways it reinscribes queer political progress within the image of the heteronormative family. To be sure, the code is but one step in an ongoing process of trans/queer people's negotiations with the state for better lives.

It should come as no surprise that trans/queer people, women, Afrodescendants, *reparteros*, and poor folks were among those who paid most dearly for the willful myopia of Cuba's turn to tourism after the fall of the Soviet Union. And yet, what I wish to document here, and what I hope to have shown throughout *Transformismo*, is not solely this inequity or even the ways that trans/queer people are making do in these circumstances or imagining better futures. Instead, I have tried to foreground the ways that trans/queer culture workers are, through their work and ideas, cultivating liberatory possibilities right now, in the present.

Despite the incredible challenges trans/queer people face in this hemisphere, then, goals that are supposedly impossible to reach are already being achieved every day by ordinary people: providing dignity and possibility to people despite stultifying precarity and scarcity, marrying revolutionary nationalism and trans/queer politics, going beyond normative understandings of gender and sexuality, and living out the urgent social interventions of Black feminism. If it is unlikely that Cuba will find its way out from underneath the weight of US imperialism anytime soon, there will always be the meeting of the social project in the repartos, the unlicensed house party, the sweaty basement level of the queer nightclub. I don't mean this in any dreamy sense; I mean it in the real, material way that people can actually access to find themselves immersed in an alternative system of value.

Transformismo Beyond Cuba

These issues trans/queer Cubans face and the work they do to address them are not specific to the island, to be sure, and instead describe trans/queer life and politics throughout the Americas. I have tried throughout *Transformismo* to deal with Cuba on Cuban terms, the way the vast majority of Cubans will always have to.[4] Here, however, I want to situate trans/queer Cuban culture works in a broader hemispheric context of intensifying racial capitalism, resurgent trans/homophobia, tepid LGBT rights discourses, and radical efforts to imagine otherwise. In doing so, I mean to recognize the ongoing and historic flight of Cubans from the island and to point more directly to some of the ways the contents of this book might inform efforts toward trans/queer liberation throughout the hemisphere.

The worlds and dynamics I described in the preceding chapters were probably familiar to anyone who cares about trans/queer (night)life in the Americas. Throughout Latin America, drag queens are at work every night performing to songs by Spanish-language singers from Mexico, Spain, Puerto Rico, and Cuba and Black divas from the US. Many of those shows are not unlike the ones that dot cities and towns in the US, especially in Latinx spaces. At the same time, everywhere in this hemisphere, trans/queer people navigate LGBT rights discourses that are primarily invested in the accumulation of capital; that erase racial and economic formations from narratives of sexual subjectivity; that privilege the metropole; that sideline certain kinds of trans people; and that turn away from the political imperatives long articulated by Black, woman-of-color, and Third World feminisms.

Take, for example, the history I recounted in chapter 1, and the ways the Cuban state—the very same one that imprisoned trans/queer people from the 1960s through the early 2000s—coopted a radical history of underground trans/queer performance in order to sell it to foreigners for a profit. Just as I was beginning to appreciate this—on an early research trip that coincided with the 2016 Jornada that opened *Transformismo*—I headed back to Boston, where I was in graduate school, and went to a Pride march with some fellow PhD students. And what did we see there, in the same city that was home to the Combahee River Collective in the 1970s, except for the police, a bank, and a major consulting firm marching by with us trans/queer people? Throughout the hemisphere, histories of trans/queer liberation are submerged in favor of LGBT rights discourses that work to secure the dystopian and uninhabitable present rather than transforming the very basis on which it rests.

But just as these struggles are hemispheric, so, too, do trans/queer people everywhere push back against them by conjuring better futures while working to cultivate affirming situations for themselves and their people in the present. The transformistas in chapters 2 and 3, for example, are participating in hemispheric struggles to provide sustenance for racially, geographically, and economically marginalized trans/queer people in the face of an LGBT rights movement that has always valorized the experiences and circumstances of Euro-descendant urban elites. Though their political discourses might be distinct, I see their work as part of a collective that includes the Trans Justice Funding Project, the Sylvia Rivera Law Project, Familia: Trans/Queer Liberation Movement, and the countless smaller or nameless projects throughout the hemisphere that insist that trans/queer liberation is for all of us and must be based in dismantling broader structures of global racial capitalism, white supremacy, and US imperialism.

Similarly, I see the kinds of expansive possibilities that transgender transformistas are imagining and living out in Cuba, which I detailed in chapter 4, reflected in the brilliant and pathbreaking interventions that travesti movements are making throughout Latin America. Sometimes these ties have been explicit, as in the participation of Conurbanes por la Diversidad, a trans/queer organization in Buenos Aires, in the 2016 Jornada, where they took up space to remember the legacies of their travesti sisters Diana Sacayán and Lohana Berkins. At other times I have caught glimpses of corners of the movement that recalled the performative moves of Blaccucini, Ángel Daniel, and Titi, as when I saw the radical Ecuadorian travesti performance art duo Pacha Queer perform in Mexico City in 2019. Though their distinctly anti-imperialist *trava sudaca* lexicon differs from that of Cuba's transgender transformistas, both are cultivating vital and necessary lifeways for trans and travesti people in the Americas.

And, of course, the Black lesbian feminist vision of Argelia and her co-performers resonates archipelagically with other drag kings and Black/queer social projects throughout the hemisphere. If indeed lesbian women, Black people, and poor people are marginalized within LGBT spaces not just in Cuba but throughout the Americas, drag king performance has been a crucial tool for more radical interventions. In *The Drag King Book*, Del LaGrace Volcano and Jack Halberstam (1999, 139–40) suggest that drag kinging in the US emerges explicitly out of Black and working-class sexual cultures. In Mexico City, Nancy Cázares links her drag king performance practice to the struggle against femicide and broader efforts to "take back political spaces to defend our labour, sexual, and reproductive rights" (*Left Voice* 2017). I see the work of Havana's transformistas masculinos, then, as one example in a long line of Black and Latinx lesbian feminist labor—from the Combahee River Collective to *This Bridge Called My Back* to Black Lives Matter—that articulates a vision for racial, sexual, and economic justice, one that would bring collective liberation.

A Hemispheric Trans/Queer Conga

At a talk at UC Berkeley devoted to Afro-transfeminism in June 2022, Odaymar of the hip-hop duo Krudxs Cubensi spoke with a group of mostly undergraduate students about how the moves they make with their body intervene in a global history of antiblackness, whether they find themselves in Havana, where they were born; in Austin, Texas, where they were based for fifteen years; or in the San Francisco Bay Area, where they currently reside. Their commentary on the futures they imagine for each of these places spoke to a collective and hemispheric racial, sexual, and economic transformation that we could call trans/queer liberation.

How might we learn from Cuba's trans/queer culture workers as we build it? Cuba's Afrofeminist/trans/queer movement demonstrates the possibility of struggling against global racial capitalism and US imperialism while acknowledging the shortcomings of existing structures of revolutionary nationalism to fully address the racial-sexual-economic histories of the Americas. In concert with their counterparts throughout the Caribbean and Latin America, Cubans are keenly aware of the ravages of US imperialism, of the impossibilities of life in our current world system. But they are also perhaps more aware than most of the limitations of revolutionary nationalism for the project of Black/trans/queer liberation. From the Afrofeminist/trans/queer movement we can learn not a third way, one that equivocates on the moral distinctions between capitalism and socialism, but rather one that emerges from the particular historical circumstances of the Americas to demand redress, reparation, and reprieve.

Cuba's Afrofeminist/trans/queer movement further shows us that this liberatory future will need to be, to return to the words of Afibola Sifunola, "escandalosa, colorida" ("scandalous, colorful"), as she said of the 2019 march. In the face of revolutionary nationalist movements that have either repressed or reluctantly accommodated sexual rebels, this trans/queer liberatory one would emerge from these oppositional subjectivities to actually address the sexual legacies of colonialism, slavery, and capitalism.

To revisit the chapters of *Transformismo*, such a future would need to emerge from the repartos, from the provinces, from working-class trans folks, from Black lesbian feminists—which is to say, from the racial, sexual, economic, and geographic margins of Cuba, the Caribbean, and the Americas. It would be a hemispheric conga in which this trans lesbian Latina, this daughter of a Cuban mother, would give everything to march.

Toward a Glossary

While I want to offer a collection of key terms, translations, and acronyms here, I am also mindful of this book's and its informants' rights to a certain level of opacity. Moreover, some of the terms I "define" here I trouble considerably in the preceding chapters. So, I hope this will be a helpful resource for readers while also resisting any impulse to pin down ideas that are meant to be messy and free.

Afro-: The prefix Afro- is used in many activist circles in Cuba, and you will find it here in both English and Spanish, such as Afrodescendiente (Afrodescendant/Afrodescendent), Afrofeminism, Afroqueer, Afrotransformismo, etc.

Artivista/Artivismo: Literally "artivist/artivism," from artist-activist and art-activism. This term is used by many Cubans, especially in Afrodescendent movements, whose artistic work is caught up with their activism.

Babalawo: A kind of priest in the Afrocuban religion Regla de Ocha.

CENESEX: The Centro Nacional de Educación Sexual (National Center for Sex Education) in Cuba. This is a primary state voice for sexual diversity on the island, and among other things it manages trans care, organizes the projects that include transformismo, and puts on the yearly Jornada Contra la Homofobia y la Transfobia (see below).

Centro Habana: Central Havana. Along with La Habana Vieja and El Vedado, one of the three coastal municipalities in the center of the city. It is perhaps less manicured than El Vedado and less transformed by tourism than La Habana Vieja.

CNP/CPP: The Centro Nacional de Prevención de las ITS-VIH/sida (CNP, National Center for the Prevention of STIs and HIV/AIDS) is another state public-health group doing sexual health work on the island. It is divided into the CPPs or Centros Provinciales de Prevención de las ITS-VIH/sida (Provincial Centers for the Prevention of STIs and HIV/AIDS).

Conga: Refers literally to the music and dance of the *comparsas* or parades in Cuba. In *Transformismo* this refers mostly to the yearly Conga Contra la Homofobia y la Transfobia that takes place during the Jornada (see below).

CUC: The *peso convertible* (convertible peso), a now-defunct tourist currency that was pegged to the US dollar. During the primary research for this book, 1 CUC was worth 25 Cuban pesos, the local currency.

Cumpleaños de santo: The anniversary of one's initiation into Regla de Ochoa.

Gala: In *Transformismo*, this generally refers to the Gala Contra la Homofobia y la Transfobia, a nationally televised performance that takes place during the Jornada (see below).

La Habana Vieja: Old Havana. This is the historic center of the city of Havana and, with Centro Habana and El Vedado, one of its three central coastal municipalities. Though it is home to some of Havana's most blighted neighborhoods, this municipality has been aggressively restored and invested in as part of Cuba's tourism campaign, as evidenced by the cruise ships that dock in its port.

HSH: Hombres que tienen sexo con hombres, which corresponds with the often-used phrase "men who have sex with men" or "MSM" in public health discourse in English. Some public-health networks historically oriented toward gay men in Cuba carry this name.

Humorista: Literally "comedian." In most of *Transformismo*, this refers to a comedic drag performer.

Jornada: In *Transformismo*, this is mostly used to refer to the yearly Jornada Contra la Homofobia y la Transfobia (Conference Against Homophobia and Transphobia), which could be seen as Cuba's version of Pride. It is put on by CENESEX and includes panels by scholars and activists, parties, performances, and a Conga through downtown Havana.

July 11: In 2021, Cubans throughout the island took to the streets on July 11 to demonstrate against material scarcity, unequal access to goods, and economic hardship. The Cuban state responded severely to the protests, while the US used the protests to support their representation of the Cuban Revolution as a failure.

Latinx: Throughout *Transformismo*, I use gender-neutral language with terminal x. Though many commentators in the Spanish-speaking Americas suggest that this construct is only used in the US, trans and queer Cubans—like their counterparts throughout the hemisphere—deploy all kinds of creative gender-neutral language. I honor that here while attempting to intervene in the trans/homophobia so present in discussions about the term "Latinx."

Madrina: Literally "godmother." In Cuba, this often refers specifically to one's godmother in Regla de Ocha. Trans and queer Cubans will also use madrina to refer to the person who brought them into transformismo or served as their trans mother.

El Malecón: The famous seawall and boulevard that extends from La Habana Vieja to El Vedado. Sometimes referred to as the longest couch in Havana, El Malecón is a cherished place to meet and spend time in the evening.

Maricón: Literally "faggot." Okay, I guess literally, "big little María." But it is used similarly to how "faggot" is used in the English-speaking world. And I suppose "Mary," too. Maricón refers to any male-identifying person who is attracted to other men, but it is particularly used to describe femme-presenting people assigned male at birth who are attracted to men. Though still used pejoratively, it has been reclaimed by queer people, like Cinthya in chapter 3 of this book.

Miramar: Along with Playa (below), one of the coastal municipalities on the west side of Havana known for its economically privileged residents.

Moneda Nacional: In contrast to the now-defunct CUC (above), this is the local currency of Cuba, also known as the *peso cubano* (Cuban peso) or CUP. During the primary research for this book, the peso was pegged to the dollar such that 25 CUP had the same purchasing power as 1 CUC (roughly 1 USD). At the time of this writing, however, it would take more than 300 CUP to buy 1 USD.

OREMI: Also Grupo (Group) OREMI, the CENESEX network for lesbian and bisexual women. OREMI emerged particularly out of Black lesbian organizing in the early 2000s, and Tanya Saunders (2008) has argued that CENESEX limited its scope after explosive interest in its early days.

Peligrosidad social: Literally "social danger," a vague term that has been used to criminalize certain ways of being in Revolutionary Cuba, especially for Black and trans/queer people.

Peña: Generally, something like "group." Among my interlocutors, however, this term was mostly used to refer to transformismo performances that took place during the daytime and generally did not involve compensation.

Playa: Along with Miramar (above), one of the coastal municipalities on the west side of Havana known for its economically privileged residents.

Proyecto: Literally "project." In *Transformismo*, this refers both to the community-based projects often organized in the Afrofeminist/trans/queer movement and to the state-run groups of transformistas and other artists who perform at official queer nightclubs.

Proyecto TransCuba: The trans network of CENESEX.

La Rampa: Literally "The Ramp," a nickname given to the stretch of Calle 23 nearest the Malecón, long the queer hub of Havana.

Reparto: A section of the city's *municipios* (municipalities). More informally, this refers to the neighborhoods of Havana away from the more affluent tourist-centric areas on the coast. For example, Párraga is a reparto in the municipio Arroyo Naranjo. See chapter 2.

Transformismo/Transformista: In the Cuban context, these roughly correspond to drag performance/drag performer.

Transformismo femenino/masculino: Drag queen performance/drag king performance.

Transformista femenina/masculino: Drag queen/king.

Transgénero/Transexual: Transgender/transexual.

Travesti: A term used throughout the Spanish-speaking Americas to refer to a femme-identified person assigned male at birth. This term aligns and clashes with "transgénero" or "transgender" in a number of ways; it generally tends to describe poor and/or racialized trans and gender-nonconforming people as well as those with a subjective, ideological, and/or political opposition to the gender binary. See chapter 4 and Machuca Rose (2019, 242).

El Vedado: A central coastal municipality in Havana also known as Plaza de la Revolución. This is now a touristy part of the city, if not quite as manicured for the foreign gaze as La Habana Vieja. This is also where my mother was born and spent the first six years of her life.

Notes

Preface

1. Beyond being my wife, Kerry is a fellow student of gender and sexuality in Cuba and a key social, political, and intellectual interlocutor throughout this book. See White (2017, 2023).

2. You can see Diarenis's embedded narration of her neighborhood in "San Miguel del Padrón" (2020).

3. When I say "in the US" here, I am referring to the racial formation of *latinidad*, not the use of the trans/queer "Latinx." Contrary to popular belief, "Latinx" is not only used in the US. You can hear all kinds of gender-neutral (-e and -x) as well as modified feminine (-a instead of -o or a consonant) in trans/queer space throughout Cuba and Latin America. Some examples include *amora* instead of *amor* (love), *cuerpa* instead of *cuerpo* (body), *amigxs* instead of *amigos* (friends), and many more.

4. This conversation is reconstructed from my field notes.

5. Travesti is a term of gender subjectivity deployed throughout Latin America. I discuss this further in chapter 4.

6. These remarks, too, are reconstructed from fieldnotes.

7. In saying "white queer people in Cuba," I am referring to people who would be seen as such by Cubans on the island. To be sure, such people's racial subjectivities, like my own, are more complicated in a broader hemispheric perspective.

8. I agree wholeheartedly with Yarimar Bonilla when she says that "[g]overnment forms often clarify that Latino is not a race but rather a racially diverse panethnic group. And yet in practice, we are routinely racialized and treated as nonwhite" (2023).

9. Tavia Nyong'o has explained that Muñoz, for example, "emphatically thought of himself as a student of the Black radical tradition, which is to say, an analytic that places orthodox Marxism in constant tension with slavery and its afterlives" (2021).

10. More recently, Som-Mai Nguyen (2022) criticized the "blunt force ethnic credibility" of the diasporic author.

11. By "femme," I refer to feminized people, to women, to "the sissies, the cry babies, those of us who chose adornment as a reminder that we are worthy, the quiet

ones whose introvertness is taken as 'passive' and therefore feminine, those who perform taken-for-granted labor, those of us who must hold the world before we can hold ourselves, and those of us whose gender is just that: femme" (Pelaez Lopez 2018). In calling this project a "diasporic femme ethnography," I am gesturing toward the Diasporic Femme Collective, alongside whom I write and think about race, sex, and diaspora. The members of this group—Krystal Klingenberg, Laurie Lee, Tamar Sella, and myself—met while in graduate school in the Harvard University Department of Music, and this book is an outgrowth of our work together.

Introduction

1. I will use performers' and other people's actual names when they have asked me to or when they are well-known public figures. Otherwise, I have concealed my interlocutors' identities.

2. Like "transformista masculino" here, throughout *Transformismo* terms in Spanish will generally appear italicized the first time and then in regular roman in subsequent uses.

3. In this way, Castro cruised around El Vedado as tourists do, sitting atop the back seat of a classic car with the top town.

4. Throughout *Transformismo*, I use "trans/queer" to refer to a broad array of nonheteronormative and gender-nonconforming people, performances, and subjectivities. I juxtapose these categories of sexual subjectivity to recall the ways that gender and sexuality have historically been caught up with one another, as I will discuss further in chapter 4. Like Eric Stanley (2021, 5), I want to "think of trans/queer as tendencies and not codified identities as both a theoretical intervention and a fact of history." See Leslie Santana (2022, 58–59) for more context.

5. I write this, for example, shortly after the state of Tennessee criminalized public drag performance.

6. In the American context, these shortcomings include investments in heteronormativity and empire (through marriage and the military), ongoing and intensifying transphobia and femmephobia, alliances with global capital, and unchecked white supremacy. The hemispheric conversation about our trans/queer alternatives includes Gossett, Stanley, and Burton (2017); Santana (2019); Wayar (2018); and many others.

7. This includes Lumsden (1996), Bejel (2001), Sierra Madero (2006), Allen (2011), Stout (2014), and Saunders (2015).

8. One exception is Morad (2015). On the importance of the cultural sphere in Cuban politics, see Fernandes (2006), de la Fuente (2008, 2012), Fusco (2015), Saunders (2015), and Perry (2015).

9. For me, this lineage includes earlier ethnomusicological work on performance (e.g., Frisbie 1967; Hood 1969; McLeod and Herndon 1980; Seeger 1987), critical reflections over the years on ethnomusicology as a discipline (e.g., Kisliuk 1998; Wong 2014); and more recent ethnomusicological scholarship that challenges the definition of musical study (e.g., Wang 2018; Pilzer 2022, 14–16; Putcha 2022, xvi–xvii).

10. In this way, *Transformismo* also participates in the development of a trans/queer ethnomusicology alongside Hayes (2010), Morcom (2013), Amico (2014), Morad (2015), and Barz and Cheng (2019).

11. Robert Cox (1983, 166–67) described how Gramsci's trasformismo "can serve as a strategy of assimilating and domesticating potentially dangerous ideas by adjusting them to the policies of the dominant coalition and can thereby obstruct the formation of class-based organised opposition to established social and political power." There is a kind of sexual trasformismo present in Cuba's official LGBT rights movement, then, reflected obliquely in Negrón-Muntaner's (2008) discussion of "mariconerías" ("faggotries") of the state and Sierra Madero's (2014) understanding of a "travestismo" ("transvestism") of the state.

12. I refer here to the writers of the travesti movement in Argentina, including Lohana Berkins, Marlene Wayar, and Susy Shock; the recent interventions into trans/queer studies in *Transgender Studies Quarterly* ("Trans Studies en las Américas") and the *Gay and Lesbian Quarterly* ("Cuir/Queer Américas"); and a host of books that engage sexual subjectivity in the hemisphere by Rosamond King, Lyndon Gill, Marcia Ochoa, Lawrence La Fountain-Stokes, and several others. See, for example, Berkins ([2007] 2015), Wayar (2018), Shock (2011), Rizki et al. (2019), Pierce et al. (2021), King (2014), Ochoa (2014), Gill (2018), and La Fountain-Stokes (2021).

13. Here I follow in particular Namaste (2000) and Valentine (2007).

14. While I don't necessarily situate *Transformismo* within the North American literature on drag, it is certainly inspired by Newton ([1972] 1979) and in dialogue with Rupp and Taylor (2003) and Peña (2013, 157–76).

15. Transformistas often refer to smaller, regular afternoon performances as "peñas," or gatherings. Cumpleaños de santo are the anniversaries celebrated in the Afrocuban religion Regla de Ocha that mark a practitioner's reception of their corresponding orisha or saint.

16. The intimacies between race and sex stem not only from how the social realm is "lived" but also from how such categories have been historically and materially produced in relation to one another. See, for example, Somerville (2000).

17. When I refer to the Afrofeminist movement, I mean to call to mind the women of projects such as Afrocubanas, which I will discuss later, and other Black feminist efforts throughout Cuba's history. When I reference the Afrofeminist/trans/queer movement, I mean to include not only those women but also the many overlapping artists and activists who have brought Afrofeminism to bear on the lives of trans/queer people. Collectively, these movements include projects like NOSOTRXS, Afrocubanas, Afrodiverso, and many others. They have produced a wide body of work, including the book *Afrocubanas* (2011), the database Directorio de Afrocubanas, blogs and periodicals like *Negra cubana tenía que ser* and *Afrocubanas – La Revista*, and much more. See, for example, Guillard Limonta (2016), *IPS Cuba* (2020), Benson (2020), and *Cubadebate* (2021).

18. On the history of Black feminism in Cuba, see Brunson (2021, 92–117).

19. Think, for example, of Gloria Anzaldúa, Cherríe Moraga, Rosario Morales, Chirlane McCray, and Merle Woo.

20. See, for example, the statement of the Colectivo Cuba Liberación Negra, which links a Black/queer analysis of the July 11 movement to Black/queer activism against police and prison violence in the US (Cuesta, Álvarez, and López 2021).

21. As Merriam's acknowledgment makes clear, a more transparent account of these collaborations transforms understandings of the role of women in the ethnographic enterprise. See Wayne (1985), for example, for a discussion of the influence of various women on Malinowski's work.

22. In chapter 1, I describe other grassroots trans/queer organizations that did related work in the 1990s and 2000s.

23. In the face of similar exclusions within mainstream feminism in Cuba, Benson (2020, xxii) suggests that Afrofeminism in Cuba emerged out of the Afrodescendant movement more than the feminist movement.

24. Throughout *Transformismo*, I capitalize "Revolution" and "Revolutionary" when they are explicitly related to the Cuban Revolution, its ideas, or its practices, and I use "revolution" and "revolutionary" when deploying these terms in their broader senses. I do so in order to reflect a distinction some of my interlocutors made between revolutionary possibilities in Cuba and the Americas and the realities of the Cuban Revolution.

Chapter 1

1. Arguably, Tate's discussion of "the American music industry's never-ending quest for a white artist who can competently perform a Black musical impersonation" (2003, 4) can be read as a description of the Americas, not just the US.

2. In reality this was one of the songs of choice of Musmé's fellow transformista Omar Ferrán. The two of them were particularly known for singing in their own voices. See Marquetti (2018) for more context on both transformistas.

3. Yucayo is the indigenous name for the city of Matanzas in western Cuba, and the Yumurí is one of two rivers that runs through the city.

4. I draw here from Hartman (2008, 11–12). Throughout *Transformismo* I deploy divergent narrative strategies to represent the lives and work of people like Musmé, whom humanities and social science scholars have historically elided.

5. See Thomas (2008, 86–90) for more context about the social meanings of Montaner's performance of racialized gender.

6. In fact, Anckermann, whose music transformista Omar Ferrán was known for singing, was a composer for the very theatrical traditions I mention here and above.

7. My use of "narrating class" draws from Nadine Hubbs, who described "the professional middle class" in the US in the 21st century as "the narrators of working-class life and reality, because they are the narrating class: the analysts and experts, the language, representation, and knowledge specialists for the whole society" (2014, 37). In turn-of-the-century Cuba, such a formation would have included the lawyers, doctors, and journalists who helped build the panic around gender and sexual transgression.

8. See Marqués de Armas (2014) for a broader discussion of homophobia and nation-making in Cuba.

9. See Sierra Madero (2006, 28–31) and González Pagés (2012) for more context on the case of Enriqueta Favez.

10. For more context on the Cuban Revolution's engagement with sex workers, see Guerra (2012, 277–23) and Hynson (2020, 149–200).

11. For more context on the UMAP camps, see Sierra Madero and Guerra (2016), Lumsden (1996, 65–71), Bejel (2001, 100–110), Guerra (2012, 227–55), and Benson (2016, 118).

12. See, for example, Roque Guerra (2011, 220–21), Fernández Robaina (2005), and Benson (2016, 235–40).

13. Roque Guerra (2011, 222) also suggests that GNTES was providing gender-

affirming care to at least one trans woman as early as 1972. See Kirk (2020) for a genealogy of sexual health education on the island.

14. Later, during the 1994 *balsero* crisis, the camp set up in the US naval base in Guantanamo Bay for Cubans returned to the island by the US would also become a center for transformismo. One gay Cuban man who stayed there recalls, "Al principio que llegamos a Guantánamo prepararon un show. . . . Era un show de homosexuales en el campamento de hombres" (*Perra!* 1995, 7; ["Right when we got to Guantánamo, they put on a show. . . . It was a homosexual show in the men's camp."]).

15. For more on the Special Period and its social effects see de la Fuente (2001, 315–34).

16. For more information on the "fiestas de diez pesos" scene, see Morad (2015), Allen (2011, 167–70), Sierra Madero (2006, 225–51), and Lumsden (1996, 141–57).

17. Admittedly, the term "working-class" is a complicated one to use to describe the Cuban context, and Marxists and other class scholars will likely quibble with it. In using it, I am not trying to make a claim about class structure on the island or to euphemize poverty. I am instead distinguishing between those who primarily live within the local, domestic economy and those with greater access to foreign capital. I am trying to translate the language of social class to the context of a post-socialist tourism economy.

18. 2008 was also the culmination of several years of growth in the influence and scope of CENESEX, including the creation of a network for gay men in 2000 and the hosting of the Sixteenth World Congress of Sexology in Havana in 2003 (Roque Guerra 2011, 225).

19. Critics of the Cuban state would understand this shift toward acceptance as an effort to bring trans/queer people under their control and purview, and the shortcomings of government efforts like OREMI or the Agencia Cubana de Rap indeed lend credence to these analyses. See Negrón-Muntaner (2008), Sierra Madero (2014), and Saunders (2015, 314–16).

20. CUC refers to the Cuban convertible peso, a tourist currency pegged to the US dollar that was phased out in 2021.

21. As in the rest of Latin America, travesti as a category is "classed and raced" (Machuca Rose 2019, 242). I will discuss this and other categories of trans subjectivity in Cuba in chapter 4.

22. Cuba's reliance on tourism and remittances is not exceptional but rather situates it within a Caribbean context of US imperialism and global racial capitalism. See, for example, Alexander (2005, 26–27).

23. As elsewhere, tipping is an important practice within Cuban transformismo. The size of the tip, the way the tip is placed, and the accompanying gestures all speak to characteristics of the transformista, their audience, and the space they are performing in. Sarah Hankins (2015) has suggested that tipping highlights drag as a form of sex work, and indeed in Cuba transformismo is tied up with various forms of sexualized labor. See, for example, Hodge (2014).

24. The bolero itself was born of working-class Black and mixed-race musicians in the eastern tip of the island, drawing on rhythms from Haiti. See Sublette (2004, 252–53).

25. I mean here to situate Cuba and its transformismo within a hemispheric context of national cooptation and white theft of Black creativity. See, for example, Rose (1994, 3–5), Neal (1999, 16–17), and Tate (2003, 4).

26. If the *humorista* aligns to some degree with blackness and the "linda" with whiteness, then *temperamentales* like Devora occupy the space of *la mulata*. To a certain extent, then, they perform la mulata's psychic excesses in much the same way that humoristas like Blankita perform Black women's perceived physical excesses.

27. In doing so, Blankita was also—I imagine consciously—recalling a scene from *Mariposas* in which Maridalia implores her audience to stop throwing change at her and instead throw "un Washington" (coins from the US). When someone finally does so, she catches it in her high heel and dramatically faints, to her public's delight.

28. I will admit, for example, that the shows offered me, from those alongside me in the audience, some of my first experiences of trans recognition and sisterhood.

29. Popular conceptions of *jineterismo* (hustling) among foreigners tend to overstate the formality of the practice and its relation to sex work more generally. To me, Cubans are more likely to see jineterismo as a broad spectrum of practices that are better understood as diverse forms of hustling that involve foreigners. For some young queer people, this might mean dancing with a foreigner and then asking them for a drink or a cigarette. For others, it might mean getting a foreigner to pay their entrance to the nightclub or to take them out somewhere another night. For still others, it could mean finding a foreigner to have sex with, perhaps including the exchange of some money. And, finally, others have their sights on finding a foreigner who will invite them to visit them abroad, who will write them a letter of invitation to another country where they might be able to stay for a while or for the rest of their lives. In this way, then, jineterismo can be seen as a spectrum that begins to resemble heterosexual courtship and marriage more generally. That is to say, in some ways the discourse of jineterismo merely sensationalizes and exoticizes practices that economically marginalized people—including, historically, white women in the United States and Europe—have always engaged in to secure their material well-being into the future. For further discussion, see Stout (2014), Hodge (2001, 2014), and Allen (2011, 157–85). For a broader Caribbean context, see Padilla (2007).

30. Here I take some license, as this song was not released until September 2018. But I could not help myself, and it indeed has become the reigning final song of the night at queer nightclubs, telling the audience that it is time to go home.

31. My use of "otherwise" here and throughout the manuscript draws from Crawley (2017). Crawley explains that "[o]therwise, as word—otherwise possibilities as phrase—announces the fact of infinite alternatives to what *is*" (2017, 2; emphasis for "*is*" in the original). Like Crawley, I use *otherwise* "to underscore the ways alternative modes, alternative strategies, alternative ways of life already exist, indeed are violently acted upon in order to produce the coherence of the state" (6–7).

Chapter 2

1. See, for example, Espina Prieto (2008) for a description of Black Cubans' overrepresentation in traditional sectors of the economy, which pay in *moneda nacional* and are therefore considerably less lucrative than the tourism sector. Moreover, as I explained in the introduction, women overall are underrepresented in the private sector (see Torres Santana 2020, 12).

2. To be sure, this is not unique to Cuba but is instead reflective of the salience of subnational regionalism more broadly. See, for example, Gopinath (2018, 19–58).

3. I would later learn that Apocalipsis was on the same street where my abuela grew up, just a block or so away.

4. See Berry (2021) for a Black feminist discussion of the guaguancó.

5. The full ensemble, coincidentally, provides the musical backing for the once yearly Conga Contra la Homofobia y la Transfobia that opened this book.

6. Each orisha has their own characteristics, symbols, and domain. Oyá is associated with storms, lightning, and wind; Yemayá and Ochún with the ocean and the river, respectively; and Obbatalá with the head and the mind. See Cabrera ([1954] 2018; [1974] 1996) and Bolívar Aróstegui ([1990] 2017).

7. The notion of a transformista performing in drag as an orisha disturbs some popular notions about Regla de Ocha as homophobic. For a nuanced discussion of Regla de Ocha beyond the homophobic/tolerant binary, see Vidal-Ortiz (2008). For another example of mixing Afrocuban religious performance and transformismo, see Thorne (2019).

8. As Esther Newton ([1972] 1979, 59–61) suggested in *Mother Camp*, the gay-straight distinction between bars and performance spaces was more about social expectations and class positions than who necessarily was in the audience. For Chalet, this meant that there was no problem with me and Kerry attending as translesbians, but we were not in trans/queer space.

9. "Dura" is a very trans/queer word in Cuba, used especially to compliment an exemplary transformismo performance.

Chapter 3

1. The monument to the armored train ("el tren blindado") captured in 1958 by Revolutionary forces led by Che Guevara is another important symbol of the Revolution in Santa Clara.

2. For more information on El Mejunje, see Ravsberg (2007), Castañeda Pérez de Alejo (2010), and Gori (2021).

3. Rockers, along with queer people, were seen as ideologically problematic in Revolutionary Cuba. See, for example, Torre Pérez (2023).

4. The symbolism of the virile, industrious New Man did important ideological work in early Revolutionary Cuba, just as it did in other communist nations. See Sierra Madero (2022) and Guerra (2012, 227–55).

5. Kerry and my interview with Cinthya/Javier was memorable and impactful, and I carry her vision of *mariconería* with me in my everyday life. I was devastated to learn that he passed in January 2020, and I reproduce his words here as a testament to his inspiring work and life.

6. Note, for example, that the name of the newspaper of the Unión de Jóvenes Comunistas (Communist Youth Union) is *Juventud Rebelde*.

7. Curiously, we share a day in Cuba: May 17 is both El día del campesino and the International Day Against Homophobia, with which the Jornada is scheduled to coincide.

8. See, for example, Frederik (2012, 21–23) and Martin (1994, 129–32).

9. Multiple transmasculine people in Cuba continued to use discourses of lesbophobia and misogyny when describing their experiences as trans men to me. This reflected, for me, an ongoing investment in feminism even as they embrace a more masculine presentation and subjectivity. See, for example, Mitjans Alayón (2020).

10. Previously, we had seen Cinthya out of drag at the show at El Mejunje discussed above, and in drag, from a distance, during the Gala during the Jornada Contra la Homofobia y la Transfobia in Santa Clara in 2017.

11. Following Zulema, I use feminine pronouns to refer to Omega. I can't say how Omega understood and described herself; Silverio described him as a boy, but both Zulema and Laura used feminine pronouns.

12. Due in no small part to the US blockade, it is exceedingly difficult for trans people to access adequate medical and surgical care in Cuba. Informal treatments and procedures—unlicensed breast implants and silicone injections, hormones from the street—and the risks that come with them are common on the island.

13. I am reminded here of Jacob Mallinson Bird's description of an interlocutor's "particularly memorable [lip-synch] performance in which the music resonated around them, where the vibrations of the track were felt within their body, making it seem, if only in a moment of 'magical realism,' that the voice was emanating from them" (2020, 58).

Chapter 4

1. As David Valentine has said, "the insistence in mainstream accommodationist gay and lesbian activism that homosexuality is not inflected by gender variance is at root an attempt to argue for the validity of *male* homosexuals as *men* and to erase the stigma that attaches to femininity in male-bodied people" (2007, 236).

2. See Saunders (2009) and Guillard Limonta (2016).

3. See, for example, Berkins ([2007] 2015) and Wayar (2018).

4. And even more films produced off the island on the topic, including the documentary *Mariposas en el andamio* (1996) and the feature film *Viva* (2015). And documentaries such as *Bocarrosa* (2000), *Máscaras* (2014), and *Batería* (2016).

5. I am here paraphrasing transfeminist scholar Viviane Namaste (1996, 186–87), who noticed an inconsistency in queer studies around the relationship between performance and subjectivity.

6. See also Valentine (2004). Rupp and Taylor also discuss a particular drag performance that offered "a powerful and confusing lesson about sex, gender, sexual desire, and identity, communicating among other things that when men dress in drag, their apparent transgression is a performance, not an essential identity" (2003, 132).

7. Ellison, for example, deploys "Black femme flight" to describe "the re/appearances of queer femininity that disorganize and confound the categories we often use to make sense of the world" (2019, 8).

8. See chapter 3 for an in-depth discussion of El Mejunje and its place in trans/queer culture in Cuba.

9. Black performing artists in Cuba experience a similar dynamic to Black musicians in the US: Though their performances are often cited as national culture, blackness is often erased in national imagery. Umi Vaughan, for example, suggests that in the wake of the fall of socialism "Afro-Cubans [were] excluded from meaningful roles in Cuban television and other media while Afro-Cuban folklore was commercialized for the tourist market" (2012, 71).

10. I draw here from Marlon Bailey's (2013, 23) approach to participants in the ballroom scene in Detroit.

11. "Reparto" refers both to the divisions of Havana's municipalities into neighborhoods and to the neighborhoods away from Havana's coast, toward and on the periphery of the city. See chapter 2 for more detail.

12. To draw a transnational connection, his analysis here reminds me of the way

US drag king k. bradford has talked about their drag persona Johnny T. as a "filter, a mode that allows my gender variance to come into sharper focus, tighter action" (2002, 23).

13. As I will discuss further in chapter 5, this connection between drag kinging and Black lesbian and transmasculine feminist praxis is not unique to Cuba but can be observed, too, in the US. See, for example, Tinsley (2018, 52) and Richardson (2013, 70–74). I understand this as evidence of broader possibilities toward Black lesbian feminist and transgender collectivity (see Green and Ellison 2014).

14. This, too, has analogues in US politics and culture. See, for example, Namaste (1996, 186–87) and Rupp and Taylor (2003, 31–44).

15. In this case, "madrina" refers to one's drag/trans mother.

16. See Vidal-Ortiz (2008) for a discussion of competing notions of Regla de Ocha as either homophobic or tolerant.

Chapter 5

1. Crucially, the *son* is a distinctive Cuban genre with working-class Black origins. See Moore (1997, 89–91) and Sublette (2004, 336–38).

2. Like the son, the rumba is a thoroughly Cuban genre with Black working-class origins. See Daniel (1991).

3. The *guaguancó* is a variant of the rumba that involves partner dances featuring mixed-gender couples. See Daniel (1995).

4. Scholars of Black lesbian life have discussed the daytime gathering as a possibility that accommodates the particular needs of Black women in the city, including security, transportation, and childcare. See, for example, Adeyemi (2022, 136) and Saunders (2009, 178).

5. Curiously, this was before I even met my own family members in Cuba, which I did on my second trip to Havana six months later.

6. Though I didn't know it then, I would meet other members of Havana's Afro-feminist/trans/queer movement through Argelia who would become my chosen family. Consequently, my relationship with them and their networks had a profound impact on my own self-realization as a translesbian.

7. Though it never had an erotic charge, I certainly developed a strong personal and emotional connection with Argelia, not unlike Esther Newton's (1993) relationship with her own lesbian "best informant."

8. I offer this tremendously abbreviated account of Argelia's life story in the face of the fact that there are "still few Caribbean women's life histories of any class background" (Wekker 2006, 2). A more thorough biography of Argelia is sorely needed, and no one is better poised to write it than she.

9. In this case, the transformista played an indirect role in a case involving an underage sex worker. The Cuban state's exorbitant punishment for "corrupción de menores de edad" (corruption of minors) links up with a hemispheric (and global) rise in the criminal management of sex during a time of so-called LGBT rights. See Halperin and Hoppe (2017).

10. This pairing recalls Maya Berry's suggestion of "a black feminist choreographic aptitude . . . between rumberas" that "speaks to an embodied engagement with the pointedly gendered valances of worsening racialized class inequality in contemporary Cuba" (2021, 29).

11. You can watch this performance on YouTube; see Addis DD (2017).

12. In the Cuban context, the racial-sexual figure of *la mulata* captures this tension between invisibility and hypervisibility. If Black women are invisibilized in Cuban popular culture, *la mulata*—the mixed-race woman—is omnipresent as the central symbol of the Cuban nation. See Kutzinski (1993), Blanco Borelli (2016), and Fraunhar (2018).

13. It was actually an unforgettable moment in the interview when I asked whether there had been more lesbian parties in the 1990s and all of the transformistas masculinos exclaimed in the strongest collective unison of the day as they recalled the foregone scene.

14. To be sure, there is good reason to complicate dominant readings of reggaetón as sexist and/or homophobic, as it has long been a language of feminist/trans/queer Caribbean people. See, for example, Rivera-Servera (2016).

15. In his analysis of Toni Morrison's *Sula*, Roderick Ferguson details "women of color and black lesbian feminist desires for modes of agency that departed from nationalist articulations of coalition" (2004, 133). Chela Sandoval's (2000) elaboration of "differential consciousness" relies on related creative and purposeful coalitions.

16. As Tinsley said of Dréd, Argelia and her co-performers deploy "creative, pliable self-descriptors that trouble masculine/feminine, butch/femme, king/queen binaries," enacting "the importance of expressing a black femmeness, curviness, bejeweled-ness, open-thighed-ness that never has to be erased . . . *not even while working your daddy mack*" (2018, 36; emphasis in the original).

Coda

1. Tellingly, there was not another Conga Contra la Homofobia until 2023. The 2020 and 2021 Congas were canceled due to the COVID-19 pandemic, and though 2022 was finally set to see one, the tragic explosion of the Hotel Saratoga led to its cancellation, too.

2. All of the quotations in this paragraph come from contemporaneous Facebook posts. Curiously, both the independent trans/queer actors and their state critics took to the US social media platform to air their grievances.

3. See, for example, Krudas Cubensi (2021). For more on the context and significance of the events of July 11, see LeoGrande, Kirk, and Brenner (2021).

4. Thanks to Alejandro de la Fuente for offering me this framing during graduate school.

References

Abreu Arcia, Alberto. 2020. "Soy, me pienso y hablo como homosexual negro." *Hypermedia Magazine*, August 12. https://www.hypermediamagazine.com/sociedad/soy-me-pienso-y-hablo-como-homosexual-negro/

Abu-Lughod, Lila. 1991. "Writing Against Culture." In *Recapturing Anthropology: Working in the Present*, edited by Richard G. Fox, 137–62. Santa Fe: School of American Research Press.

Addis DD. 2017. "Habana Quartet in 10th JCCHT—Karl Marx Gala 2017." YouTube, July 24. https://www.youtube.com/watch?v=tVmpGbAL6aM

Adeyemi, Kemi. 2022. *Feels Right: Black Queer Women and the Politics of Partying in Chicago*. Durham: Duke University Press.

Aizura, Aren. 2018. *Mobile Subjects: Transnational Imaginaries of Gender Reassignment*. Durham: Duke University Press.

Alexander, M. Jacqui. 2005. *Pedagogies of Crossing: Meditations on Feminism, Sexual Politics, Memory, and the Sacred*. Durham: Duke University Press.

Allen, Jafari S. 2011. *¡Venceremos? The Erotics of Black Self-Making in Cuba*. Durham: Duke University Press.

Allen, Jafari S. 2013. "Race/Sex Theory 'Toward a New and More Possible Meeting.'" *Cultural Anthropology* 28 (3): 552–55.

Allen, Jafari S. 2016. "One View from a Deterritorialized Realm: How Black/Queer Renarrativizes Anthropological Analysis." *Cultural Anthropology* 31 (4): 617–26.

Amerise, Atahualpa. 2022. "'Tengo a mis tres hijos en la cárcel': La Güinera, el barrio de Cuba con decenas de jóvenes en prisión por las protestas del 11-J." *BBC News Mundo*, July 11. https://www.bbc.com/mundo/noticias-america-latina-62110528

Amico, Stephen. 2014. *Roll Over, Tchaikovsky: Russian Popular Music and Post-Soviet Homosexuality*. Urbana: University of Illinois Press.

Bailey, Marlon M. 2013. *Butch Queens Up in Pumps: Gender, Performance, and Ballroom Culture in Detroit*. Ann Arbor: University of Michigan Press.

Bailey, Marlon M. 2014. "Engendering Space: Ballroom Culture and the Spatial Practice of Possibility in Detroit." *Gender, Place, and Culture* 21 (4): 489–507.

Barz, Gregory, and William Cheng, eds. 2019. *Queering the Field: Sounding Out Ethnomusicology*. Oxford: Oxford University Press.

Batería. 2016. Directed by Damián Sainz. Produced by Javier Ferreiro.
Behar, Ruth, ed. 1995. *Bridges to Cuba/Puentes a Cuba.* Ann Arbor: University of Michigan Press.
Behar, Ruth. 1996. *The Vulnerable Observer: Anthropology that Breaks Your Heart.* Boston: Beacon Press.
Bejel, Emilio. 2001. *Gay Cuban Nation.* Chicago: University of Chicago Press.
Benson, Devyn Spence. 2016. *Antiracism in Cuba: The Unfinished Revolution.* Chapel Hill: University of North Carolina Press.
Benson, Devyn Spence. 2020. "Editor's Introduction." In *Afrocubanas: History, Thought, and Cultural Practices,* edited by Devyn Spence Benson, Daisy Rubiera Castillo, and Inés María Martiatu Terry, xvii–xxvii. London: Rowman and Littlefield.
Berkins, Lohana, ed. (2007) 2015. *Cumbia, copeteo y lágrimas: Informe nacional sobre la situación de las travestis, transexuales y transgeneros.* Buenos Aires: Madres de Plaza de Mayo.
Berry, Maya J. 2016. "'Salvándose' in Contemporary Havana: Rumba's Paradox for Black Identity Politics." *Black Diaspora Review* 5 (2): 24–31.
Berry, Maya J. 2021. "Black Feminist Rumba Pedagogies." *Dance Research Journal* 53 (2): 24–48.
Bird, Jacob Mallinson. 2020. "Haptic Aurality: On Touching the Voice in Drag Lip-Sync Performance." *Sound Studies* 6 (1): 45–64.
Blanco Borelli, Melissa. 2016. *She Is Cuba: A Genealogy of the Mulata Body.* Oxford: Oxford University Press.
Blau, Jnan. 2009. "More than 'Just' Music: Four Performative Topoi, the Phish Phenomenon, and the Power of Music in/and Performance." *TRANS-Revista Transcultural de Música* 13. https://www.sibetrans.com/trans/article/44/more-than-just-music-four-performative-topoi-the-phish-phenomenon-and-the-power-of-music-in-and-performance
Bocarrosa. 2000. Directed by Henry Eric Hernández and Iván R. Basulto. Produced by Producciones Doboch.
Bodenheimer, Rebecca M. 2015. *Geographies of Cubanidad: Place, Race, and Musical Performance in Contemporary Cuba.* Jackson: University Press of Mississippi.
Bolívar Aróstegui, Natalia. (1990) 2017. *Los orishas en Cuba.* La Habana: Editorial José Martí.
Bonilla, Yarimar. 2023. "Enrique Tarrio and the Curious Case of the Latino White Supremacist." *New York Times,* August 19. https://www.nytimes.com/2023/08/19/opinion/enrique-tarrio-proud-boys-latinos-racism.html
Borrero Batista, Darcy. 2022. "Havana's 'La Guinera' Barrio: Punished after July 11th." *Havana Times,* March 16. https://havanatimes.org/features/havanas-la-guinera-barrio-punished-after-july-11th/
bradford, k. 2002. "Grease Cowboy Fever; or, the Making of Johnny T." In *The Drag King Anthology,* edited by Donna Troka, Kathleen Lebesco, and Jean Noble, 15–30. New York: Harrington Park Press.
Brunson, Takkara K. 2021. *Black Women, Citizenship, and the Making of Modern Cuba.* Gainesville: University of Florida Press.
Cabrera, Lydia. (1954) 2018. *El Monte.* Havana: Editorial Letras Cubanas.
Cabrera, Lydia. (1974) 1996. *Yemayá y Ochún: Kariocha, Iyalorichas y Olorichas.* Miami: Ediciones Universales.
Capó, Julio, Jr. 2010. "Queering Mariel: Mediating Cold War Foreign Policy and U.S. Citizenship among Cuba's Homosexual Exile Community, 1978–1994." *Journal of American Ethnic History* 29 (4): 78–106.

References · 183

Capó, Julio, Jr. 2017. *Welcome to Fairyland: Queer Miami before 1940*. Chapel Hill: University of North Carolina Press.

Casal, Lourdes. 1976. "Para Ana Veltfort." *Areíto* 3 (1): 52.

Casal, Lourdes. 1995. "For Ana Veldford." In *Bridges to Cuba/Puentes a Cuba*, edited by Ruth Behar, 22. Translated by David Frye. Ann Arbor: University of Michigan Press.

Castañeda Pérez de Alejo, Alexis. 2010. *No pido permiso para hacer*. Santa Clara: Ediciones Sed de Belleza.

Castro, Mariela. 2017. *La integración de las personas transexuales en Cuba*. La Habana: Editorial CENESEX.

Chamaco. 2010. Directed by Juan Carlos Cremata. Produced by ICAIC.

Cohen, Cathy J. 1997. "Punks, Bulldaggers, and Welfare Queens: The Radical Potential of Queer Politics?" *GLQ* 3 (4): 437–65.

Collazo, Bobby. 1987. *La última noche que pasé contigo: 40 años de farándula cubana*. San Juan, Puerto Rico: Editorial Cubanacán.

Cox, Robert W. 1983. "Gramsci, Hegemony and International Relations: An Essay in Method." *Millennium* 12 (2): 162–75.

Crawley, Ashon T. 2017. *Blackpentecostal Breath: The Aesthetics of Possibility*. New York: Fordham University Press.

Cubadebate. 2021. "Dar es dar: Nosotrxs y la suma de las diferencias." January 19. http://www.cubadebate.cu/especiales/2021/01/19/dar-es-dar-nosotrxs-y-la-suma-de-las-diferencias-video/

Cuesta, Odaymar, Sandra Álvarez, and Marlihan López. 2021. "Declaración del Colectivo Cuba Liberación Negra." *Negra cubana tenía que ser*, August 8. https://negracubanateniaqueser.com/2021/08/08/declaracion-del-colectivo-cuba-liberacion-negra/

Daniel, Yvonne Payne. 1991. "Changing Values in Cuban Rumba, A Lower Class Black Dance Appropriated by the Revolution." *Dance Research Journal* 23 (2): 1–10.

Daniel, Yvonne Payne. 1995. *Rumba: Dance and Social Change in Contemporary Cuba*. Bloomington: Indiana University Press.

de Jesús Fernández, Teresa, Sara Más, and Lirians Gordillo Piña. 2020. *Libres para amar*. Havana: Editorial Caminos.

de la Fuente, Alejandro. 2001. *A Nation for All: Race, Inequality, and Politics in Twentieth-Century Cuba*. Chapel Hill: University of North Carolina Press.

de la Fuente, Alejandro. 2008. "The New Afro-Cuban Cultural Movement and the Debate on Race in Contemporary Cuba." *Journal of Latin American Studies* 40 (4): 697–720.

de la Fuente, Alejandro. 2012. "'Tengo una raza oscura y discriminada.' El movimiento afrocubano: hacia un programa consensuado." *Nueva Sociedad* 242: 92–105.

Dilla Alfonso, Haroldo. 2008. "La reestructuración especial en Cuba." *Cuadernos del CENDES* 25 (68): 55–70.

Ellison, Treva. 2019. "Black Femme Praxis and the Promise of Black Gender." *Black Scholar* 49 (1): 6–16.

Espina Prieto, Mayra. 2008. "Viejas y nuevas desigualdades en Cuba: Ambivalencias y perspectivas de la reestratificación social." *Nueva Sociedad* 216: 133–49.

Espina Prieto, Mayra. 2010. "La política social cubana para el manejo de la desigualdad." *Cuban Studies* 41: 20–38.

Espinosa, Norge. (1987) 2006. "Vestido de Novia." *Revista Encuentro* 41/42: 122–23.

Espinosa, Norge. 2019. "¿Mariconga o Marimarcha? Lo que puede venir tras el 11 de

mayo." *La Tizza, Medium*, May 21. https://medium.com/la-tiza/mariconga-o-mar imarcha-175b253465d4
Fátima o el Parque de la Fraternidad. 2014. Directed by Jorge Perrugoría. Produced by ICAIC.
Ferguson, Roderick A. 2003. *Aberrations in Black: Toward a Queer of Color Critique*. Minneapolis: University of Minnesota Press.
Fernandes, Sujatha. 2006. *Cuba Represent! Cuban Arts, State Power, and the Making of New Revolutionary Cultures*. Durham: Duke University Press.
Fernández Robaina, Tomás. 2005. "El proyecto revolucionario y los homosexuales." *Revista Consenso* 1.
Fleetwood, Nicole. 2011. *Troubling Vision: Performance, Visuality, and Blackness*. Chicago: University of Chicago Press.
Fowler Calzada, Víctor. 1998. *La maldición: una historia de placer como conquista*. Havana: Editorial Letras Cubanas.
Fraunhar, Alison. 2018. *Mulata Nation: Visualizing Race and Gender in Cuba*. Jackson: University Press of Mississippi.
Frederik, Laurie. 2012. *Trumpets in the Mountains: Theater and the Politics of National Culture in Cuba*. Durham: Duke University Press.
Fresa y chocolate. 1993. Directed by Tomás Gutiérrez Alea and Juan Carlos Tabío. Produced by ICAIC.
Frisbie, Charlotte Johnson. 1967. *Kinaaldá: A Study of the Navaho Girl's Puberty Ceremony*. Middletown: Wesleyan University Press.
Fusco, Coco. 2015. *Dangerous Moves: Performance and Politics in Cuba*. London: Tate.
Gallo, Rubén. 2022. "Missing in Havana." *Brooklyn Rail*, June. https://brooklynrail .org/2022/06/criticspage/Missing-in-Havana
Gill, Lyndon Kamaal. 2018. *Erotic Islands: Art and Activism in the Queer Caribbean*. Durham: Duke University Press.
González González, Lázaro. 2014. "Máscaras." Undergraduate thesis, University of Havana.
González Pagés, Julio César. 2012. *Por andar vestida de hombre*. Havana: Editorial de la Mujer.
González Rego, René A. 2018. "La Habana: dinámica socio especial de las formas urbanas." *PatryTer* 1 (1): 1–12.
González Rego, René A. 2019. "Dinámica socioespacial de La Habana, Cuba, posterior a 1990." *PatryTer* 2 (4): 63–74.
Gopinath, Gayatri. 2018. *Unruly Visions: The Aesthetic Practices of Queer Diaspora*. Durham: Duke University Press.
Gori, Yanina. 2021. "Re/mediating Revolution: Cultivating Solidarity in a Queer Cuban Community." PhD diss., UCLA.
Gossett, Reina, Erica A. Stanley, and Johanna Burton, eds. 2017. *Trap Door: Trans Cultural Production and the Politics of Visibility*. Cambridge: MIT Press.
Green, Kai M., and Treva Ellison. 2014. "Tranifest." *TSQ* 1 (1–2): 222–25.
Guerra, Lilian. 2012. *Visions of Power: Revolution, Redemption, and Resistance in Cuba, 1959–1971*. Chapel Hill: University of North Carolina Press.
Guillard Limonta, Norma R. 2016. "To Be a Black Woman, a Lesbian, and an Afro-Feminist in Cuba Today." *Black Diaspora Review* 5 (2): 81–97.
Halperin, David, and Trevor Hoppe, eds. 2017. *The War on Sex*. Durham: Duke University Press.

Hankins, Sarah. 2015. "'I'm a Cross between a Clown, a Stripper, and a Streetwalker': Drag Tipping, Sex Work, and a Queer Sociosexual Economy." *Signs* 40 (2): 441–66.
Hartman, Saidiya. 2008. "Venus in Two Acts." *Small Axe* 12 (2): 1–14.
Hayes, Eileen M. 2010. *Songs in Black and Lavender: Race, Sexual Politics, and Women's Music*. Urbana: University of Illinois Press.
Herring, Scott. 2010. *Another Country: Queer Anti-Urbanism*. New York: New York University Press.
Hodge, G. Derrick. 2001. "Colonization of the Cuban Body: The Growth of Male Sex Work in Havana." *NACLA Report on the Americas* 34 (5): 20–28.
Hodge, G. Derrick. 2014. "'Dangerous' Youth: Tourism Space, Gender Performance, and the Policing of Havana Street Hustlers." *Journal of Latin American and Caribbean Anthropology* 19 (3): 441–72.
Hood, Mantle. 1969. "Ethnomusicology." In *Harvard Dictionary of Music*, 2nd ed., edited by Willi Apel, 298–300. Cambridge: Harvard University Press.
Hubbs, Nadine. 2014. *Rednecks, Queers, and Country Music*. Berkeley: University of California Press.
Hynson, Rachel. 2020. *Laboring for the State: Women, Family, and Work in Revolutionary Cuba, 1959–1971*. Cambridge: Cambridge University Press.
IPS Cuba. 2020. "Nosotrxs: cubanas negras y queer alzan sus voces." June 22. https://www.ipscuba.net/genero/nosotrxs-cubanas-negras-y-queer-alzan-sus-voces/
Jiménez Enoa, Abraham. 2019. "Argelia Fellove es una dura." *El Estornudo*, September 3. https://revistaelestornudo.medium.com/argelia-fellove-es-una-dura-5cba496b5226
Johnson, E. Patrick. 2018. *Black. Queer. Southern. Women: An Oral History*. Chapel Hill: University of North Carolina Press.
King, Rosamond S. 2014. *Island Bodies: Transgressive Sexualities in the Caribbean Imagination*. Gainesville: University of Florida Press.
Kirk, Emily. 2020. "Cuba's National Sexual Education Program: Origins and Evolution." *Cuban Studies* 49: 289–309.
Kisliuk, Michelle. 1998. "A Response to Charles Keil." *Ethnomusicology* 42 (2): 313–15.
Krudas Cubensi. 2021. "Que esta pasando en cuba: What is happening in cuba l." Facebook, July 14. https://www.facebook.com/KrudasCubensi/videos/que-esta-pasando-en-cuba-what-is-happening-in-cuba-l/1914818065352661
Kutzinski, Vera M. 1993. *Sugar's Secrets. Race and the Erotics of Cuban Nationalism*. Charlottesville: University Press of Virginia.
La Fountain-Stokes, Lawrence. 2021. *Translocas: The Politics of Puerto Rican Drag and Trans Performance*. Ann Arbor: University of Michigan Press.
Lane, Jill. 2005. *Blackface Cuba, 1840–1895*. Philadelphia: University of Pennsylvania Press.
Lane, Jill. 2008. "ImpersoNation: Toward a Theory of Black-, Red-, and Yellowface in the Americas." *PMLA* 123 (5): 1728–31.
Left Voice. 2017. "The Trotskyist Drag King of Mexico City." August 26. https://www.leftvoice.org/the-trotskyist-drag-king-of-mexico-city/
LeoGrande, William M., John M. Kirk and Philip Brenner, eds. 2021. "The Road Ahead: Cuba after the July 11 Protests" (website). https://www.american.edu/centers/latin-american-latino-studies/the-road-ahead-cuba-after-the-july-11-protests.cfm

Leslie Santana, M. Myrta. 2022. "*Transformista, Travesti,* Transgénero: Performing Sexual Subjectivity in Cuba." *Small Axe* 68: 46–59.

Lumsden, Ian. 1996. *Machos, Maricones, and Gays: Cuba and Homosexuality.* Philadelphia: Temple University Press.

Machuca Rose, Malú. 2019. "Giuseppe Campuzano's Afterlife: Toward a Travesti Methodology for Critique, Care, and Radical Resistance." *TSQ* 6 (2): 239–53.

Madison, D. Soyini. 2005. *Critical Ethnography: Method, Ethics, and Performance.* Thousand Oaks: SAGE Publications.

Madrid, Alejandro. 2009. "Why Music and Performance Studies? Why Now? An Introduction to the Special Issue." *TRANS-Revista Transcultural de Música* 13. http://www.sibetrans.com/trans/articulo/1/why-music-and-performance-studies-why-now-an-introduction-to-the-special-issue

Mariposas en el andamio. 1995. Directed by Margaret Gilpin and Luís Felipe Bernaza. Produced by Kangaroo Productions.

Marqués de Armas, Pedro Luis. 2014. *Ciencia y poder en Cuba: racismo homofobia, nación (1790–1970).* Madrid: Editorial Verbum.

Marquetti, Rosa. 2018. "Con todos ustedes, Musmé, el transformista más famoso de Cuba." *Colección Gladys Palmera,* May 28. https://gladyspalmera.com/coleccion/el-diario-de-gladys/musme-en-vinilo/

Martin, Randy. 1994. *Socialist Ensembles: Theater and State in Cuba and Nicaragua.* Minneapolis: University of Minnesota Press.

Máscaras. 2014. Directed by Lázaro González.

McLeod, Norma, and Marcia Herndon, eds. 1980. *The Ethnography of Musical Performance.* Norwood, PA: Norwood Editions.

Merriam, Alan. 1964. *The Anthropology of Music.* Evanston: Northwestern University Press.

Mitjans Alayón, Tito. 2020. "Audre Lorde Now: Letter to Audre Lorde from the Future." https://www.centerforthehumanities.org/distributaries/letter-to-audre-lorde-from-the-future

Moore, Robin. 1997. *Nationalizing Blackness: Afrocubanismo and Artistic Revolution in Havana, 1920–1940.* Pittsburgh: University of Pittsburgh Press.

Morad, Moshe. 2015. *Fiesta de diez pesos: Music and Gay Identity in Special Period Cuba.* Surrey: Ashgate.

Morcom, Anna. 2013. *Illicit Worlds of Indian Dance: Cultures of Exclusion.* New York: Oxford University Press.

Muñoz, José Esteban. 1999. *Disidentifications: Queers of Color and the Performance of Politics.* Minneapolis: University of Minnesota Press.

Muñoz, José Esteban. 2009. *Cruising Utopia: The Then and There of Queer Futurity.* New York: New York University Press.

Muñoz, José Esteban. 2020. *The Sense of Brown,* edited by Joshua Chambers-Letson and Tavia Nyong'o. Durham: Duke University Press.

Naga, Noor. 2022. *If an Egyptian Cannot Speak English.* Minneapolis: Graywolf Press.

Namaste, Viviane. 1996. "Tragic Misreadings." In *Queer Studies: A Lesbian, Gay, Bisexual, and Transgender Anthology,* edited by Genny Beemyn and Mickey Eliason, 183–203. New York: New York University Press.

Namaste, Viviane K. 2000. *Invisible Lives: The Erasure of Transsexual and Transgendered People.* Chicago: University of Chicago Press.

Neal, Mark Anthony. 1999. *What the Music Said: Black Popular Music and Black Public Culture.* New York: Routledge.

Negrón-Muntaner, Frances. 2008. "'Mariconerías' de Estado: Mariela Castro, Los Homosexuales Y La Política Cubana." *Nueva Sociedad* 218: 163–79.

Newton, Esther. (1972) 1979. *Mother Camp: Female Impersonators in America*. Chicago: University of Chicago Press.

Newton, Esther. 1993. "My Best Informant's Dress: The Erotic Equation in Fieldwork." *Cultural Anthropology* 8 (1): 3–23.

Nguyen, Som-Mai. 2022. "Blunt-Force Ethnic Credibility." *Astra*, June 30. https://astra-mag.com/articles/blunt-force-ethnic-credibility/

Nyong'o, Tavia. 2021. "José Muñoz, Then and There." *The Baffler*, February 10. https://thebaffler.com/latest/jose-munoz-then-and-there-nyongo

Ochoa, Marcia. 2014. *Queen for a Day: Transformistas, Beauty Queens, and the Performance of Femininity in Venezuela*. Durham: Duke University Press.

Padilla, Mark. 2007. Caribbean Pleasure Industry: Tourism, Sexuality, and AIDS in the Dominican Republic. Chicago: University of Chicago Press.

Pelaez Lopez, Alan. 2018. "The X in Latinx Is a Wound, Not a Trend." *ColorBloq*. https://www.colorbloq.org/article/the-x-in-latinx-is-a-wound-not-a-trend

Peña, Susana. 2013. *Oye Loca: From the Mariel Boatlift to Gay Cuban Miami*. Minneapolis: University of Minnesota Press.

Pérez, Juan. 1996. "A través de los 'travestis,' ¿Cuba se transforma?" *El Nuevo Herald*, January 23, 1C.

Perra. 1995. "Los balseros." December 1995, 7–8, 21. Cuban Heritage Collection, University of Miami.

Perry, Marc. 2015. *Negro Soy Yo: Hip Hop and Raced Citizenship in Neoliberal Cuba*. Durham: Duke University Press.

Pierce, Joseph M., María Amelia Viteri, Diego Falconí Trávez, Salvador Vidal-Ortiz, and Lourdes Martínez-Echazábal, eds. 2021. "Cuir/Queer Américas: Translation, Decoloniality, and the Incommensurable." Special issue, *GLQ* 27 (3).

Pilzer, Joshua. 2022. *Quietude: A Musical Anthropology of "Korea's Hiroshima."* New York: Oxford University Press.

Pineda, Leticia. 2022. "La Güinera, el barrio pobre de La Habana epicentro de las protestas de julio de 2021." *France 24*, July 8. https://www.france24.com/es/minuto-a-minuto/20220708-la-güinera-el-barrio-pobre-de-la-habana-epicentro-de-las-protestas-de-julio-de-2021

Puar, Jasbir. 2005. "Transversal Circuits: Transnational Sexualities and Trinidad." In *A Companion to Feminist Geography*, edited by Lise Nelson and Joni Seager. Hoboken, NJ: Blackwell Publishing.

Putcha, Rumya Sree. 2022. *The Dancer's Voice: Performance and Womanhood in Transnational India*. Durham: Duke University Press.

¡Quba! 2024. Directed and produced by Kim Anno.

Ramírez, Marta María. 2010a. "De Fuller a Musmé: Tras sus huellas (1918–1959)." *TransCuba*, August 25. https://transcuba.wordpress.com/2010/08/25/defullera musme/

Ramírez, Marta María. 2010b. "Y en eso llegó Fidel o el transformismo de resistencia (1959–1968)." *TransCuba*, August 24. https://transcuba.wordpress.com/2010/08/24/transformismo-de-resistencia/

Ramírez, Marta María. 2010c. "Transformismo revolucionario (1968–1997)." *TransCuba*, August 24. https://transcuba.wordpress.com/2010/08/24/transformismo-revolucionario/

Ravsberg, Fernando. 2007. "'El Mejunje' de Silverio." *BBC Mundo*, July 23. http://news.bbc.co.uk/hi/spanish/latin_america/newsid_6903000/6903057.stm

Richardson, Matt. 2013. *The Queer Limit of Black Modernity: Black Lesbian Literature and Irresolution*. Columbus: Ohio State University Press.

Ríos, Anett. 2009. "Meca del transformismo cubano cumple 25 años." *El Nuevo Herald*, January 25. https://www.elnuevoherald.com/ultimas-noticias/article1971356.html

Rivera-Servera, Ramón H. 2016. "Reggaetón's Crossings: Black Aesthetics, Latina Nightlife, and Queer Choreography." In *No Tea, No Shade: New Writings in Black Queer Studies*, edited by E. Patrick Johnson, 95–112. Durham: Duke University Press.

Rizki, Cole, Juana María Rodríguez, Claudia Sofía Garriga-López, and Denilson Lopes, eds. 2019. "Trans Studies en las Américas." Special issue of *Transgender Studies Quarterly* 6 (2).

Rodríguez, Juana María. 2003. *Queer Latinidad: Identity Practices, Discursive Spaces*. New York: New York University Press.

Rodríguez, Juana María. 2014. *Sexual Futures, Queer Gestures, and Other Latina Longings*. New York: New York University Press.

Rodríguez, Juana María. 2023. *Puta Life: Seeing Latinas, Working Sex*. Durham: Duke University Press.

Roque Guerra, Alberto. 2011. "Sexual Diversity in Revolutionary Times, 1959–2009." *Cuban Studies* 42: 218–26.

Rosaldo, Renato. 1993. *Culture & Truth: The Remaking of Social Analysis*. Boston: Beacon Press.

Rose, Tricia. 1994. *Black Noise: Rap Music and Black Culture in Contemporary America*. Middletown, CT: Wesleyan University Press.

Rubiera Castillo, Daisy, and Inés María Martiatu Terry, eds. 2011. *Afrocubanas: historia, pensamiento, y prácticas culturales*. Havana: Editorial de Ciencias Sociales.

Rupp, Leila J., and Verta A. Taylor. 2003. *Drag Queens at the 801 Cabaret*. Chicago: University of Chicago Press.

Sandoval, Chela. 2000. *Methodology of the Oppressed*. Minneapolis: University of Minnesota Press.

San Miguel del Padrón, por Diarenis Calderón Tartabull. 2020. Directed by Roberto García Suárez. Produced by Michele Hardesty and Roberto García Suárez. https://vimeo.com/495521739

Santana, Dora Silva. 2019. "*Mais Viva!* Reassembling Transness, Blackness, and Feminism." *TSQ* 6 (2): 210–22.

Saunders, Tanya. 2009. "Grupo OREMI: Black Lesbians and the Struggle for Safe Social Space in Havana." *Souls* 11 (2): 1–19.

Saunders, Tanya. 2015. *Cuban Underground Hip Hop: Black Thoughts, Black Revolution and Black Modernity*. Austin: University of Texas Press.

Seeger, Anthony. 1987. *Why Suyá Sing: A Musical Anthropology of an Amazonian People*. Urbana: University of Illinois Press.

Shock, Susy. 2011. *Relatos en canecalón*. Buenos Aires: Editorial Nuevos Tiempos.

Show: La revista de los expectáculos. 1958. "Night Clubs." May 1958, 74. Cuban Heritage Collection, University of Miami.

Sierra Madero, Abel. 2006. *Del otro lado del espejo: La sexualidad en la construcción de la nación cubana*. La Habana: Casa de las Américas.

Sierra Madero, Abel. 2014. "Del Hombre Nuevo Al Travestismo de Estado." *Diario de Cuba*. http://www.diariodecuba.com/cuba/1390513833_6826.html

Sierra Madero, Abel. 2020. "*Queering the archive*. La historia del Bataclán Universitario." *Hypermedia Magazine*, May 29. https://www.hypermediamagazine.com/columnistas/fiebre-de-archivo/queering-the-archive-la-historia-del-bataclan-universitario/

Sierra Madero, Abel. 2022. *El cuerpo nunca olvida: Trabajo forzado, hombre nuevo y memoria en Cuba (1959–1980)*. Santiago de Querétaro: Rialta Ediciones.

Sierra Madero, Abel, and Lilian Guerra. 2016. "Lo de las UMAP fue un trabajo 'top secret': Entrevista a la Dra. María Elena Solé Arrondo." *Cuban Studies* 44: 357–66.

Somerville, Siobhan B. 2000. *Queering the Color Line: Race and the Invention of Homosexuality in American Culture*. Durham: Duke University Press.

Spade, Dean. 2015. *Normal Life: Administrative Violence, Critical Trans Politics, and the Limits of Law*. Durham: Duke University Press.

Stanley, Eric A. 2021. *Atmospheres of Violence: Structuring Antagonism and the Trans/Queer Ungovernable*. Durham: Duke University Press.

Stout, Noelle. 2014. *After Love: Queer Intimacy and Erotic Economies in Post-Soviet Cuba*. Durham: Duke University Press.

Strongman, Roberto. 2019. *Queering Black Atlantic Religions: Transcorporeality in Candomblé, Santería, and Vodou*. Durham: Duke University Press.

Sublette, Ned. 2004. *Cuba and Its Music: From the First Drums to the Mambo*. Chicago: Chicago Review Press.

Tate, Greg, ed. 2003. *Everything But the Burden: What White People Are Taking from Black Culture*. Westminster: Crown.

Thomas, Susan. 2008. *Cuban Zarzuela: Performing Race and gender on Havana's Lyric Stage*. Urbana: University of Illinois Press.

Thorne, Cory W. 2019. "'Man Created Homophobia, God Created *Transformistas*': Saluting the *Oríchá* in a Cuban Gay Bar." In *Queering the Field: Sounding Out Ethnomusicology*, edited by Gregory Barz and William Cheng. Oxford: Oxford University Press.

Tinsley, Omise'eke Natasha. 2018. *Ezili's Mirrors: Imagining Black Queer Genders*. Durham: Duke University Press.

Torre Pérez, Carmen. 2023. "'Los Frikis': Resistance through Underground Cultures in 1980s Cuba." *Journal of Popular Music Studies* 35 (1): 85–108.

Torres Santana, Ailynn. 2020. "Regímenes de bienestar en Cuba: Mujeres y desigualdades." *Cuban Studies* 49: 6–31.

Valentine, David. 2004. "The Categories Themselves." *GLQ* 10 (2): 215–20.

Valentine, David. 2007. *Imagining Transgender: An Ethnography of a Category*. Durham: Duke University Press.

Vaughan, Umi. 2012. *Rebel Dance, Renegade Stance: Timba Music and Black Identity in Cuba*. Ann Arbor: University of Michigan Press.

Vazquez, Alexandra T. 2013. *Listening in Detail: Performances of Cuban Music*. Durham: Duke University Press.

Venegas Delgado, Hernán. 2001. *La región en Cuba: Un ensayo de intepretación historiográfica*. Santiago de Cuba: Editorial Oriente.

Vestido de Novia. 2014. Directed by Marilyn Solaya. Produced by ICAIC.

Vidal-Ortiz, Salvador. 2008. "'The Puerto Rican Way Is More Tolerant': Constructions and Uses of 'Homophobia' among Santería Practitioners Across Ethno-Racial and National Identification." *Sexualities* 11 (4): 476–95.

Viva. 2015. Directed by Paddy Breathnach. Produced by Treasure Entertainment.

Volcano, Del LaGrace, and Jack Halberstam. 1999. *The Drag King Book*. London: Serpent's Tail.

Wang, Yun Emily. 2018. "Sung and Spoken Puns as Queer 'Home Making' in Toronto's Chinese Diaspora." *Women and Music* (22): 50–62.

Wayar, Marlene. 2018. *Travesti: una teoría lo suficientemente buena*. Buenos Aires: Editorial Muchas Nueces.

Wayne, Helena. 1985. "Bronislaw Malinowski: The Influence of Various Women on His Life and Works." *American Ethnologist* 12 (3): 529–40.

Wekker, Gloria. 2006. *The Politics of Passion: Women's Sexual Culture in the Afro-Surinamese Diaspora*. New York: Columbia University Press.

White, Kerry. 2017. "Cruising Havana: Affective Spaces, Public Gestures, and the Worlds They Make in a Contemporary Cuba." Master's thesis, University of Florida.

White, Kerry. 2023. "*La Caldosa*: Afro-Lesbian Space Making and Transnational Politics in Havana." *Small Axe* 72: 32–48.

Wong, Deborah. 2014. "Sound, Silence, Music: Power." *Ethnomusicology* 58 (2): 347–53.

Zurbano, Roberto. 2014. "The Country to Come: And My Black Cuba?" *Afro-Hispanic Review* 33 (1): 71–72.

Index

Abakuá religion, 44, 54. *See also* African diaspora; Regla de Ocha
"Abrázame muy fuerte" (Juan Gabriel), 71, 105
Abreu Arcia, Alberto, 112
Abu-Lughod, Lila, xviii
Adeyemi, Kemi, 39, 54, 142, 150, 152
African diaspora: cultural production of, 44, 142; religions of, 49, 55–56, 126; religious performances of, 62, 73. *See also* diaspora, Cuban
Afrocuban: music, 44–45, 59, 135, 142, 178n9; religious performance, 20, 23, 51, 59–61, 64, 177n7
Afrocubanas (Martiatu Terry, et al.), 9
Afrocubanas – La Revista, 173n17
Afrodescendants (Afrodescendientes), 26–28, 56–57, 72, 140, 154, 167; movement, xvii, 12, 52, 140, 161, 174n23
Afrofeminism, 9, 108, 126, 140, 174n23; Afrocubanas Project, 12, 173n17; Afrodiverso, 141, 161, 173; Afroqueer movement, 2–3, 18, 125, 167; Afrotransfeminism, 165; Afrotransformismo, xvi–xvii, 167; artivism, 17, 136–42; hip-hop and, 31. *See also* Black feminism; Black lesbians; Black women; feminisms; NOSOTRXS
Agencia Cubana de Rap, 175n19
AIDS, 28–30, 136, 152, 168. *See also* HIV
Airbnb, 14

Aizura, Aren: *Mobile Subjects*, 138
Alberto (transformista), 1–2, 57–59, 61, 66, 133–45, 151, 155. *See also* Fellové Hernández, Argelia
Albita: "¿Que culpa tengo yo?," 85–86
Alfonso, Lizt, 63
"Alguien" (García), 154
Alianys, 56–65, 73. *See also* Esmeralda (transformista)
Allen, Jafari, xix, 112–14
Almodóvar, Pedro, 30, 96
Altahabana, 139
Amanecer (nightclub), 144, 146, 150
Amigas (musical), 63
"El amor" (Massiel), 90
Anckermann, Jorge, 22, 174n6
Andersen, Bibi, 30
"And I Am Telling You . . ." (Carlés), 40–42
androgyny, 73. *See also* gender nonconformity
Angela Nefer (transformista), 3
Ángel Daniel, 55–59, 68, 106–7, 140–44, 164; exclusionary experiences of, 148–50, 152–53; gender experience of, 120–27, 131–32. *See also* Dany (transformista); transformismo masculino movement
Anno, Kim, 80, 87
The Anthropology of Music (Merriam), 10
Antony, Marc, 134

Anzaldúa, Gloria, 173n19
"A puro dolor" (Son by 4), 122
Argelia. *See* Fellové Hernández, Argelia
Argentina, 109, 164
Arroyo Naranjo, 50, 52, 55, 61
Asamblea Municipal del Poder Popular (Municipal Assembly of Popular Power), 80
"Así fue" (Juan Gabriel), 19–20
Asociación Cubana de las Naciones Unidas, 161
"Ay Mamá Inés" (Rodríguez), 23

Babalawos, 53, 129, 167. *See also* Regla de Ocha
Bacallao, Juana, 3; "Yo soy Juana Bacallao," 22, 81–82
Bailey, Marlon, 8, 79, 120, 178n10
ballroom, 120, 178n10
balsero crisis, 175n14
Barnet, Miguel, 30, 110
Bataclán Universitario, 25
Batería (documentary), 178
Behar, Ruth, 7; *Bridges to Cuba*, xviii–xix
Bejel, Emilio, 26, 111
"Bembelequa" (Cruz), 49
Benitez, Lucecita, 63
Benson, Devyn Spence, 12
Berkins, Lohana, 164, 173n12
Berry, Maya, 179n10
Beyoncé, 39; "Listen," 155; "Single Ladies," 106
Biden, Joseph, 160
Bird, Jacob Mallinson, 178n13
Bisbal, Davíd: "Dígale," 137, 145
bisexuality, xvii, 31, 137, 141, 169. *See also* lesbianism; OREMI
Bismarck, Gunilla von, 29
Blaccucini (transformista), 43, 85–86, 161, 164; gender, 106, 114–22, 124–27, 131–32; as a *humorista*, 80–82, 89, 105
Black Cubans, 12, 44, 50, 53, 68–72; economic experiences of, 176n1
blackface, 23, 38–43, 69, 116. *See also* racialized performances of gender
Black feminism, xvii, 3, 162–64, 177n4; Black lesbians and, 108, 136, 152, 159, 179n13; histories of, 8–9, 173n18; transformismo masculino and, 16–17, 125–26; visibility and, 142–44. *See also* Afrofeminism
Black lesbians, 10, 56–59, 135, 138; Black feminism and, 108, 136, 152, 159, 179n13; exclusion of, 14, 147–50, 164–65; femininity and, 139, 155–56; transformismo masculino and, 16–17, 125–26, 141; visibility of, 3, 142–44. *See also* Fellové Hernández, Argelia; transformismo masculino movement
Black Lives Matter, 164
Black men, 67, 70, 112
Black music, 38–39, 142, 174n1, 178n9. *See also* African diaspora; Afrocuban; *folklor*
Black transformistas, 44, 63–64, 66, 115–16; transgender, 16, 106, 114
Black women, 21, 38–39, 139; as audience members, 57–61, 69–72; economic experiences of, 12–13, 15, 20, 176n1; exclusion of, 51, 147–50, 158–59; positive depictions of, 50, 82, 155; racist depictions of, 42–43, 69, 176n26; visibility of, 143–44. *See also* Black lesbians
Blanca Nieves (transformista), 43, 68–71
Blankita (transformista), 34, 40–44, 68–71, 82, 161, 176nn26–27
Bocarrosa (documentary), 178n4
bolero, 22, 39, 63, 175n24
Bonilla, Yarimar, 171n8
El Bosque, 93, 97
bradford, k., 179n12
Brazil, 45, 132
Bridges to Cuba (Behar), xviii–xix
Brown, James, 37
Burke, Elena, 39, 63

Cabaret Las Vegas, 19–23, 32–34, 67, 69, 123
cabaret scene, 3, 24–27, 30, 40, 47, 51–52
Cabaret Tropicana, 22, 49–50, 57
Café Cantante (nightclub), 33, 45, 161
"La cafetera" (Yoruba Andabo), 61, 135, 147
Caibarién, 80, 114
Calderon Tartabull, Diarenis, xvi–xvii, 14–15, 171n2; "Alas," ii
Calle 23, 1, 108, 157. *See also* La Rampa

Calle Humboldt, 21
Calle Infanta, 21
Calzada de Güines, xvi
Camagüey, 87, 114
Camajuaní, 114
campesinos, 82–83, 85, 177n7
el campo, 82, 87–89, 93
Candiani, José, 23
cantos, 59–60, 64–65, 126–27, 134. *See also* Regla de Ocha
capital, foreign, 13–15, 23, 38–40, 44–45, 55, 68, 175n17
capitalism, 36–37, 172n6; global racial, 4, 160–65, 175n22
Capó, Julio, 79
Carbonell, Walterio, 28
"Careless Whisper" (Michael), 96
Carlés, Maggie, 38; "And I Am Telling You . . . ," 40–42
Carnaval, 23, 25, 85
Carneiro, Sueli, 9
Carteles (magazine), 25–26
Casal, Lourdes, xviii; "Para Ana Veltfort," xv, xix
Castro, Fidel, 2, 11, 28, 37, 78
Castro, Raúl, 11–12
Castro Espín, Mariela, 2–3, 158, 172n3
Cázares, Nancy, 164
La Cecilia, 141, 150
CENESEX (Centro Nacional de Educación Sexual), 3, 13, 28, 167–70, 175n18; "campaign for respect toward free sexual orientation" ("campaña por el respeto a la libre orientación sexual"), 13; criticisms of, 31, 158; Diversity is Natural (La Diversidad es Natural), 31–32; events, 120, 136–37; sexual health campaigns, 39–40; transformistas and, 106, 109, 122–23, 139–40. *See also* Conference Against Homophobia and Transphobia (Jornada Contra la Homofobia y la Transfobia); Conga Against Homophobia and Transphobia (Conga Contra la Homofobia y la Transfobia); Gala Contra la Homofobia y la Transfobia; Proyecto TransCuba
Centro Habana, 157
Centro Nacional de Prevención de las ITS-VIH/sida, CNP (National Center for STI-HIV/AIDS Prevention), 136, 168
Centro Provincial de Prevención (Provincial Center for Prevention, CPP), 93–94
El Cerro, xvi
Céspedes, Francisco: "Vida loca," 151
El Chacal: "No te enamores de mi," 151
Chamaco (film), 110
"Chandelier" (Sia), 35
Changó, 60
Chantal (transformista), 153–55
chants, 59–60, 64–65, 126–27, 134
Chappottín y sus Estrellas: "Yo sí como candela," 134
Chicago, 54, 142, 150, 152
Chocolate MC: "Guachineo," 35
Cimafunk, 46, 176n30
Cine Acapulco, 120, 122, 133, 140, 151, 153
Cinthya (transformista), 75, 78, 80–85, 89, 92–93, 98–99, 102, 115, 177n5, 177n10
class, 68, 113; narrating, 25, 174n7; working, 175n17
coalitions, 85, 95, 107, 114; intergenerational, 16, 93, 97–98, 103; lesbian, 151–53, 180n15; politics of, 76, 79, 142, 147, 156; transformismo masculino and, 135–36
Código de la Familia (Family Code), 13, 158, 161–62
Cohen, Cathy, 79, 152
Cole, Nat King, 22
Colectivo Cuba Liberación Negra, 173
Collazo, Bobby, 25
colonialism, 8, 165; Spanish, 23. *See also* imperialism (Spanish); imperialism (US)
colonization, 53
Combahee River Collective, 163–64
comedians, 88–89, 92, 168. *See also humoristas*
communism, 82–84. *See also* Cuban Revolution; socialism
Communist Youth Union (Unión de Jóvenes Comunistas), 177n6
"Cómo decirle" (García), 94

Compañía Futuro, 87, 91, 97, 101–2
Comparsa de la FEU, 59
Compay Segundo, 70–71
"comunidad gay," 82–83
Conference Against Homophobia and Transphobia (Jornada Contra la Homofobia y la Transfobia), 13, 31, 88, 158, 167–68, 177n7, 177n10; 2016, 2–3, 142–43, 163–64
conga, 59, 168
Conga Against Homophobia and Transphobia (Conga Contra la Homofobia y la Transfobia), 157, 177n5, 180n1; 2016, 1–2, 142–43
Conjunto Folklórico Nacional, 130
Conquergood, Dwight D., 8
Conurbanes por la Diversidad, 164
coperformative witnessing, 8
"corruption of minors," 45, 179n9
COVID-19 pandemic, 5, 7, 17, 52, 159–61
Cox, Robert, 173n11
criminalization: of gender nonconformity, 25–30; of transformismo, 29–32
critical ethnographies, 8, 11
cross-dressing, 23, 25, 47. *See also* gender nonconformity; transformismo; travestis
Cruz, Celia, 38; "Bembelequa," 49; "Yo viviré," 37
Cuarteto Habana, 140–41, 143–47, 149–50, 152
Cubanacán, 97–103, 105
Cuban diaspora. *See* diaspora, Cuban
Cuban independence, 4, 23
Cuban pesos, 71, 101, 169
Cuban Revolution, 6, 16, 86–87, 174n24; homophobia in, 84; impact on trans/queer people, 26–30; reforms of, 78–79; sex workers and, 174n10; support for, 82–84; transformismo and, 84–85; trans/queer vitality and, 78, 80. *See also* communism; Revolutionary discourses; socialism
CUC, 71, 168, 175n20
Cuervo, Caridad, 49–50
Cuir/Queer Americas, 173n12
CUP, 169
currencies, 11–12, 29, 175n20; foreign, 32, 43–44, 71, 176n27; local, 43–44, 71. *See also* CUC; CUP; *moneda nacional*; *peso convertible*; *peso cubano*; tourism

dancing, social, 67, 99, 105–6, 155–56; at Apocalipsis, 56–62; at nightclubs, 35, 45–46, 72
Dany (transformista), 57–59, 61, 66, 120–26, 134–35, 144, 151. *See also* Ángel Daniel
"Danza Ñáñiga" (Valdés), 44
Danza Voluminosa, 3
deaths from surgical complications, 99–100
defectors, 36
de la Fuente, Alejandro, 7, 180n4
de la Uz, Laura, 3
Delgado, Soledad, 30
"De mis recuerdos" (Formell), 63
desconocimiento, 85
Detroit, 79, 178n10
Devora (transformista), 19–20, 34, 37–39, 42–43, 146–47, 161, 176n26
Deyanira (transformista), 62, 126–31, 161. *See also* Titi
El Día del Campesino, 177
Diamantes, Cucu, 3
diaspora, Cuban, xvii–xix, 7–9, 17, 38
diasporic ethnographies, xvii, xix, 8, 172n11
"Dígale" (Bisbal), 137, 145
Dilla Alfonso, Haroldo, 52–53
Dion, Celine: "My Heart Will Go On," 69
Directorio de Afrocubanas, 173n17
El discreto encanto del transformismo (documentary), 28
El Divino, 35–36, 45, 161
documentaries: *Batería*, 178n4; *Bocarrosa*, 178n4; *El discreto encanto del transformismo*, 28; *Mariposas en el andamio*, 19–20, 30, 51–52, 63, 111, 178n4; *Máscaras*, 178n4; *¡Quba!*, 80; *Un episodio en la vida de Truca Pérez*, 28
dollarization, 11. *See also* currencies
drag competitions. *See festivales*
The Drag King Book (Volcano and Halberstam), 164
drag kings, 146, 164, 179nn12–13. *See also* transformistas; transformistas masculinos

drag performances. *See* transformismo
Dreamgirls (musical), 40, 155
"Dura" (term), 70, 101, 177n9
Dúrcal, Rocío, 39
Duval, Rubén (transformista), 24
Duvall, Alex: "¿Por qué no le dices?," 94

economic struggles in Cuba, 4–5, 29, 52, 71, 86–87, 115–16, 157–60
economic transformation in Cuba, 11–13, 53
Ecuador, 164
Edgar, Kika: "Ojalá que no puedas," 96
Elegguá, 49–50, 59–60, 64–65, 143
"Elegguá: Rey del mal y el bien" (Grupo Abbilona), 64
Elejalde, Ignacio, 143
Ellison, Treva, 131–32, 178n7
época de oro (transformismo), 92, 98
"Eres" (Massiel), 90
Escambray Mountains, 89
Esmeralda (transformista), 49–50, 56–57
Espina Prieto, Mayra, 176n1
Espinosa, Norge, 158; "Vestido de novia," 109–10
"Estrellita" (Ponce), 133
ethnographic research, xvi–xix, 4, 6–8, 10–11, 20–21, 111, 138, 173n21
ethnographies, xvii, xix, 8, 11, 172n11
ethnomusicology, 4, 51, 172nn9–10
"Evidencia" (Pantoja and Los 4), 72, 81
"Exkiusmi Yusmi" (Krudxs Cubensi), 141

faggotries, 20, 173n11. *See also* mariconerías
Family Code (Código de la Familia), 13, 158, 161–62
Fátima o el Parque de la Fraternidad (film), 110
fatphobia, 95
Favez, Enriqueta, 25, 174n9
Federación Estudiantil Universitaria (Federation of University Students), 59
Federation of Cuban Women (Federación de Mujeres Cubanas) (FMC), 28, 83
Fellové Hernández, Argelia, 7, 64, 68; Afrofeminism and, 9, 161, 164; transformismo and, 1–4, 17, 39, 55–59, 95, 121–22, 135–56. *See also* Afrofeminism; Alberto (transformista); transformismo masculino movement
feminisms, xvii, 177n9; Third World, 79–80, 163; woman-of-color, xvii, 8–9, 163. *See also* Afrofeminism; Black feminism
femme (term), 171n11, 172n6
Ferguson, Roderick, 180n15
Fernández, Daniel, 28
Fernández Robaina, Tomás, 27, 31
Ferrán, Omar (transformista), 24, 174n2, 174n6
Festival de Afrotransformismo, 161
Festival de Transformismo Gunilla, 30
festivales, 51, 62–67, 73
fiestas, 73; *de diez pesos*, 29, 175n16; *gay*, 21, 32, 50–51
filin, 143
First Congress on Education and Culture (Primer Congreso de Educación y Cultura), 27–28
Fleetwood, Nicole, 144
"Flor de Yumurí" (Anckermann), 22
folklor, 51, 55–57, 73, 128–31; dancers, 143; music, 59–61, 64–65
foreign capital, 13–15, 23, 38–40, 44–45, 55, 68, 175n17
foreign currencies, 71, 176n27. *See also* currencies
foreigners, 14, 34–36; Black women and, 43; catering to, 45, 51; in Santa Clara, 78–79; sex work and, 12–13, 176n29; as tourists in Havana, 52–53
foreign music, 3, 5, 37–38, 63, 69, 163
Formell, Juan: "De mis recuerdos," 63
Fowler, Víctor, xviii
Franklin, Aretha, 37, 38
Fresa y Chocolate (film), 30, 110
Frye, David, xv
"Fuera de mi vida" (Sosa), 154
funk carioca, 45

Gala Contra la Homofobia y la Transfobia, 3, 5, 142, 144, 146, 177n10
Gallo, Rubén, 32
García, Kany: "Alguien," 154; "Cómo decirle," 94

garzonismo, 25
Gaultier, Jean Paul, 30
gay (term), 111, 113–14
Gay and Lesbian Quarterly, 173n12
gay men, 14, 33–39, 57, 77, 94, 111, 175n18
Gaynor, Gloria, 38; "I Will Survive," 37, 42
gender-affirming: care, 175n13; surgeries, 28, 99–100, 111–12, 178n12
gender and sexuality, 108–14
gender-expansive language, 36, 106–20, 128, 167–70
gender nonconformity, 107–14, 178n1; criminalization of, 25
Gerestant, MilDred "Dréd," 146, 180n16
Ginestá, Guillermo, 29–30
global racial capitalism, 4, 160–65, 175n22
golden age of transformismo, 92, 98
Gopinath, Gayatri, 79
"La gozadera" (Yoruba Andabo), 57, 155
Gramsci, Antonio, 6, 173n11
Grupo Abbilona: "Elegguá: Rey del mal y el bien," 64; "Yemayá: Reina del mundo," 65
Grupo Nacional de Trabajo de Educación Sexual, GNTES (National Working Group on Sex Education), 28, 32, 174–75n13
Grupo OREMI, 31, 136–38, 140, 169, 175n19
La Gruta, 2–3
"Guachineo" (Chocolate MC), 35
guaguancó, 57–59, 135, 177n4, 179n3
Guanabacoa, 53
Guantanamo Bay, 175n14
Guerrero, Juan José, 23
Guevara, Ernesto "Che," 76–78, 84, 177n1
Guillard Limonta, Norma, 2, 136–37, 143
La Güinera, 30, 52

La Habana Vieja, 157, 168, 170
Haiti, 175n24
Halberstam, Jack: *The Drag King Book*, 164
"Hallelujah" (Massiel), 90
Haniff, Nesha, xviii

Harvard University Department of Music, 172n11
Havana Hilton, 37
health care, 29, 39–40; transgender, 28, 167, 178n12. *See also* gender-affirming
Heifetz, Jascha, 133
"Hermosa Habana" (Los Zafiros), 143–44
Hernández, Adela, 80–85
Herring, Scott, 79
heterosexuality, 54, 57, 68, 70, 84, 108, 144, 176n29
hip-hop movement, 31, 53–54
HIV, 28–29, 39, 152. *See also* AIDS
Hola Gente (magazine), 31
Holguín, 99–102
Holliday, Billie, 42
"El Hombre Nuevo" ("The New Man"), 77, 177n4
homoeroticism, 109–10, 113
homophobia, 15, 85, 129, 150, 174nn7–8, 177n7; Cuban Revolution and, 77, 84; experiences of, 82–83; movements against, 31, 89–90; resurgence of, 162–63. *See also* criminalization; UMAP camps
homosexuality, 107–10, 178n1
Hotel Habana Libre, 37
Hotel Nacional, 1
Hotel Saratoga, 180n1
Houston, Whitney, 3, 39
"Hoy me emborraché por ti" (Juan Gabriel), 72–73
HSH (hombres que tienen sexo con hombres), 93–95, 168
Hubbs, Nadine, 174n7
Hudson, Jennifer, 39
Humboldt, 45, 137
humoristas, 43, 68–71, 80–82, 105, 115–16, 168, 176n26. *See also* Blaccucini (transformista); Blankita (transformista)
Hurricane Irma, 46, 80
hustling (*jineterismo*), 45, 176n29

Iberostar, 36
If an Egyptian Cannot Speak English (Naga), xv, xix
Iglesia de Santa Bárbara, 55, 59, 61, 67
immigration out of Cuba, 17, 160–61. *See also* migration

Index · 197

imperialism (Spanish), 37
imperialism (US), 4–5, 8, 18, 36, 158–60, 164–65, 175n22; Cuban Revolution and, 26. *See also* sanctions (US)
Imperio (transformista), 3, 161
incarceration, 3, 28, 54, 128, 140, 163, 173n20. *See also* criminalization; UMAP camps
La India, 113
intergenerational connections, 16, 93, 97–98, 103
International Day Against Homophobia (IDAHO), 13, 31, 177n7
International Decade for People of African Descent, 140
Irakere, 44
"I Will Survive" (Gaynor), 37, 42
"Iyaoromi" (Síntesis), 134

"Jardin con enanitos" (Melendi), 65
Javier (Cinthya), 84, 177n5. *See also* Cinthya (transformista)
jineterismo (hustling), 45, 176n29
Johnny T., 179n12
Jornada Contra la Homofobia y la Transfobia (Conference Against Homophobia and Transphobia), 13, 31, 88, 158, 167–68, 177n7, 177n10; 2016, 2–3, 142–43, 163–64
Juan Gabriel, 20; "Abrázame muy fuerte," 105–6; "Así fue," 19; "Hoy me emborraché por ti," 72–73; "Perdona si te hago llorar," 75; "Te lo pido por favor," 134
July 11 movement, 7, 17, 52, 159–60, 173n20
Jurado, Rocío: "Maniquí," 98; "¿Quién te crees tú?," 98
Juventud Rebelde (newspaper), 177

Karabalí, 33–35, 41, 44–46, 67
Key West, 120
King, Rosamond, 113, 173n12
Kiriam (transformista), 31, 40, 161
Krudxs Cubensi, 13, 31, 165, 180n3; "Exkiusmi Yusmi," 141

La Fountain-Stokes, Lawrence, xviii, 7, 113, 173n12

Lane, Jill, 23
Lanfang, Mei, 23, 25
language, gender-expansive, 36, 106–20, 128, 167–70
La Niña Rita o La Habana en 1830 (zarzuela), 23
Lao-Montes, Agustín, 9
La Palma, 122
Lara (transformista), 68–69, 71–73
Las Tunas, 126
Las Vegas (nightclub), 19–23, 32–34, 67, 69, 123
Latin America, 9–10, 20, 39, 108, 140, 163–65, 171n3; travestis in, 171n5, 175n21
Latinx (term), xvi, 171n3
Laura Marlen (transformista), 87–92, 100
Lecuona, Ernesto, 44
legality of transformismo, 29–32. *See also* criminalization; UMAP camps
lesbianism, 10, 14, 77, 122, 138, 149, 151–53. *See also* Black lesbians
lesbian women, 56–57, 68, 85, 94–95, 142, 144–45
lesbophobia, 4, 18, 94, 146, 177n9; of transformistas femeninas, 147–50
LGBT mainstream, 51, 103, 108–9, 139–40, 158–59; inequity in, 14–17, 68; limitations of, 56, 73, 79–80, 142; El Mejunje exceeding, 76; racist ideologies in, xvii, 4; transformismo masculino and, 151
LGBT rights, xvii, 17; in Cuba, 11, 13, 31–32, 34–35, 173n11; discourses, 83–84, 88–89, 114, 131–32, 162–64; politics, 4, 6, 51
liberalization, 12, 29, 32, 86
liberation, trans/queer, 6, 9, 14, 17, 80, 136, 159; revolutionary nationalism and, 21, 162–65. *See also* Afrofeminism; Revolutionary discourses; revolutionary nationalism
Lili/Octavio, 112–14
Lima, José Lezama, 110
*linda*s, 43, 176n26
"Listen" (Beyoncé), 155
Listening in Detail (Vázquez), 5
literacy campaign, 84–85

Lorde, Audre, 9, 125, 143
Los 4: "Evidencia," 72, 81
Los Cocos sanatorium, 29
Los Zafiros: "Hermosa Habana," 143–44
Lukumí, 126–27
Lumsden, Ian, 111
La Lupe, 38
Luyanó, xvi

"Madame Caridad" (Mompié), 65, 130
Madame Musmé (transformista), 22–23, 26, 38, 174n2, 174n4
Madame Pompadour (transformista), 24
Madero, Abel Sierra, 23, 25, 111, 173n11
Madrid, Alejandro, 5
"Mala costumbre" (Soler), 121, 151
Malecón, 2, 46, 113, 157, 169–70
Malinowski, Bronisław, 11, 173n21
Malú, 72, 131
Manicaragua, 85, 89
"Maniquí" (Jurado), 98
Mantilla, 55–56, 68–69, 71–72, 122
Margot (transformista), 3, 43, 161
maricón (term), 20, 67, 70, 83–84, 99, 110, 119, 169
mariconerías, 173n11, 177n5
Maridalia (transformista), 19–20, 23, 176n27
Mariel boatlift, 28
Mariposas en el andamio (documentary), 19–20, 30, 51–52, 63, 111, 176n27, 178n4
Márquez, Edith, 72
marriage, 13, 25, 161–62, 172n6, 176n29
Martí, José, 88
Martiatu Terry, Inés María, 9
Martin, Lili, 88
Marxism, 171n9, 175n17
Máscaras (documentary), 178n4
masculinity, transgender, 121–24
Massiel, 63, 89–91
Mastrozzimone, Julie, 28
Matanzas, 55, 114
May 11, 2019: 157–58
McCray, Chirlane, 173n19
Medina, Mirtha, 38
"Me Incluyo," 88
El Mejunje, 16, 29, 75–76, 114; history of, 77–79, 177n2

Melendi: "Jardin con enanitos," 65
Meliá, 36–37
Mercury, Freddie, 77, 87
Merriam, Alan, 173n21; *The Anthropology of Music*, 10
Merriam, Barbara, 10
Mexico, 63, 163–64
Miami, 46, 79, 86, 88, 161; drag scene, 28
Miami Herald (newspaper), 76
Michael, George: "Careless Whisper," 96
migration, 47, 53. *See also* immigration out of Cuba
"La miki y la repa" (La Reyna y La Real), 53–54
military, 172n6
Military Units to Aid Production (UMAP), 26–28, 38. *See also* UMAP camps
Ministerio de Cultura, 30–32
Ministerio del Interior, 157
Miramar, 143, 169
misogyny, 129, 146, 177n9
Miss Cuba competition (2016), 99
Mitjans Alayón, Tito, 125
"Mi vida por un hombre" (Naranjo), 3
Mobile Subjects (Aizura), 138
Mompié, Haila, 126; "Madame Caridad," 65
moneda nacional, 43–44, 71, 176n1. *See also* currencies
Montaner, Rita, 23, 38, 174n5
Moraga, Cherríe, 173n19
Morales, Rosario, 173n19
Morrison, Toni: *Sula*, 180n15
Mother Camp (Newton), 120, 177n8
MSM (men who have sex with men), 168
mujer transgénero, 110
"la mulata," 12, 138, 176n26, 180n12
Municipal Assembly of Popular Power (Asamblea Municipal del Poder Popular), 80
Muñoz, José Esteban, xviii, 171n9
music: Afrocuban, 12, 44–45, 59, 135, 178n9; Black, 38–39, 142, 174n1, 178n9; criticism, 21; foreign, 3, 5, 37–38, 63, 69, 163; industry, 174n1; studies, 4–5, 172n9. *See also* folklor
"My Heart Will Go On" (Dion), 69

Naga, Noor: *If an Egyptian Cannot Speak English*, xv, xix
Namaste, Viviane, 113, 178n4
Naranjo, Mónica: "Mi vida por un hombre," 3
narrating class, 174n7
National Center for Sex Education. *See* CENESEX
National Center for STI-HIV/AIDS Prevention, CNP (Centro Nacional de Prevención de las ITS-VIH/sida), 136, 168
nationalism, revolutionary, 4, 21, 162, 165
National Working Group on Sex Education, GNTES (Grupo Nacional de Trabajo de Educación Sexual), 28
Nefer, Angela (transformista), 3
Negra cubana tenía que ser, 173n17
"The New Man" ("El Hombre Nuevo"), 77, 177n4
Newton, Esther, 179n7; *Mother Camp*, 120, 177
New York City, 46, 79
Nguyen, Som-Mai, 171
nightclubs: Amanecer, 144, 146, 150; Café Cantante, 33, 45, 161; Cubanacán, 97–103, 105; La Gruta, 2–3; Karabalí, 33–35, 41, 44–46, 67; Las Vegas, 19–23, 32–34, 67, 69, 123; Tropical, 126; Tropicana, 22, 49–50, 57; XY, 36, 38, 146–47, 150
"No querías lastimarme" (Trevi), 99–102
NOSOTRXS, 14–15, 152, 157, 161, 173n17
"No te enamores de mí" (El Chacal), 151
El Nuevo Herald (newspaper), 29
Nuevo Vedado, 133
Nyong'o, Tavia, 171

Obama, Barack, 149, 160
Obbatalá, 59–60, 129–31, 177n6
Ochoa, Marcia, 173n12
Ochún, 59, 65, 126–27, 130–31, 177n6
Odaymar, 165
Oggún, 59
"Ojalá que no puedas" (Edgar), 96
Old Havana, 71, 168
Oliva, Carlos: "You are Unique," 80
Omega (transformista), 99–102, 178n11

OREMI, 31, 136–38, 140, 169, 175n19
Organización Nacional de Entendidos (ONE), 31
orishas, 59–61, 64–65, 73, 126–31, 133, 143, 177nn6–7. *See also* Regla de Ocha
Oyá, 59–60, 177n6

Pabellón Cuba, 2–3
Pacha Queer, 164
La Palma, 55
Pantoja, Isabel, 19–20, 39, 63; "Abrázame muy fuerte," 71, 105; "Para sobrevivir," 64; "Perdona si te hago llorar," 75
Pantoja, Tania: "Evidencia," 72, 81
"Para Ana Veltfort" (Casal), xv, xix
"Para sobrevivir" (Pantoja), 64
Parque Central, 157
Parque Vidal, 93–94, 105
Párraga, 49–51, 55, 67
Parrandas, 87
Paseo del Prado, 157
Paz, Senel, 30
Peláez, Amelia, 37
peligrosidad social, 3, 170
Peña de Olga Navarro, 123
peñas, 152, 173n15, 179n4
pepillismo, 25
"Perdona si te hago llorar" (Juan Gabriel), 75
El Perequitón, 30
performance ethnographies, 8, 11
performance studies, 6–8, 113, 172n9, 178n4
Período Especial en Tiempos de Paz (Special Period in Times of Peace), 11, 29, 40, 43, 160, 175n15
peso convertible, 168. *See also* CUC; currencies
peso cubano, 169
pimping (*proxenetismo*), 45
Pinar del Río, 55
Piñera, Virgilio, 110
Placetas, 87
Playa, 57, 113, 150, 169–70
Plaza de la Revolución, 170
police, 137, 163; repression, 30–32, 46, 52, 67, 106; violence, 173n20
political organizing, 97

Ponce, Manuel, 133
"¿Por qué no le dices?" (Duvall), 94
postracial discourses, 116
postsocialism, 6, 52, 159, 175n17; criticisms of, 12, 18
Premio Nacional de Literatura, 30
Primer Congreso de Educación y Cultura (First Congress on Education and Culture), 27–28
prison, 3, 28, 54, 128, 140, 163, 173n20
private sector, 12–14, 28, 32, 46, 76, 176n1
protests, 52, 157–58, 160, 168–69. See also July 11 movement
provinces. See regionalism
Provincial Centers for the Prevention of STIs and HIV/AIDS (Centros Provinciales de Prevencion de las ITS-VIH/sida), 93–94, 168
proxenetismo (pimping), 45
Proyectos, 39, 170; Bravissimo, 33; Divino, 33, 35–36; Ibiza, 33, 145; Yo Me Incluyo (PYMI), 75, 84–85, 87–93
Proyecto TransCuba, 31, 40, 109, 170
Puar, Jasbir, 113
Puerto Rico, 45, 63, 113–14, 163

quartet. See Cuarteto Habana
¡Quba! (documentary), 80
"Que bueno que no fui Lady Di" (Trevi), 69
"¿Que culpa tengo yo?" (Albita), 85–86
queer (term), 113–14, 119–20
queer studies, 4–6, 16, 51, 76–79, 112–13, 173n12, 178nn4–5
"¿Quién te crees tú?" (Jurado), 98
quinquenio gris, 27–28

racelessness, 4, 89
postracial discourses, 116
racial impersonation, xvi, 9, 40–43, 174n1. See also blackface
racialization, xviii; of Latinx, 171n8
racialized performances of gender, 15, 23, 38–43, 112, 174n5, 176n26
racist iconography, 40–43
Ramírez, Marta María, 25–27, 29
La Rampa, 1, 170. See also Calle 23
rebeldía, 84, 177n6

reeducation centers, 26–27. See also UMAP camps
reggaetón, 35, 45, 65, 94, 149, 151, 180n12
regionalism, 16, 76–79, 89, 176n2
Regla de Ocha, 53, 59, 126–29, 167–69, 173n15, 177nn6–7; homophobia in, 179n16; performance and, 134. See also orishas
Remate de Ariosa, 16, 75–76, 87–91, 93, 103
Remedios, 87, 114
repartos, 15–16, 18, 49–55, 159, 170
Republican era, 47
resorts, 36–37, 78–79
respectability politics, 4, 34, 83–84, 107
Revolution, Cuban. See Cuban Revolution
Revolutionary discourses, 16, 76–77, 82–84, 159, 174n24; trans/queer, 83–84, 87, 89, 102–3
revolutionary nationalism, 4–6, 21, 162, 165
anti-Revolutionary rhetoric, 86
La Reyna y La Real: "La miki and la repa," 53–54
rockers, 77–78, 177n3
Rodríguez, Alfredo: "Ay Mamá Inés," 23
Rodríguez, Juana María, xviii
Rosaldo, Michelle, 11
Rosaldo, Renato, 11
rumba, 42, 61, 85, 142, 147, 150, 155, 179n2; *guaguancó*, 57–59, 135, 177n4, 179n3
RuPaul, 63

Sacayán, Diana, 164
Sahira (transformista), 3
salsa, 37, 65, 72, 135
same-sex-couple adoption, 161–62
same-sex marriage, 13, 161–62
same-sex-parent adoption, 13
San Basilio, Paloma, 96
Sánchez, Marta, 3
sanctions (US), 7, 149, 157–60
Sancti Spiritus, 128
Sandoval, Chela, 79, 180n15
San Miguel del Padrón, xvi
Santa Clara, 7, 16, 29, 55, 76–100, 114

Santana, Dora Silva, 132
Santiago, Héctor, 26
Sarduy, Severo, 110
Saunders, Tanya, 169
Schieffelin, Bambi, 11
Schieffelin, Edward, 11
Segundo, Compay, 70–71
Selena, 92
Seligman, Brenda, 11
Seligman, Charles, 11
La Semana (magazine), 25
sex tourism, 10, 13, 20
sexual health: campaigns, 39, 150; education, 93, 175n13. *See also* CENESEX
sexual impersonation, 40–43
sexuality and gender, 108–14
"sexual revolution," 13–14, 143. *See also* CENESEX
sexual subjectivity, 16, 107, 110–14, 139, 163, 173n12; performance and, 5–6, 119–22, 127–32, 172n4; travestis and, 107
sex work, 176n29; drag as, 107, 175n23; state repression of, 45
sex workers, 26, 31, 107–9, 179n9; Cuban Revolution and, 174n10
Shock, Susy, 173n12
Show (magazine), 24–26
Sia: "Chandelier," 35
Sifunola, Afibola, 14, 157, 165
Silverio Gómez, Ramón, 77–78, 80–85, 87–88, 101–2; performance as Carmita, 80. *See also* El Mejunje
"Single Ladies" (Beyoncé), 106
Síntesis: "Iyaoromi," 134
"Si una vez" (Villarreal), 92
Sixteenth World Congress of Sexology, 175n18
slavery: legacy of, xviii, 4, 8, 18, 165, 171n9; persistence of, 23
Social (magazine), 23, 25
socialism, 3–4, 9, 11, 20–21, 32, 47, 53, 72. *See also* Cuban Revolution; postsocialism
Solaya, Marilyn, 110
"Soledad" (Torres), 65
Soler, Pastora: "Mala costumbre," 121, 151
Son by 4: "A puro dolor," 122

Sosa, Natalia: "Fuera de mi vida," 154
Soviet Union, 11, 29, 32, 37, 47, 53, 78
Spain, 63, 163
Special Period in Times of Peace (Período Especial en Tiempos de Paz), 11, 29, 40, 43, 160, 175n15
Stanley, Eric, 172
state-run establishments, 13, 147; transformismo in, 20, 32–33
Stout, Noelle, 111
straight men, 111
strippers, 33, 45
Sula (Morrison), 180n15
surgeries, gender-affirming, 28, 111–12, 178n12; deaths from, 99–100
Swann, Valetta, 11
Sylvia Rivera Law Project, 164

Tañón, Olga, 72
"Te amo" (Massiel), 90
Teatro América, 30
teatro bufo, 23, 40–44
Teatro Karl Marx, 142–43
Teatro La Caridad, 105
Teatro Nacional José Martí, 3, 33
"Te lo pido por favor" (Juan Gabriel), 134
temperamentales, 43, 176n26
theater, community, 89
Third World feminism, xvii, 8–9, 79–80, 142, 163. *See also* feminisms
This Bridge Called My Back, 164
Tinsley, Omise'eke, 146, 155, 180n16
tipping, 71, 96, 131, 137–38, 175n23, 176n27; act of, 37, 42–43, 71, 101, 134, 145, 154
Titanic (film), 69
Titi, 62–63, 65–67, 106–7, 126–32, 164. *See also* Deyanira (transformista)
Torres, Leoni: "Soledad," 65
Torres, Lourdes, 25, 39
Torres Santana, Ailynn, 12
tourism, 4, 12–15, 21, 29, 32; in Havana, 52–53; negative effects of, 89; postsocialist, 175n17; racism and, 43; in Santa Clara, 78–79; sex, 10, 13, 20; stratification because of, 53–54; transformismo and, 13–15, 34–36, 47; trans/queer spaces beyond, 76, 79–80

202 · Index

trans (term), 113–14
transformismo: criminalization of, 20, 172n5; defined, 4–6, 118–19; economics of, 13–15, 130; exclusion in, 94–95; feminist, 146; golden era of, 29–30; history of, 21–32; mainstream spaces, 20–21; as mutual care, 50–51, 61–62; as a performance complex, xvi–xvii, 3; race and, xvi–xvii, 20, 22–23, 40–44, 68–69; as a theatre of resistance, 26–30, 175n14; transgender, 109; in Villa Clara, 75–103. *See also festivales*
transformismo masculino movement, 1–3, 9, 31, 39, 95, 120–26, 133–56, 159, 164; struggles of, 147–50
transformista (term), 107–14, 118–19, 128
transformistas, 3, 43, 176n26; Alberto, 1–2, 57–59, 61, 66, 133–45, 151, 155; Angela Nefer, 3; Blaccucini, 43, 80–82, 85–86, 89, 105–6, 114–22, 124–27, 131–32, 161, 164; Blanca Nieves, 43, 68–71; Blankita, 34, 40–44, 68–71, 82, 161, 176nn26–27; Carmita, 80; Chantal, 153–55; Cinthya, 75, 78, 80–85, 89, 92–93, 98–99, 102, 115, 177n5, 177n10; Dany, 57–59, 61, 66, 120–26, 134–35, 144, 151; Devora, 19–20, 34, 37–39, 42–43, 146–47, 161, 176n26; Deyanira, 62, 126–31, 161; Esmeralda, 49–50, 56–57; Imperio, 3, 161; Kiriam, 31, 40, 161; Lara, 68–69, 71–73; Laura Marlen, 87–92, 100; Madame Musmé, 22–23, 26, 38, 174n2, 174n4; Madame Pompadour, 24; Margot, 3, 43, 161; Maridalia, 19–20, 23, 176n27; Omar Ferrán, 24, 174n2, 174n6; Omega, 99–102, 178n11; Rubén Duval, 24; Sahira, 3; Uma Rojo, 44, 161; Víctor Víctor, 94, 139; Zulema, 75–78, 88, 91–102, 105–6, 161, 178n11
transformistas femeninas, 3, 94–95, 133–35
transformistas masculinos, 1–3, 9, 16–17, 55, 153; struggles of, 94–95. *See also* Alberto (transformista)
transgender: men, 120–26, 140, 177n9; transformistas, 16, 92, 106, 112–13, 159; women, 84, 114
transgender (term), 120

Transgender Studies Quarterly ("Trans Studies en las Americas"), 173n12
transgénero (term), 5, 107–14, 117, 128, 170
Trans Justice Funding Project, 164
translesbianism, xvii, 177n8, 179n6
transmasculine people, 94–95, 177n9
transphobia, 15, 18, 25, 68, 129, 172n6, 174n7; experiences of, 113; resurgence of, 162–63; struggles against, 89–90; in transformismo, 34
trans/queer: coalitions, 152; definition, 172n4; liberation, 87, 102–3, 147; performance, 79; spaces, 78–80; studies, 4–6, 16, 51, 76–79, 112–13, 173n12, 178nn4–5; subjectivity, 113
transvestite (term), 111
trasformismo (Gramsci), 6, 173n11
travesti (term), 107–20, 128
travestis, xvii, 5, 117, 164, 175n21; in Argentina, 109; in Brazil, 132; discrimination against, 34–35, 68; movements, 30–31, 164, 173n12; repression of, 128–30; as sex workers, 107–9; as transformistas, 62–63, 65–66
travestismo, 23–25
Trevi, Gloria, 3, 39; "No querías lastimarme," 99–102; "Que bueno que no fui Lady Di," 69
Trinidad, 113
Tropical (nightclub), 126
Tropicana (nightclub), 22, 49–50, 57
Trump, Donald, 157, 159

UC Berkeley, 165
UMAP camps, 26–28, 38, 40, 44, 77, 174n11
Uma Rojo (transformista), 44, 161
Un episodio en la vida de Truca Pérez (documentary), 28
Unidades Militares de Ayuda a la Producción (UMAP), 26–28. *See also* UMAP camps
Unión de Jóvenes Comunistas (Communist Youth Union), 177n6
University of Florida, 9
University of Havana, 25, 59
USSR, 11, 29, 32, 37, 47, 53, 78

Valdés, Chucho, 44
Valdés, Mayra Caridad: "Danza Ñáñiga," 44
Valentine, David, 120, 178n1, 178n6
Vaughan, Umi, 178n9
Vázquez, Alexandra: *Listening in Detail*, 5
El Vedado, xvi, 1, 21–23, 32–33, 55, 57, 61, 67, 126, 157, 170
Venegas Delgado, Hernán, 54–55
Vestido de novia (film), 109–10
"Vestido de novia" (Espinosa), 109–10
Víctor Víctor (transformista), 94, 139
"Vida loca" (Céspedes), 151
VIH. *See* HIV
Villa Clara, 16, 55, 75, 78–79, 87, 114, 159
Villarreal, Alicia: "Si una vez," 92
violence: police, 173n20; against trans/queer people, 97–98
Virgen del Camino, xvi
visibility, 142–47, 156, 180n12
Viva (film), 90, 178n4
Volcano, Del LaGrace: *The Drag King Book*, 164

Wayar, Marlene, 173n12
white Cubans, 12, 44, 53, 86, 149, 171n7
white supremacy, xviii, 172n6
white women, 176n29
woman-of-color feminism, xvii, 8–9, 163
women, Black. *See* Black women
Woo, Merle, 173n19
working-class, 30, 175n17

XY (nightclub), 36, 38, 146–47, 150

Yemayá, 59–61, 65, 73, 128, 130, 134, 177n6
"Yemayá: Reina del mundo" (Grupo Abbilona), 65
Yoruba Andabo, 59, 130; "La cafetera," 61, 135, 147; "La gozadera," 57, 155
"Yo sí como candela" (Chappottín y sus Estrellas), 134
"Yo soy Juana Bacallao" (Bacallao), 81–82
"You Are Unique" (Oliva), 80
"Yo viviré" (Cruz), 37
Yuri, 63
Yuridia, 19–20, 72

Zulema (transformista), 75–78, 88, 91–102, 105–6, 161, 178n11
Zurbano, Roberto, 12